NEW WOMEN OF EMPIRE

NEW WOMEN of EMPIRE

Gendered Politics and Racial Uplift in Interwar Japanese America

CHRISSY YEE LAU

UNIVERSITY OF WASHINGTON PRESS
Seattle

New Women of Empire was made possible in part by a grant from the Capell Family Endowed Book Fund, which supports the publication of books that deepen the understanding of social justice through historical, cultural, and environmental studies.

Composed in Iowan Old Style, typeface designed by John Downer

26 25 24 23 22 5 4 3 2 1

Printed and bound in the United States of America

UNIVERSITY OF WASHINGTON PRESS
uwapress.uw.edu

LIBRARY OF CONGRESS CATALOGING-IN-PUBLICATION DATA
Names: Lau, Chrissy Yee, author.
Title: New women of empire : gendered politics and racial uplift in interwar Japanese America / Chrissy Yee Lau.
Description: Seattle : University of Washington Press, [2022] | Includes bibliographical references and index.
Identifiers: LCCN 2021056893 (print) | LCCN 2021056894 (ebook) | ISBN 9780295750514 (hardcover) | ISBN 9780295750521 (paperback) | ISBN 9780295750538 (ebook)
Subjects: LCSH: Japanese American women—California—Los Angeles—Social conditions—20th century. | Japanese Americans—California—Los Angeles—Social conditions—20th century. | Japanese Americans—Cultural assimilation—California—Los Angeles. | Los Angeles (Calif.)—Social conditions—20th century. | United States—Race relations—History—20th century. | Japan—Relations—United States.
Classification: LCC F869.L89 J3385 2022 (print) | LCC F869.L89 (ebook) | DDC 973/.04956—dc23/eng/20220214

LC record available at https://lccn.loc.gov/2021056893
LC ebook record available at https://lccn.loc.gov/2021056894

♾ This paper meets the requirements of ANSI/NISO Z39.48-1992 (Permanence of Paper).

For daughters of immigrant families

CONTENTS

ACKNOWLEDGMENTS

This book has been an intellectual and political journey for the past ten years. Every inch of this book has been shaped and nurtured by the labors of love of many, many people.

First and foremost, I must thank Paul Spickard, who taught an undergraduate course on Asian American history that changed my life. As chair of my dissertation committee, he never ceased to amaze me with his deep well of encouragement. I owe my love of women's studies to my three brilliant dissertation committee members for their trailblazing feminist scholarship and honest mentorship: Eileen Boris, Grace Chang, and erin Khuê Ninh. Thank you to the Department of Asian American Studies at the University of California, Santa Barbara, for creating an intellectual home: Jim Lee, Celine Parreñas Shimizu, Diane Fujino, and Xiaojian Zhao. I was surrounded by amazing women of color who held me up as we navigated graduate school together: Mimi Khúc, Melissa Kwon, Lily Anne Welty Tamai, Niccole Coggins, Rosie Kar, Cristina Serna, and Tara Villalba.

I am thankful for the mentorship I received that broadened my scholarly interests in the final stages of graduate school. My interests in the study of Asian American religions blossomed in a wonderfully supportive and collaborative scholarly circle called Asian Pacific American Religions Research Initiative. Thank you to Chris Chua, Rudy Busto, Jane Iwamura, Carolyn Chen, Khyati Joshi, David Yoo, Russell Jeung, Sylvia Chan-Malik, and Benny Liew. My love for public history expanded when I shadowed Noriko Sanefuji at the National Museum of American History.

I became a better historian and educator by being a visiting assistant professor in Asian American studies and history at Cornell University. Thanks to the faculty and staff who provided mentorship, expanded my thinking on comparative race, and offered good company: Derek Chang, Shelley Wong, Viranjini P. Munasinghe, and Vladimir Micic. I thank my former students who taught me firsthand about youth organizing and coalitional politics: Diana Li, Linda He, Emily Dong, Taylor Wong, Esther Hwang, and Moseh Cho.

I valued my three years at Texas A&M University–Corpus Christi, where my research broadened transnationally as I taught at the nexus of US history and Asian history. Many thanks to my colleagues in the history department: Sandrine Sanos, Laura Muñoz, Peter Moore, David Blanke, Robert Wooster, Anthony Quiroz, Claudia Rueda, Jen Brown, Eliza Martin, Beth Robinson, Adam Costanzo, and Timothy Scott Johnson. I also thank members of the English department for their support of my research, including Kelly Bezio, Jason Farr, Kathryn Santos, and Jenni Sorenson. I am grateful to interlibrary loan librarian Brent Day for obtaining crucial primary sources. I was also changed by the incredible students there: Harley Matthews, Humberto Garcia, and Bridgette Ramirez among others.

At California State University, Monterey Bay, I have found my niche in US women's history. I was lucky to come home to California to the welcome arms of loving friends, Phuong and Betty Nguyen, who have always showered me with encouragement, food, and companionship. I am so thankful I have found a wonderfully supportive writing group of brilliant and humorous colleagues: David Reichard, Kyle Livie, Dustin Wright, and Fred Vermote. I am thankful to call this place home with colleagues like Rebecca Bales, Amanda Pullum, Sara Salazar Hughes, Tolga Tozan, and the Ethnic Studies Working Group.

Interdisciplinary workshop spaces and conference panels have contributed immensely to the development of this manuscript. I thank the organizers of the Association of Asian American Studies junior faculty workshop, and my group: Daryl Maeda, Dana Nakano, and Andrew Leong. I am indebted to university archivists like Kaoru Ueda, who organized the Hoji Shinbun Digital Collection and the Japanese Diaspora Initiative workshop. I thank my go-to panel co-organizers, Michael Jin and Meredith Oda, for creating space and generating conversations about new directions in

Japanese American history. I thank the organizers of the AAPI (Asian Americans and Pacific Islanders) History Group at the Huntington Library, Art Museum, and Botanical Gardens, David Yoo, Constance Chen, Lon Kurashige, and the scholars who provided insightful comments: Valerie Matsumoto, Cindy I-Feng Cheng, and Jane Hong. I thank Heike Friedman, Albert Manke, and Soren Urbansky for organizing the Mobilities, Exclusion, and Migrants' Agency in the Pacific Realm workshop. Finally, thank you to my Wabash peer mentoring group who provided sisterhood during the COVID-19 lockdowns and restrictions: Christine Hong, Samira Mehta, Jung Choi, JanJan Lin, Roshan Iqbal, Cuilan Liu, Sailaja Krishnamurti, Harshita Kamath, Zayn Kassam, and Su Pak.

This scholarship has been supported by many fellowships: UC Pacific Rim Research Program; Goldman Sachs Multicultural Junior Fellowship at the Smithsonian Institute; Wagenschein Fellowship in Women's, Gender, and Sexuality Studies; James and Sylvia Thayer Short-Term Research Fellowship at UCLA Special Collections; the Sophia Smith Travel-to-Collections Fellowship; CSUMB start-up funds; and the Citizens and Scholars Early Career Fellowship Program. Parts of this book were originally published in an anthology edited by Judy Tzu-Chun Wu and Catherine Ceniza Choy.

I am incredibly grateful for the local librarians and family members of the people in this book who assisted the final stages of research during a pandemic. Thanks to the Monterey County Free Libraries for access to Ancestry.com. I thank archivist Sue Payne at the California Room in the Feldheym Library for her generous research in local databases. Thank you to Ronald Fujiyoshi and Roger Endo for their insights, photos, and sharing of primary sources. Thanks also to Sara Gray and Elizabeth Fisher for finding photographic gems at the Asilomar Historic Photo archives.

Thanks to the team of editors at the University of Washington Press. Thank you to Mike Baccam for being an endlessly gracious and problem-solving acquisitions editor throughout the review process, Chad Attenborough, Joeth Zucco, and others. Thanks to my peer reviewers, who asked all the right questions and even provided some answers. Thanks to Deborah Oliver for copyediting and Jordan Gonzales for indexing.

Throughout the years, Lily Wong and Quynh Nhu Le have been loving sisters, the best of friends, and the most inspiring and challenging conversation partners. I thank them for reading endless drafts, rallying in times of need, and modeling generosity. Lily Wong and Yan Zheng provided me with housing, food, and friendship when I was an itinerant adjunct for several years and gave me the cutest caregiver: Bunny. Thanks to Becky Romano for our lifelong friendship. Thanks to Jeffrey Trevino, who asks about the people I am writing about, reminds me to take walks on the beach, and listens to my antiracist feminist analyses.

Finally, I thank the strong women in my family who have filled my world since my mother passed away from cancer when I was twelve years old. I especially thank Auntie Betty Hee for her generosity, Auntie Margie Jew and Auntie Helen Lee for their care, and Po Po for her tenacity and strong will. My mother's death, and the subsequent family narratives about her, generated the haunting questions about womanhood and agency that inspire this book. This book is also dedicated to my mother, Alice S. Lau.

NEW WOMEN OF EMPIRE

Introduction

COMING OF AGE in Los Angeles during the 1910s, Lily Satow believed she was in "the unenviable position of belonging to two national groups." The Satows deliberately moved to a white neighborhood uptown to disassociate themselves from the "degrading influence of the crowded downtown Japanese community." Satow became well acquainted with high white culture, accessing a local school and attending a Protestant church. At school, her teachers lavished her with praises and held her up as an example to her white peers. Encouraged by her mother to never bring home anything short of an A, Satow excelled and graduated when she was fifteen years old. At church, Satow embraced Christianity and even dreamed of becoming a missionary. But she often faced racial discrimination. Once, at high tea, she felt embarrassed when her Sunday school teacher gasped at the fact that she did not know how to properly butter her bread. At conventions, some white Christians avoided sitting next to her. Incidents like these led Satow to waver between wishing she had never been born and making it her life's mission to prove them wrong. In her boldest moments, she declared, "Sometimes the haughty demeanor of an American so piqued me that I, too, have tilted up my nose and sat up stiffly with a superior manner, saying to myself, 'Someday, Madame American, you are going to respect me.'"[1]

Satow decided instead to embrace her Japanese roots. She began reading books on Japan and was attracted to the "naiveness and charm of the Japanese." However, what she read did not quite reflect the realities of the downtown Japanese community. She began attending the Japanese Union

Church in downtown Los Angeles. But Satow felt that she did not quite fit in with her Japanese American peers. She was much further along in her studies and she joined a club of young women older than herself rather than join a club made up of her peers. Satow's peers had considered her to be "stuck-up" and a "goody-goody girl." They elected Satow as president of their youth group, the Intermediate Christian Endeavor Society, shouldering her with the responsibility that none of her peers had wanted. Craving friendship, however, Satow tried to mix with the young people at church in their "frivolous pleasures." She proceeded to change into a "wild wicked flapper." She attended parties and played basketball but did not dance because she believed it was the devil. Eventually, she became disgusted by their attitudes of only "having a good time" and "taking it easy." She felt destined for a greater purpose.

Satow became determined to uplift young women in the downtown community. She drew from Japanese and US ideologies. When teaching piano to youths, she engaged in discussions with Japanese immigrant parents, who taught her that she must "rise above the American." She listened to speeches by Stanford historian Yamato Ichihashi, who implored to youths to observe the elder generation's advice and become cultural bridges. Satow wanted to combine the best of both worlds. Envisioning herself as a future mother, she planned to teach her children to "be loyal to America, its flag, and its constitution, and to inculcate them with American ideals," but also the "best" parts of Japanese culture, including "respect for elders, obedience to authority, and politeness."

Satow also read books by prominent Black leaders. She read works by Booker T. Washington and became familiar with his vision of racial uplift among Black communities in the US South, or the responsibility of educated Black people to lift up their race. Washington believed in overcoming racism through trade-based education, with a focus on gradual elevation through accumulation of wealth. She drew inspiration from Ida Jackson, the first Black educator in California, at a Young Women's Christian Association (YWCA) student conference, who supported higher education. She came to a similar approach to racial uplift: "to eliminate prejudice, the standards of the Japanese must be raised and their conditions improved." Satow was attracted to the YWCA Girl Reserves movement that uplifted young women through Christian New Woman values. She had a newfound mission: to become a YWCA social worker and shape the next generation of young Japanese American women.

Histories of US-Pacific relations often center on how immigrant male elites—the first generation of settlers seeking land, economic and ideological expansion—advanced Japanese settler colonialism in the United States. Satow's story reminds us, however, that transnational New Women—a new generation of young women negotiating new and modern Japanese and US gender roles—were central to reshaping the Japanese imperial project to the next generation. When immigrant elites passed down Japanese settler ideologies to the next generation, young women like Satow constantly negotiated their inheritances from the elder generation. Moreover, she drew from the YWCA Girl Reserves and Black scholars to adopt new models of womanhood and respectability. Drawing from both Japanese settler ideologies as well as US imperial movements, Satow developed her vision of a Japanese American New Woman. Satow was part of a new generation of young women and men that negotiated overlapping projects of US and Japanese imperialism to racially uplift Japanese American youths through new gender roles.

New Women of Empire: Gendered Politics and Racial Uplift in Interwar Japanese America excavates the lives of Los Angeles Japanese American reform-minded and reform-affected youth organizers during the first three decades of the twentieth century. The youths came of age during a period of anti-Japanese legislation, including the 1907–8 Gentlemen's Agreement between the United States and Japan, the 1913 and 1920 California Alien Land Laws, and the 1924 Immigration Act. They inherited Japanese elders' hopes and wishes to expand Japan's international reputation and to preserve Japanese modern culture. They were mentored by white Protestant progressives who introduced them to ideas of internationalism, interracial justice, and world friendships. The guiding question of this book is: How did young Japanese American women and men negotiate between overlapping US and Japanese gender-based imperial projects? These young people utilized select components of these imperial ideologies that best fit their vision of community and society building. They became college students, youth-group leaders, recreational coaches, social workers, newspaper journalists, business entrepreneurs, and civic organizers. Young women and men played significant roles as intellectual, spiritual, recreational, and civic reform-minded leaders of their communities who developed a gendered and racial interimperial politics that met the shifting terrains of Japanese and US imperialism.

The first premise of this book is that youth leaders approached the racial uplift of the Los Angeles Japanese American community as part and parcel of the projects of US and Japanese imperialisms. Youth leaders learned and debated over these imperial visions through a variety of ways: reading literature by US and Japanese authors, discussing hot topics in youth groups at ethnic churches, obtaining college degrees in sociology, reading and writing ethnic newspapers, and listening to prominent speakers at conferences. Many youth leaders invested in racial uplift: the responsibility of educated Japanese American youths to lead and develop their communities morally, spiritually, physically, and intellectually. They envisioned racially uplifting their peers through a wide array of alignments as "cultural bridges" between the Japanese and US imperial ideologies. Some envisioned building their intellectual reputation as part of their role in Japanese settler colonialism. Others envisioned advancing the US imperial project of spreading the progressive values to Asia. This book distills the range of alignments, how they intersected in, or were at odds with, racially uplifting youth communities.

The second premise of this book is that young women and men racially uplifted youths through new gender roles. Youth leaders believed the modern woman or New Woman was a central component to the expansion of both Japanese and US imperial projects. Young women inherited and developed their values of the Japanese modern women of "good wife, wise mother" from Japanese settler colonialism and anti-immigrant white nativism. At the same time, young women participated in new movements that advanced the US New Woman: a tidal change in women's roles that enabled young women to maintain respectability while increasing their entrance into the public sphere. Debates over the modern and New Woman, as well as anti-Japanese legislation, also sparked a masculinity crisis among young Japanese American men. Young men had to reconceptualize their masculinity as the expansion of women's roles and racial exclusion challenged and limited settler colonial masculinity. This book argues that an array of transnational New Women and New Men emerged. Some women continued to understand the modern woman as a reiteration of "good wife, wise mother," while others took up a public voice and political role. Meanwhile, some men continued to preserve ideologically radical masculinity while others developed New Men as patriotic and physically fit.

GENDERING EMPIRE IN JAPANESE AMERICAN HISTORY

New Women of Empire centers young women and men as both inheritors and agents of empire. Historians have typically used the terms "Nisei" or "second generation," which originated as part of Japanese settlers' attempts to rewrite history for the purposes of empire building and later by Nisei Week festival planners to encourage young women and men to invest in Japanese American small businesses, to describe a younger set of people, particularly daughters and sons of immigrant families, coming of age in the 1920s and 1930s.[2] Either studied through the lens of US assimilation theory or as a "problem" of Japanese empire building, studies on the youths have understood young women and men as inheritors of cultures within a generational teleology. The generational framework privileges the perspectives of how the first generation or the Issei viewed the second generation or the Nisei, and it leaves the Nisei in their infantile state until their coming to power during World War II. My research shows that a variety of terminology based on age, place of birth, and generation was used to describe young women and men. Their identification varied from "young people" to "American-born" and "second-generation." That their identity vis-à-vis the first Japanese settler male migrants in the 1920s was not yet set in stone is my entry into exploring the messiness and the multiple narratives of how young women and men appeased, pushed back, and redefined empire building.

From the 1920s to the 1930s, young women and men developed their identities and communities under what Eiichiro Azuma calls a period of "adaptive settler colonialism." Azuma defines the Japanese settler colonialism of the late nineteenth century to the first three decades of the twentieth century as "frontier" male migrants as consisting of an ideology and practice of moving to a location external to the home archipelago, engaging in wage labor as a preliminary stage to primitive accumulation, sinking roots by way of farming and building a family, usurpation of land and other fundamental modes of production, development of commercial agricultural economy and the rise of a transplanted "national"/"racial" community often referred to as a "new Japan."[3] In the United States, as elsewhere, migrant communities had to negotiate the colonial metropole with the local political economy at different points in history, or what Azuma calls "adaptive settler colonialism." Because the US, state, and local governments passed racist laws targeting Japanese immigrants, including the 1920 California Alien Land Law, which disallowed "aliens ineligible for citizenship" to own land, and the 1924 US Immigration Act, which disallowed "aliens ineligible for citizenship" to migrate, parts of Japanese settler colonialism were no longer possible, including migration and farming. By the 1920s, during the period of Japanese exclusion, young women and men focused on reforming their communities in the United States, particularly by building a family, developing a commercial agricultural economy, and the rise of a transplanted national/racial community referred to as a "new Japan."

But racism alone does not fully flesh out our understanding of how youths participated in empire building, rather this book heeds the call for gendering the transpacific. Seeking to promote an intersectional analysis of gender and race, historians ask how racialization is a gendered project and how genderization is a racial project.[4] In order to better understand what Azuma calls "private" forms of adaptive settler colonialism within the United States, the historical category of gender provides a useful lens in resituating anti-Japanese legislation. The 1924 Immigration Act was not just a defining moment of racial exclusion but also a gendered one.[5] The 1924 Immigration Act solidified the normative gender roles preceded by earlier immigration policies like the 1907–8 Gentlemen's Agreement, which banned the future migration of male laborers, who were assumed to be the only gender fitting under the category of "laborers," though it enabled the migration of family members under the assumption that migrant women would not be "laborers." However, when immigrant women who were trained to become housewives instead labored in the fields, anti-Japanese agitators built their case for exclusion around the protection of the white nuclear family. Although Japanese community leaders worked with the Japanese government to stop issuing visas to picture brides, policy makers passed the 1924 Immigration Act and disallowed the future migration of all Japanese immigrants. The 1924 Immigration Act solidified in the minds of elites that acceptable immigrant women remained in the home.

New Women of Empire argues the 1924 Immigration Act, and anti-Japanese sentiment, in general, catalyzed the reshaping of gender roles for youths. Elites adapted women's roles to US racism by promoting uplift in two ways: encouraging Americanization (code for proper domesticity) in the home among elder women, and discouraging Americanization (code for expanding gender roles) outside the home among young women. Japanese associations' reform programs targeted immigrant women. Sidney Lu researched how the Japanese government trained emigrant women as *ryōsai kenbo*, "good wife, wise mother," both to serve the Japanese empire abroad and to assuage US racism.[6] Shiori Nomura argues that Japanese immigrant motherhood and birth control were shaped by the charge to establish a healthy and civilized Japanese immigrant community acceptable to US society.[7] In contrast, young women were often warned against becoming "too Americanized" or of stepping outside of the purview of "good wife, wise mother." Elite parents discouraged young women from entering men's professions, instead directing them to enter acceptable women's occupations. Young women learned proper domesticity through US institutions. Community leaders discouraged young women from new courtship practices, such as dating and dancing, and from divorce.

This was also a time of changing roles for young men. While Japanese elders responded to the 1924 Immigration Act by disciplining young women into acceptable women's spheres, Japanese elders expanded and encouraged new avenues of masculinity. The 1924 act emasculated a new generation of young men by foreclosing economic avenues of pioneering manhood to young Japanese immigrant men without US citizenship. The 1920 California Alien Land Law and the US Supreme Court case of Takao Ozawa—which maintained that Japanese immigrants were in fact "aliens ineligible for citizenship"—foreclosed Japanese settlers from fulfilling their charge to farm new settlements. Elites adapted to the racial exclusion by redirecting young men to build their masculinity in two arenas that were not bound to US borders or citizenship: intellectualism and athleticism. Elders encouraged young men to seek self-respect measured not by national citizenship but by the world. Moreover, young men imagined a new hierarchy: the United States and Japan would be the two leading empires of the world.

While young women and men inherited adaptive Japanese settler colonial gender roles, they were also shaped by the gendered moral uplift projects of US imperialism abroad. Historians have identified that, from the 1920s to the 1930s, although the US government adopted isolationist policies, Christian progressives continued to expand the US empire through moral uplift outside the United States. Ian Tyrrell argues that the YMCA was among the many US organizations that began to try to establish a US "moral empire," or cultural hegemony, around the globe.[8] During the 1920s, YMCA organizers worked abroad to spread muscular Christianity—what Clifford Putney argues as the ideal Christian manliness shaped by competitive sports and physical education—in Japan. Ikuo Abe argues that Japanese Christians created a hybrid form of muscular Christianity.[9]

From the 1920s to the 1940s, the global crossings of missionaries who spread protestant Christian values in parts of Asia arose in conjunction with teachers and Christian leaders that turned to focus on Americanizing children of immigrants in the United States. Sarah Griffith has studied how US YMCA workers traveled across the Pacific and later brought their ideologies back to inform their civil rights organizing in the United States.[10] YMCA secretaries from Japan traveled to give speeches to young Japanese American boys in the United States and inspired them to partake in Y work. Because of the interest and organizing of young boys, teachers and social workers of the kindergarten movement as well as the YMCA expanded their outreach to young Japanese American boys. They created segregated schools, clubs, and facilities for the purposes of raising young men to become acquainted with democratic governance, self-discipline, and masculine athleticism. Young men participated in US moral reform through modern sports and the YMCA.

Young women's participation in US moral reform departed from that of young men. The scholarship on US women's history suggests that women's movements like the YWCA embraced internationalism from the 1920s to the 1930s. Historians have researched how organizations and groups of women from different nations built friendship or bonds across borders, identified common issues, addressed interracial justice, and worked toward affecting diplomacy. However, US internationalists often exercised their own forms of cultural imperialism, such as imposing ideas of progress, modernity, femininity onto others. Still, young women in colonial outposts or communities of color within the colonial metropole embraced women's organizations for their own subversive goals.[11] For instance, Rumi Yasutake argues that when viewed from the perspectives of urban middle-class women activists in Japan, the internationalist movement of the Women's Christian Temperance Union (WCTU) provided opportunities for improving the status of Japan.[12] Japanese immigrant churchwomen sought to create resources for middle-class women, disassociate themselves from prostitutes, and participate in building a better international reputation for their local Japanese immigrant community.

By the 1920s, young Japanese American women learned a new international model of girlhood through the YWCA Girl Reserves movement. This book extends the research of Kristine Alexander, who argues that the Girl Guides of the 1920s and 1930s attempted to create a conservatively modern ideal of imperial and international girlhood.[13] Born from anxieties around young women's changing roles who preferred leisure to domesticity as well as debates over immigration and Americanization, the YWCA Girl Reserve movement sought to create a cohesive national community of girls that were trained in Christian and patriotic values. By the 1920s, YWCA social workers reached out to daughters of immigrant families and women of color, who would be a cultural bridge to influencing immigrant mothers. Women of the YWCA saw themselves as a cosmopolitan organization that sought to spread progressive and democratic values. They worked toward a future world of promoting anti-imperialism and interracial justice. At the same time, this book builds on the scholarship of Valerie Matsumoto, who argues that YWCA girls' clubs served as bulwarks against racial discrimination as well as a resource to gain skills.[14] Young women utilized girls' clubs to expand their freedoms by mediating the parental pressures they faced at home as well as racism at school. The Japanese American Girl Reserves movement provided vital support and a measure of agency for youths who faced racial segregation, which prevented their full participation in US society.

New Women of Empire argues that both US and Japanese imperial projects intersected and overlapped to cultivate young women and men into modern gendered ideals. To solve both US anxieties around the flaming youths—a name derived from popular literature and film and often used by observers or critics commenting on a new generation of youths who desired expansions of sexual freedom—as well as what Japanese elites called the second-generation problem, Japanese Christian elites and white Christian social workers combined their efforts to uplift Japanese American youths as moral, disciplined, and both American and Japanese. Japanese elites and white social workers emphasized developing young men as patriotic, masculine, and muscular. Meanwhile, they encouraged young women to embrace domesticity, social hygiene, and service. Through such modern gender ideals, young women and men would become the cultural bridges to mend and build better relations between the United States and Japan.

This book emphasizes the agency of young women and men who negotiated the differently modern gendered ideals of both Japanese elites and white social workers. Many embraced leadership positions as Y secretaries and club presidents that helped shape modern gender roles. Young women found that what both Japanese elites and white social workers viewed as modern gendered ideals were not one and the same, especially when it came to the ideals of the New Woman. Young women received the brunt of the criticism when they began girls' clubs and defended their club activities like holding dances. When Japanese elites wrote editorials criticizing the emergence of youth clubs, young women wrote back to defend the purpose of such clubs. Young women and men held community town halls to discuss with parents, social workers, and community elites who had concerns about too much dancing and divorce. Through constant negotiation, young women and men created modern gendered alignments that simultaneously encouraged conservative and progressive qualities.

Young women and men negotiated between these overlapping projects of the US and Japanese empires to create a wide range of transnational gendered alignments and imagined alternative futures throughout the interwar period. As young women and men began to build their local and global communities, they entered into these imperial projects from different access points based on gender, citizenship and immigration status, class and occupational or professional status, and family lineage. Social workers cared deeply about the reform of their peers while others were less invested. Some were more invested in US internationalism while others promoted Japanese empire building. Some envisioned more peaceful relations between the US and Japan, while others saw the United States and Japan as the two coleading empires of the world. These gendered uplift projects also had to adapt and shift alongside the economic and political changes across the decades, including the Roaring Twenties, the Great Depression and the New Deal, and the rise of the Sino-Japanese War. This book examines just a sampling of the New Women and New Men that emerged during the growing empires of the United States and Japan in the 1920s and 1930s.

A TRANSNATIONAL APPROACH TO THE NEW WOMAN

New Women of Empire applies a transnational approach to the study of the New Woman. Historians have typically studied the New Woman as a modern conception of femininity within a regional or national context. I use transnationalism to focus on the interconnections between two nations bordering the Pacific ocean and their growing imperial visions.[15] A transnational framework encourages us to reimagine the Japanese American woman's experience, not simply as adaptation and integration into the US nation-state, but to explore the persistent connections with their or their parents' homeland, other diasporic communities, and shared or divergent ideologies. I take a transnational approach in three main ways. First, I examine what shaped the emergence and qualities of the New Woman: the social and cultural factors in the United States, US relations with Japan, and Japan's policies and practices toward the diasporic communities outside of Japan. Second, whereas social and political movements typically associated with the New Woman, such as temperance, suffrage, and progressivism have been studied as domestic ones, this book places the progressive movement as part of expanding US imperialism abroad. Finally, just as the New Woman emerged in the United States, so too did the modern girl take Japan by storm. Japanese ideologies of modern womanhood remained ever so present in parental and community raising of youths. Young women drew from multiple models of femininities.

This book examines how young women negotiated between the US imperial project of the New Woman and the Japanese imperial project of the modern woman to create the transnational New Woman. The transnational

New Woman was a social phenomenon rooted in both US and Japanese imperialism from the 1920s to the 1940s. Organizers combined racial uplift with modern femininity. Defined by her commitment to a measure of independence, but at the same time bearing the responsibility to the family, the typical transnational New Woman was college-educated and believed in women's expanded roles in the public sphere as well as a seriousness for the practice of mothering and homemaking. She was physically active as well as professionally trained in musical talents. Unlike her mother's generation of arranged marriages, she chose her marriage partner, but only with parental approval. The YWCA movement and Japanese female elders alike supported the transnational New Woman. At the same time, the transnational New Woman generated controversy. She was misunderstood and the subject of mockery by Japanese male elites. She at once challenged older models of masculinity and adapted to new ones.

This book situates the transnational New Woman in the historiography of the US New Woman. Scholars have overwhelmingly studied the New Woman as part of white middle-class feminism that sought to expand women's roles and rights both in the home and the public sphere.[16] But this book takes its cue from the multiethnic turn. Scholars of African American women's history, including Evelyn Higginsbothom, Deborah Gray White, Victoria Wolcott, and Erin Chapman, have argued that the sociopolitical factors of racism and class differences, the mobilization of ethnic nationalism, and diasporic networks shaped a woman of color's interpretation of the New Woman. For New Negro Women, because of the long history of sexual violence toward Black women and stereotypes of Black female immorality, Black middle-class reformers discouraged open sexuality—which their counterparts were not doing for New white Women. Black women combined the New Negro movement with the New Woman and developed a politics of respectability.[17] LaShawn Harris argues that Black women who were deemed unrespectable, who worked as sex workers, psychics, and numbers runners, developed their own definitions of respectability and enjoyed measures of freedom within an underground economy.[18]

New Women of Empire fills a void in the historiography of the US New Woman by examining racial uplift and the Japanese American New Woman. Japanese American women developed a politics of respectability in response to US racism. Building on the scholarship on Japanese prostitution in the United States during the late nineteenth and early twentieth centuries, my research shows that the earlier history of hypersexualization and orientalism shaped community discouragement of young women's participation in sexual expression. Amy Sueyoshi argues that representations of Japanese and Chinese women as geisha or prostitute mirrored anxieties around the expansion of gender and sexuality for white womanhood, particularly the rise of the modern woman and fear over white slavery. As discussions over explorations of gender and sexuality waned and sexual morality rose, the Chinese and Japanese subjects merged into the immoral pan Asian American caricature of an "Oriental" simultaneously geisha and prostitute in a single body.[19] Kazuhiro Oharazeki found that, by the 1910s, antiprostitution reforms removed prostitutes from the public sphere in order to protect Japan's national honor.[20] This history of US orientalism toward Japanese immigrant women, followed by the antiprostitution efforts, shaped the approach of Japanese American female reformers as well as the larger community response to the flapper. By the 1920s, many in the community discouraged young Japanese American women from participating in the expansion of sexual freedom in the proliferation of dancing, dating, and social interactions.

Young Japanese American women in Los Angeles developed multiple avenues of respectability, including an intellectual uplift culture that promoted interimperial respectability and a working woman's subculture that developed alternate respectability. By the 1920s, young women engaged with white Christian progressive reformers and the new US imperial project of the YWCA Girl Reserves by the 1920s. Young women encountered a Christian youth culture devoted to the development of their spirituality, health, discipline, and entrance into professional jobs. The Girl Reserves promoted sex education, or abstinence before marriage, and provided clubs to maintain their respectability. Young women devoted their time and energies to social service and the uplift of their communities. At the other end of the spectrum, young women engaged with a popular and global flapper youth culture. A vibrant working-class Japanese American youth culture flourished in the downtown Los Angeles community. Young women joined clubs, bobbed their hair, went to picture shows, attended dances, and listened to popular music. Young women participated in industrial or secretarial work and unapologetically enjoyed spending their money and time on their leisure.

But US racism was not the only determining factor toward Japanese American politics of respectability. Many looked askance at the flapper as an example of Japanese imperial decline. The modern girl posed a crisis to reformers, who had previously endorsed the ideology "good wife, wise mother" in Japan and Japanese emigrants. This book also situates the Japanese American New Woman in the historiography of the Japanese modern woman. Gail Bernstein has linked women's changing roles to modernization during the Meiji and Taisho periods. During the Meiji period, Japan pursued Westernization by creating a centralized government and constitution, a powerful army and navy, and a highly educated population. The Japanese government also remade gender roles by promoting the "good wife, wise mother" ideology. Departing from previous expectations that valued women for their roles as daughters-in-law and wives, for the first time in Japanese history the words "wise mother" signaled the newly recognized importance of education of all women so they could better perform their home duties and child-rearing. The new ideal woman represented a composite of the feminine virtues of various Japanese classes, including modesty, courage, frugality, literacy, hard work, and productivity—to generate a cult of productivity for the nation's growth. Politics was an inappropriate activity since women needed to concentrate on managing the home, educating their children, and promoting economic development—that was their civil service to the nation.[21]

However, as Japan entered into a period of imperial democracy in the Taisho period, women voiced their desire for new gender roles. For the first time, Japanese women themselves partook in the national conversations about defining femininity or womanhood through groups such as the Bluestockings (Seitô).[22] Writers demanded state support of family, female suffrage, and equal economic opportunity. The Taisho period was defined by the *moga*: a sexually liberated, urban consumer who symbolized new freedoms and liberations. Barbara Sato researches the everyday life of urban women and consumerism in the 1920s: the bobbed-haired, short-skirted modern girl, the self-motivated housewife, and the rational, extroverted professional working woman. Through their everyday engagement with consumerism, urban women were "redefining the modern."[23] The modern girl symbolized a national crisis for the government in Japan, as well as, I argue, empire building abroad. My research examines how Japanese imperialism and ideas of modernity shaped Japanese American women in the United States.

Young Japanese American women in Los Angeles engaged the Japanese imperial project of the modern woman in several ways. They reported and read about women's issues in Japan in the community newspaper. However, much of their engagement with the *moga* or other Japanese women writers was mediated through community guardians of true Japaneseness: parents whose stated expertise on Japanese culture determined what young women were and were not allowed to do and educated elite who discouraged flapper-associated values to promote diplomacy between United States and Japan. The Japanese imperial project of "good wife, wise mother" had deeply influenced Japanese immigrant parents and elders and their raising of young women. To avoid social stigma, parents mediated young women's expanding social interactions and sexual freedom through chaperonage, curfew, and familial obligations. Parental strictness combined with outspoken intellectual elite women, whose travels to Japan shaped their gender ideals. Intellectual elite women promoted a philosophy known as "moderation of Americanization." Japanese American modernists promoted a eugenics solution to the wholesale adoption of the flapper: to pick and choose the best traits of the Japanese and white womanly virtues for the growth of interimperial relations.

New Women of Empire examines how Japanese American elders and reform-minded youths continued to promote the modern woman as the homemaker, evolved from the Japanese imperial concept of "good wife, wise mother." Shizuko Koyama argues that *ryōsai kenbo*, "good wife, wise mother," continued to be a widely accepted notion that reflected the expectations and aspirations of many modern Japanese women in Japan.[24] It therefore asks us to revisit the US New Woman not only as a tidal change but also how the "good wife, wise mother" ideology shaped the New Woman. My research found that Japanese elites continued to encourage the "good wife, wise mother" ideologies onto young women in multiple disciplinary ways. From parental advice in line with Japanese imperial ideologies, such as deciding their choice of college education in acceptable women's fields, to a partnership with US institutions like the sex education movement and home economics, that reaffirmed the qualities of "good wife, wise mother." Young women continued to have dreams of marriage and grand weddings, thought about what kind of mother they wanted to be, and daydreamed about furnishing their dream home. Many believed it was new and modern to be women of the home.

TRANSNATIONAL CHRISTIAN YOUTH MOVEMENT

New Women and Christian youth organizations that cultivated modern gender roles contributed to what I call the long racial formation of the model minority. Historians have argued that Japanese American Christian student organizations in the prewar era contributed to the long civil rights movement.[25] While most studies have focused on national student organizations like the Japanese Student Christian Association (JSCA), this book examines off-campus local organizations for both college students and nonstudents like the youth groups of ethnic churches, such as the Christian Endeavor and Epworth League, as well as the YWCA Girl Reserves and YMCA boys' clubs. Building on the idea that the YWCA and YMCA provided both conservative and progressive possibilities, my research shows that Japanese American Christian student organizing contributed to the making of both the long civil rights movement as well as the long model minority. The model minority we come to know in the 1960s, what Ellen Wu argues as an ethnic minority viewed as well-assimilated, self-reliant, politically nonthreatening, nondelinquent and "not-Black," can be traced to community racial uplift of the 1920s.[26]

During the interwar period, reformers envisioned using Christianity to uplift Los Angeles youths. For instance, many elders believed that Christianity could be a tool to prevent the ghettoization of youths. Moreover, white youth group leaders politicized youths through group discussions on the possibilities of war between Japan and the US Japanese American youth leaders utilized Christian organizations to uplift their peers through education, fitness, and wholesome fun. They all promote a range of interimperial coalitions, from interracial justice to a global racial hierarchy. However, other young people who were the subjects of reform utilized Christian organizations for a variety of different reasons that subverted imperial ambitions. I call them "reformees" rather than "reformed" to highlight the agency and negotiation that young people practiced rather than suggest a passive acceptance of reformers' goals. Some young people used youth groups to find a community of ethnic peers. Others used it to provide and expand access to resources, such as gym facilities or opportunities for leisure. Many youths were disillusioned and disinvested from community efforts to show they were equal or superior. In examining racial uplift from the reformer and reformee perspectives, my research explores the aspect of the model minority stereotype often taken for granted: elision of class inequality and the mobilization of status shaming within the ethnic group.

New Women and New Men participated in a transnational Christian youth movement: the creation of mixed-gender communities as well as gender-based social groups to cultivate young people as ambassadors toward improved relations between the US and Japanese empires. By the 1920s, ethnic churches used "young people" to describe a younger set of people—in their teenage years and early twenties, regardless of citizenship or immigration status—that presented different spiritual needs and wants than the elder immigrant congregation. Young people yearned for a space of their own—a service in the English language, discussions and themes relevant to their lives, and a community of peers. After World War I, Young People's Societies extended their reach in the Christian internationalist movement to unite the world through peace and friendship, establishing Christian Endeavors and Epworth Leagues in churches in the United States. Ethnic churches in Los Angeles, including the Japanese Christian Institute and the Japanese Union Church, adopted the Christian Endeavor as an organizing society for young people. In the Christian Endeavor, young people and particularly young women took leadership positions and determined the programming of their youth fellowship. In contrast, the Japanese Methodist Episcopal Church adopted the Epworth League, in which women did not take leadership positions and elders took direct control over the fellowship for youths. While the Christian Endeavor societies were instrumental in recruiting youths into US social work and developing leadership skills, the Epworth League reinforced Japanese elder's vision of settler colonial projects and patriarchal gender roles.

New Women of Empire argues that the simultaneity of both conservative and progressive possibilities in Japanese American Christian youth organizing paved the way for both model minority making and civil rights organizing in gender-specific ways. Men's intellectual uplift was more closely aligned with the making of the model minority. I define the model minority in the 1920s and 1930s as an ethnic minority viewed as well-assimilated, self-reliant, politically nonthreatening, nondelinquent, and compliant with gender order. Some young men aligned conservative aspects of US Christianity with Japanese militant imperialism to reinforce a major underpinning of the model minority: patriarchal values. They believed a return to nuclear family Christian morals would resolve and maintain civic order of what he perceived to be a problem society for the Japanese diaspora. Young men expressed reactionary sentiments toward the changing roles of women. Discouraging young men from participating in activities that were criminalized, like gambling, intellectual leaders encouraged the organization of basketball, baseball, and football among Japanese American youths. The institution of the family would become the Orientalized basis for presenting Japanese Americans as the solution to racial inequality. New intelligentsia men expressed an early vision of the sociological argument of the model minority: a racial minority that did not rely on welfare and held a comparably better racial standing than other minority groups.

Between US moral reform and Japanese racial uplift, young Japanese American men developed a transnational muscular Christianity: a Christian commitment to manliness and health and a passionate attachment to ethnicity. Young reformers and young reformees approached athletics in a variety of ways. Some reformers believed athletics would discipline young men and keep them astray from other forms of leisure like gambling. Some athletes wanted to expand recreation across the Japanese American community, whether to create more resources or to find new opponents or competitors. Other athletes enjoyed the community or comradery of sports teams and clubs for leisurely reasons. Other youth leaders believed that sports provided an effective tool of impressing values of patriotic duty, manliness, and self-discipline. At the same time, elder business leaders invested in expanding the ethnic economy looked to build their new consumer base around youth athletics, as Lon Kurashige argues.[27] Youth reformers combined muscular Christianity and the ethnic economy to develop a Japanese American fraternalism around US sports.

By the 1920s, YWCA Girl Reserves developed young women through social work and as cultural ambassadors—which lent itself to the model minority and an emergent Japanese American feminism. Some young Japanese American women joined the YWCA Girl Reserves to elevate their own status as well as the status of the community, and they disassociated from the flapper lifestyle—a formula for the model minority. Young Japanese American women utilized their positions within the YWCA to build alliances with white Christian liberals and maintain the integrity of the Japanese American community's public image. Valuing virtuosity, self-improvement, abstinence, purposeful meaning for how to live, Japanese American youth leaders aimed to racially uplift young women in the cities. Nonetheless, the YWCA Girl Reserves provided a social service to develop a girl's recreation, fellowship, work, and religion. By 1926, the YWCA resolved to address racial discrimination and actively recruit more women of color into the organization and take on leadership positions. Some young Japanese American women who took on a leadership role approached the Girl Reserves as one of social service. Some participated in the YWCA Girl Reserves because they believed in the project of interracial justice—the roots of Japanese American feminism. Indeed, Valerie Matsumoto has argued that young women learned the value of civic participation and utilized club activities in the 1920s and 1930s as a building block for community organizing during World War II and the civil rights movement.[28]

This history of Japanese American youth reform reminds us why racial uplift is limited. Young Japanese American women faced racial tokenization within white Christian activist spaces. Reform movements used young Japanese American women to advance the New Woman and reform immigrant communities. Youths were expected to serve as the cultural bridges between Japanese American communities and the YWCA, particularly as interpreters to Japanese immigrant parents. Young Japanese American women were often given the diversity role at larger gatherings, and rarely ever did they move beyond tokenization. At the same time, reformers bolstered existing race, class, and gender hierarchies. Only women from higher-status families or families that prioritized racial uplift could afford to receive a higher education, participate in the activities of the Girl Reserves, and be concerned with their public image. Farmers, women and men from indebted families fixed to lowbrow economies, and women who partook in unapologetically selfish leisure did not find access to these spaces and/or were frowned upon. Racial uplift was a tool to use the unrespectable, those considered the cause of imperial decline, in ways that elided this history of intercommunity harm.

YOUNG PEOPLE

I first conceived of this book while reading life histories of young people at the Hoover Institution Archives. Funded by Christians and educated elites during the 1920s, the Survey of Race Relations is an archive of interviews conducted by sociologists with multiple racial and ethnic groups. Previous scholarship has focused on the organizers of the survey, whereas I am much more interested in the people surveyed.[29] And while other scholarship examines these youths' interviews at a broad generational scale, I take a closer look at five main youth organizers.[30] Who are these youths that sociologists chose to interview? Why are these youths selected as representatives of their communities? What was their relationship to the interviewers? And what happened to them after the interviews?

I followed the same five young people from the survey to the ethnic newspapers. Not only did the survey's white Christian organizers identify these young people as leaders of their communities, but immigrant elites and youth peers did so as well. Sources like the Japanese American Los Angeles newspaper *Rafu Shimpo* highlighted young people in leadership and participation in urban youth culture. By 1926, its editor was a transnational New Woman: Louise Suski. Suski had grown up in Los Angeles, was raised by well-to-do parents, and majored in education at the University of California, Los Angeles.[31] The *Rafu Shimpo*'s English-language section offers a youth's vision and reporting of urban youth culture in the 1920s and 1930s.

In addition to surveys and ethnic newspapers, their stories are also pieced together through bits and pieces in local newspapers, records of Christian organizations, and the US Census. These sources provide another perspective on the relationships between and among youths and local townspeople, their churches, and the state. Local newspapers provided a wealth of information about how small rural towns engaged with Japanese American youths. Christian youth organizations' records showed the activities of youths in social service organizations like the YWCA Girl Reserves as well as emerging youth groups in ethnic churches like the Christian Endeavor. Moreover, census data provided a wealth of information about young people, including family lineage, college yearbooks, residence, occupation, and voter registration.

Set in Los Angeles, this is the story of young people at the center of making the US and Japanese empires in the interwar period. Los Angeles became the leading city with the highest Japanese population and the most extensive youth networks in the 1920s and 1930s, surpassing San Francisco and Seattle. In 1920, US-born youths made up over one-fourth of the Japanese American population in Los Angeles; by 1930, they made up about half of the entire Japanese American population of Los Angeles.[32] In Los Angeles in 1936, there were "66 second generation Japanese organizations, whose members range from 18 years of age and up."[33] Youth developers contributed by modernizing the main street of Japanese immigrant quarters, lined with immigrant and later youth-run businesses. About thirteen ethnic churches in the Los Angeles area provided the main form of community and spiritual life by 1924.[34] During this era, youth groups helped to fund-raise to build resources for themselves, such as gymnasiums and church buildings. They often repurposed clubhouses, school gyms, dormitories, and churches in order to hold their own events and meetings. In addition, Los Angeles also hosted numerous colleges where a rapidly growing population of Japanese American youths began to attend, including the University of California Los Angeles, University of Southern California, Occidental College, and Los Angeles City College. And finally, Los Angeles became a major metropolitan stop for visiting Japanese university sports teams and a port from which young people set sail for tours of Japan.

This book is organized thematically across five chapters. In each chapter I focus on one young person and utilize their life story as a window into a reform movement and gender role of the interwar period. The reforms centered on farming, intellectualism, modesty, athletics, and social work. Each theme reflects a young person's entry point to major institutions, including the ethnic church, universities, local businesses, municipal government, but the themes also reflect the person's engagement with major social movements, including Christian internationalism, the Americanization movement, the Progressive movement, and Japanese imperialism. Youths were heterogeneous in their vision for how to racially uplift their communities—sometimes they agreed, and in other moments they were at odds. By focusing on one young person, each chapter maps the changes and shifts to their lives, as well as the changes they brought about, over the course of the Roaring Twenties and Great Depression, between the closing of the US gates and the eve of World War II. Youths developed a transnational politics that aligned with the shifting terrain of US and Japanese imperialism.

Chapter 1 begins with female reformee, the Americanized, and the figure of national debate: the farmer. Various groups refracted their political anxieties and imperatives on her ideal or expected gender role. By centering a farmer's daughter, an unlikely New Woman, in a small rural town on the outskirts of Los Angeles, Susie Yamamoto's story invites us to look at social and political movements that have long gone unexamined in relation to the New Woman. Young rural women's expected gender roles shifted between a woman's proper place in the home and a woman's entrance into men's work, depending on the prevailing political agenda of local or national movements across the decades. Various political factions, including anti-Japanese labor agitators, Japanese imperialists, country life reformers, city governance and small corporations, benefitted or had much to lose when it came to endorsing or opposing women's work in traditionally men's spheres. Young women developed ways to protect themselves alongside these competing factions and mediate their respectability. By centering the rural New Woman in local and international politics, chapter 1 illuminates the centrality of gender roles as an organizing tool in shaping immigration exclusion policies and progressive movements, as well as the agency of rural New Women.

Chapters 2 and 3 examine the reformers that closely aligned with Japanese imperialism and modern gender roles. Chapter 2 focuses on the male reformer, the academic, and the militant radical: the settler colonial journalist. This chapter examines how Masao Dodo and other young male reformers adapted Japanese imperial ideology in the aftermath of their emasculation due to the passage of the 1924 Immigration Act. No longer able to pursue settler colonial masculinity through land ownership or citizenry, reformers moved toward the remaking of young manhood through intellectualism. During the expansion of women's roles and the increasing anti-intellectualism of youths, Dodo preserved his patriarchal values and imperial ideologies through masculine-centered institutions such as the ethnic church, college fraternities, and the immigrant press. Dodo employed model minority politics when building their society alongside other settlements across the diaspora. He envisioned the United States and Japan aligning to take their rightful places as the two leading empires of the world.

Chapter 3 spotlights the female reformer who never cared for dancing, the bearer of responsibility to the family and to the church: the homemaker. This chapter excavates how young women adapted and safeguarded modern Japanese ideas of "good wife, wise mother" amid a nascent morally loose and sexually free urban youth culture. Young women negotiated between their parents' adherence to strict moral values and a quiet family home life and their peers' loosening moral values and new vibrant social and leisure life. Chiyo Otera and other young women approached Americanization through moderation, or the selection of the high culture traits of the United States and Japan. Otera adapted Japanese modern womanhood to US new womanhood in respectable ways. She safeguarded her modesty through the ethnic church's youth groups, the YWCA Girl Reserves, and marriage. As a daughter and then as a wife and mother, she also put her family first, before her community responsibilities. Ultimately, Otera enjoyed the privileges of the US adaptation of "good wife, wise mother." Through a spotlight on highbrow young women, this chapter examines the lasting influences of Japanese modern ideology of "good wife, wise mother" onto young women.

The final two chapters examine reform-minded youths that more closely aligned with US imperialism through new gender roles. Chapter 4 discusses the male reformer, the athlete, and the party-thrower: the market man. Examining the life story of Gene Sakamoto, this chapter charts how US internationalism and muscular Christianity intersected with Japanese adaptive imperialism to mold Japanese American masculinity in a second arena: athleticism. Unable to access intellectual masculinity, Sakamoto apprenticed under teachers who promoted Americanization through civic education and social workers who aimed to racially uplift young boys through organized sport. At the same time, Japanese immigrant business leaders who employed young men like Sakamoto also had a vested economic interest in developing youth sports as part of their new consumer base. This chapter examines how Sakamoto built a recreational masculinity that aligned US sports culture with an ethnic connectedness to the Japanese market. Sakamoto and other recreational leaders promoted transnational muscular Christianity—a movement around athletics that instilled in young men patriotism, discipline, and self-sacrifice to the United States while cultivating fraternalism and consumerism around Japanese goods and services.

Chapter 5 deals with the female reformer, the reluctant pianist, and lover of books: the social worker. Through an examination of the role of the Japanese American female social reformer as embodied by Lily Satow, this chapter tracks the evolving alliance between Western imperialism and Japanese modernization from the period of US imperialism to US internationalism. In contrast to earlier alliances of Western imperialism and Japanese modernization, where women's reforms focused on proper domesticity and musical education, the YWCA espoused a new model of womanhood, the Girl Reserves, in the age of US internationalism. The Girl Reserves promoted healthy, spiritual, knowledgeable, and service-oriented young women. This chapter examines how Satow led the transnational Girl Reserves movement: a model of womanhood that served as cultural ambassadors and advanced interracial justice. While this chapter shows the lasting effects of US new womanhood on young Japanese American women, it also examines the limits of US progressivism in embracing racial justice.

Collectively, these five chapters chronicle the rise of a new generation of young people that negotiated Japanese and US imperialism in dynamic complex ways. Young people's racial politics and social worlds were deeply informed by the immigration debates of the 1920s. They researched, listened, and discussed the issues at length in church settings with white social workers and Japanese leaders. At the same time, young people were not merely reflections of the immigrant elite or their parents, in fact, they felt continuously scrutinized by older members of the community who disagreed with their choices. Young people found tools to face exclusion and mediate tensions by maintaining good public relations, utilizing Christian networks, adapting Japanese imperialism, remaking American imperialism, building community recreation and leisure, and embracing new gender roles.

1

The Rural New Woman

SUSIE YAMAMOTO, A farmer's daughter from the small city of San Bernardino, opened her interview for the Survey of Race Relations by showcasing her resilience in the face of exclusion laws. Despite the recent passage of the 1924 Immigration Act, Yamamoto asserted that she had had very little trouble, and in fact she was thriving. She exclaimed, "I was born in America and have spent a great deal of my time with Americans so that I feel quite free with them and I have had no difficulties with them." Importantly, although Yamamoto had just declared that she was born in the United States, making her a US citizen, she still adhered to the prevailing assumption set by white supremacy of the time period that "American" meant "white." She established her reputation as a beloved person among small-town whites, explaining that since she was "the only Japanese girl" in San Bernardino High School, everyone knew her and treated her courteously. She boasted of her popularity around town, with the mayor frequently stopping by to say "hi" and the local judge or district attorney often calling her in for assistance in translation.[1]

The only time she felt insecure about her status was when she went on joyrides in the automobile with her white friends and witnessed Japanese immigrant women working in the fields. Anti-Japanese crusaders had weaponized women's traditional roles to rally for the renewal of the California Alien Land Law and the exclusion of Japanese immigrants in the

1924 US Immigration Act. Japanese immigrant women received the brunt of the backlash as anti-Japanese crusaders highlighted that Japanese immigrant women's work in the fields was improper and threatened whites' economic status and national goals. Yamamoto herself was running a hog farm with her mother, so in many ways, they could have been talking about her. But she did not mention once that she was in the hog farming business in the interview and instead, made a show of her disapproval of women working in the fields. She confessed that, when she went joyriding with her white friends, she felt humiliated because they saw Japanese women working in the fields. She publicly agreed with anti-Japanese critics: "I think they shouldn't work in the fields on Sunday, at any rate I don't blame the Americans for saying things about them." In fact, she told her own story that fit neatly into the anti-Japanese crusaders' rhetoric. Since Japanese women performed men's work in the fields, as anti-Japanese arguments lamented, they neglected their children and brought down the standard of living. Yamamoto reported feeling similarly: "One day when I was driving in San Bernardino with some of my American friends, as we passed a Japanese vegetable stand, the woman in charge called to me. I was greatly embarrassed because her voice seemed so loud and then her child was so very dirty."

Her embarrassment deepened when Yamamoto moved to the city of Los Angeles to attend the University of Southern California and encountered a nascent urban youth culture. She joined a youth group at the Japanese Methodist Episcopal Mission. Whenever they went to the movies, they received funny looks from white moviegoers. Yamamoto felt uncomfortable and, from then on, only went out in public with youths who were "well Americanized." To make sure that she was also well Americanized, Yamamoto began to work in a white middle-class home as a schoolgirl—that is, a young woman attending school and performing housework in a home in exchange for room and board.[2] While it was common for young Japanese American women to work for money doing domestic chores as they pursued higher education, Yamamoto did so despite the discouragement of her mother and at the cost of a status reversal. As a landowner, as a contributor to a profitable family business, as a college student, Yamamoto did not have to be a domestic worker. But she revealed the lengths she would go to protect herself: "to get rid of any of this awkwardness I am at present working in an American home just to learn their ways and their etiquette: I want to be able to go any place and not make any breaks." Yamamoto wanted to learn proper domesticity so that she could pass easily under the scrutinous eyes of white surveyors policing normative gender roles.

Yamamoto's story changes our understanding of the impact of the 1924 Immigration Act on to US womanhood. By the 1920s, middle-class white women had made significant strides for women's rights in the United States, such as the right to vote and women's increasing entrance into the public sphere. Women like Yamamoto enjoyed the newfound access to the public sphere such as riding in cars or going to the movies. However, the racist accusations of anti-Japanese agitators put a national spotlight on women's work on the farms, which Yamamoto, as a farmer's daughter, purposefully omitted in her interview. Both white liberal Christians and Japanese imperial leaders responded to racial exclusion by organizing women's roles in the home. Yamamoto even made a show of how she went against her mother's wishes to abide by white conventional understandings of gender. Unlike white middle-class women whose modernity was defined by their departure from the home, the organizing politics around Japanese exclusion defined modern for Japanese American women as their domestic role in the home.

Young Japanese American women's shift back to the home was but the first of many shifts that Yamamoto experienced between the Roaring Twenties and the Great Depression. This chapter argues that the expected gender roles of the rural young women shifted across the changing political tides between US anti-immigrant nativism, progressive movements and Japanese imperialism from the 1920s to the 1930s. White farmers, progressives, city officials, as well as Japanese imperial leaders utilized the deviance or the cosmopolitanism of the young Japanese American women farmers to advance their own political agenda at key moments. At the same time, young rural women found ways to mediate these shifting gender roles while also contesting them through lived-out gender roles. Despite being the subject of national debate, Yamamoto tried to protect herself by taking on multiple gender roles and gender code switching when necessary.

Leading up to the 1924 Immigration Act, the debates over the "Japanese Question" were mainly about the exclusion of Japanese women, population control, and the safeguarding of the home. Previous iterations of the yellow peril had once focused on the sexual deviances and economic competition of Asian men and led to the victory of Japanese men's immigration exclusion in the Gentlemen's Agreement of 1907–8. Newer anxieties about immigration, changing gender roles, and the US economy shaped the second wave of anti-Japanese crusades in the 1920s. The new political imperatives for stricter California Alien Land Laws, more comprehensive immigration reform, and even blood-based citizenship—the idea that citizenship should be based on biological inheritance rather than on place of birth—spurred newer iterations of the yellow peril discourse. The new yellow peril sensationalized women's and children's labors outside of the home as a threat to the destruction of the American home and the Japanese takeover of California.

The anxieties over the labor and reproductive labor of Japanese immigrant women appeared again and again in the activist agendas of labor unions and politicians, imagination of literary writers, and political commentary of popular magazines. In places with large Japanese farming communities such as Sacramento, local news media were instrumental in leading anti-Japanese crusades. V. S. McClatchy, a journalist for the *Sacramento Bee*, sensationalized the picture bride plan as the major pathway to a Japanese takeover in population and agriculture. He painted Japanese immigrant women as docile and submissive mobilizers of Japanese imperialism that had already taken over Hawai'i and would soon consume California.[3] In popular US literature, Wallace Irwin's *Seed of the Sun* explored the anxieties of white settler families over the Japanese question. In its plotline, a few white female characters pondered whether to purchase a farm in California, but when realizing they needed to rely on the labor of a Japanese farmer to be successful, reconsidered because they could not work like Japanese women.[4] The popular magazine, the *Literary Digest*, supported the Takao Ozawa US Supreme Court decision that Japanese immigrants were ineligible for citizenship. By featuring a picture of a Japanese immigrant woman in strawberry fields loading up a wagon, the *Literary Digest* reminded viewers why women's work directly threatened the livelihood of white farmers: "Americans cannot compete with the Japanese."[5]

In Los Angeles, the figure of the Japanese female farmer held the anxieties of privileged white businessmen who viewed Japanese immigrants as unwilling to play by their rules. According to the manager (possibly George Clements, manager of the Agricultural Department) of the Los Angeles Chamber of Commerce, Japanese farmers were purportedly successful not because of their natural abilities as "hereditary farmers" but exclusively because of their improper family roles, where all were "indefatigable workers." The manager demonstrated this among the berry industry: "The Japanese works himself, works his wife and works his whole family from three years up. In fact, I have seen at times a Japanese woman picking strawberries by lantern light with two little children on either side of her also picking, at two o'clock in the morning."[6]

Japanese elites aimed to avoid insult and establish harmonious relations by encouraging women's adoption of proper domesticity. The Japanese Associations of America (JAA), where George Shima, renowned as the potato king, served as president (1908–20s), endorsed that women adopt Western modernization and domesticity in order to maintain peaceful relations and assuage anti-Japanese sentiment.[7] They worked toward this goal in three ways. First, "The Protection of Newcomers" campaign advanced the view of some Japanese elites that adopting American ways would protect them from racism. The Japanese Associations passed out *The Guide for Newcoming Women*, a pamphlet that centered "American customs and manners, mode of living and dress, etiquette, American social structure and prevailing traditions."[8] Second, in the days leading up to the vote on the California Alien Land Law, the Central Japanese Association in the central areas of California, ratified a decree that ended "all Sunday field labor, except at critical harvest times." Following suit, in November 1919, the Los Angeles Japanese Association moved to reduce "woman's labor on Sundays in the outdoors."[9] By 1920, the JAA announced a series of decrees for the Japanese immigrant community that "adopt a policy of doing away with female labor as far as possible."[10]

Third, the San Francisco Japanese Association went one step further to ban the admission of picture brides. In a speech at the America–Japan

Society banquet in 1919, politician Charles Sherrill suggested that the Japanese should pass a Ladies' Agreement since "these 'picture brides' are being imported by Japanese laborers, they assist their husbands thus becoming laborers themselves, and therefore offsetting the loyalty to your government to the Gentlemen's Agreement."[11] In response, Shima agreed but suggested US politicians reconsider the passage of the California Alien Land Law for the sake of those Japanese Americans already in the States.[12] On March 1, 1920, the Japanese government passed the Ladies' Agreement and ceased issuing passports to picture brides.[13] The Ladies' Agreement, however, did not sway the debates over the California Alien Land Law.

In fact, in Yamamoto's hometown, the *San Bernardino Sun* came out in favor of the California Alien Land Law. The editorial team referred to a Los Angeles report stating that one-tenth of Japanese immigrants owned or leased the farming land, that they worked their women in the fields, and that the birthrate was much higher than that of the white population. They feared that if they continued to allow Japanese immigrants to "slip" across the Mexican border, then Los Angeles County would become largely Japanese.[14] Unlike the Riverside Chamber of Commerce, which publicized its opposition to the Alien Land Law, San Bernardino supported the view of the *Fresno Republican*, which argued a "no" vote would make a statement to the US government on the immigration question.[15] Anti-Japanese crusaders succeeded with the renewal of the Alien Land Law in November 1920. By a vote of 586,317 to 200,688, the California Alien Land Law of 1920 ushered in new restrictions, including doing away with three-year leases, prohibiting corporations owned by aliens ineligible for citizenship from acquiring land, and assigning a legal guardian to oversee land purchased by an underage Japanese American citizen—which many immigrant families used as a strategy to circumvent the 1913 Alien Land Law.[16]

In the years immediately after the 1920 California Alien Land Law, Japanese elites grew resentful toward farmers. The *Japanese American News*, a newspaper that had supported the Ladies' Agreement, published a series of columns by a Japanese writer using the pen name Weeping Willow and blaming farmers for anti-Japanese legislation.[17] He told a story from 1920, when the Japanese Associations learned that the US government convened a commission to investigate the plight of Japanese women working in the fields; the Japanese Associations had made an agreement with the farmers that women would not work in the fields the day of their scheduled visit. To bypass this policy, however, Japanese immigrant women dressed in men's clothing on the day of the visit so they could continue to work in the fields. The farmers approached cross-dressing as their version of "cooperation" that would resolve both their economic need with the diplomatic desires of the Japanese Associations. Missing one day of work in the fields would result in a huge loss for farmers and laborers, especially since they were competing with farmers across the city who were also working in the fields. Cross-dressing mollified the anti-Japanese complaints of women working in the fields, but at the same time it did not forfeit the agricultural and monetary needs. But some elites read the compromise of women's cross-dressing as devious. The Weeping Willow concluded, "No wonder we have land laws and failure."[18]

The California Alien Land Law had sent a message to US congressional hearings over the broader question of immigration legislation. California politicians pleaded with the federal government to pass a law banning the immigration of women from Japan. Senator James D. Phelan, a leader of the Democratic Party and anti-Japanese leader, criticized the diplomacy of the US Congress, which favored giving Japan the same quota as European immigrants. Phelan argued that since the 1908 Gentlemen's Agreement, Japan sent 38,000 Japanese women with passports as "alleged brides" and who were prolific because they "serve both as wives and laborers in the field."[19] He feared that California would become like Hawai'i—Japanese immigrants comprised a large portion of the Hawaiian population, and Phelan did not want Japanese immigrants to "reach their end goal of equality and colonization of the Pacific Coast." Factoring in the organizing of the anti-Japanese movement, the US Congress passed the 1924 Immigration Act, thereby implementing a quota-based national origins system. Pointedly, the act included a provision that prohibited "aliens ineligible from citizenship" from entering, which barred Japanese women—the only ethnic group from Asia, since the 1882 Chinese Exclusion Act prevented Chinese laborers from migrating and the 1917 Barred Zone Act barred South Asian migration, and the only gender group from Japan that could still migrate to the United States—from entering the United States following the 1907–8 Gentlemen's Agreement. This act was a bald attempt to preserve the racial composition of the United States as a white nation as well as to protect white male fragility around changing gender roles.

While anti-Japanese leaders had weaponized traditional gender roles and nuclear family values to usher in Japanese exclusion, at the local level, the Yamamotos may have resembled the worst fears of the anti-Japanese movement: two successful Japanese American women farmers. In 1905, Shotaro Yamamoto immigrated to the United States via British Columbia.[20] Shotaro and his wife, Shige Tanaka, were residing in Utah when Shige gave birth to their only daughter, Susie, in 1906.[21] After moving to California, in February 1913, Shotaro, along with his business partner, T. Toda, paid $150 for a restaurant on the 300 block of Third Street, formerly Chinatown in San Bernardino, just months before the passage of the California Alien Land Law in May.[22] Yamamoto and Toda ran the restaurant for about two years, when Shotaro died in June 1915 at the age of fifty, leaving Shige and Susie (at nine years old) to take over Shotaro's part of the restaurant, in addition to the hog ranches, which resided on a property on Mill Street.[23] Sometime after her father had died, Susie used her American citizenship to purchase land for the family farm. The Yamamotos continued to operate the restaurant located on 349 Third Street and resided above it.[24]

By 1920, the Yamamoto women ran a pig farm and obtained an exclusive garbage contract with the city. While much of the anti-Japanese sentiment in Los Angeles was directed toward truck farming and berry industries, Yamamotos established a niche in hog farming in San Bernardino.[25] In 1920, the Yamamotos were able to contract exclusively with the city to collect garbage as food for their hogs. Like many of the small towns in the United States at this time, San Bernardino used piggeries, or small hog farms, for food waste disposal. In fact, by the 1910s, the disposal method of burning one's trash was considered outdated and unsanitary. Appointed as garbage collector for the City of San Bernardino, the Yamamotos advertised their collection services in local newspapers.[26] If a townsperson wanted their garbage removed, they called Yamamoto for collection at no cost to them. The Yamamotos benefitted from collecting garbage because they would save money on hog feed and ensure a steady food source for their hogs.

Although Yamamoto had a successful hog farming business, she quickly learned the politics of anti-Japanese farming sentiment through her new church: the Japanese Methodist Episcopal Mission in Los Angeles.

The Methodist Episcopal Church had been vocal in its opposition to the 1924 Immigration Act. Once the act passed, Christian leaders of the Pacific Japanese Mission of the Methodist Episcopal Church believed the answer was to Americanize Japanese immigrants and youths. In order to assimilate them into the mainline church, however, it initially needed to maintain both English and Japanese language programs.[27] Many of its English-language programs were aimed at the youths by organizing Epworth Leagues. Youth ministries provided a space for white Christian liberals and Japanese Christian elites to politically and religiously develop the youths through their project of Americanization (fig. 1.1). These youth ministries emphasized traditional gender roles among the youths, only allowing men to take on leadership roles.

The overlapping projects of Americanization and Japanese imperialism enabled the youth group to split into two factions: a pro-US imperialism segment of youths and a pro-Japanese imperialism youth group. For instance, the Epworth League held discussions on US-Japanese relations. Youths debated over the question: If Japan and the United States went to war with one another, which side would they fight on? Yamamoto pointed out that this discussion led to the division: Japanese youths born in Japan disagreed with US-born Japanese American youths. Yamamoto fell on the side of the latter and explained: "The American-born young people do not feel any hatred toward the American on account of the recent immigration law."[28] She positioned herself among the growing majority of Americanized young people who were unoffended by the Immigration Act. Urban, cosmopolitan, educated, and young Japanese Americans felt humiliated by any public display of excludable immigrant-ness: rural, low status, unmodern, unkempt, or unclean.

Yamamoto interpreted Americanization in gendered ways. Against her mother's wishes, she had taken on the common youth labor of a schoolgirl. In her book on Japanese American women and domestic work, Evelyn Nakano Glenn argues that young, single Japanese American women entered into domestic labor while attending school for a variety of economic and social reasons. In Japan, it was customary for prosperous rural families to spend a few years serving in cultured urban households to acquire social graces. Through domestic service, daughters received training in homemaking skills while also supporting themselves and saving

1.1 The Japanese Methodist Episcopal Church created youth groups or college departments such as the Epworth League for college-aged attendees to expand their mission to youth. Courtesy of United Methodist Church.

for marriage. In the United States, that custom evolved into the schoolgirl position Japanese American rural women were largely unfamiliar with the mores of white middle-class urban culture, but domestic work provided an avenue to be trained in domesticity. Young women could acquire tailoring and sewing skills considered essential for US wives and mothers and learn something of city life, gaining sophistication and breadth.[29] Yamamoto chose the role of a schoolgirl to circumvent the white racism she had already witnessed around Japanese American women's roles.

Yamamoto's domesticity training also fit neatly into Japanese imperial response. In Japanese colonialists' imagination, women would use their higher education to become educators of the Western arts or humanities. Building on earlier reform efforts to train picture brides as good women, Japanese leaders tried to racially uplift the Los Angeles youths and encourage more and more youths to enter US universities. Japanese elites continued to advocate that young women become trained in the arts or in the home. In fact, at the end of her interview, Yamamoto noted that she planned to teach at the university and was even willing to go east. She did not declare any plans to return to her San Bernardino farm. Japanese elites and white liberals wanted educated urban youths to racially uplift other young women and become cultural ambassadors. Yamamoto's stated future plan of becoming an educator was politically aligned with both the Japanese and white liberal response to the passage of the 1924 Immigration Act.

COUNTRY LIFE REFORM, 1924 TO 1928

In the first half of the 1920s, the tightening of immigration policy nationally and Japanese imperial strategies of Americanization led Yamamoto to seek out lessons on proper domesticity in a large city. However, in the latter part of the 1920s, a thriving rebellious youth culture and the country life reform movement enabled young women like Yamamoto to portray herself as a savvy businesswoman in rural towns. In the years following the passage of the 1924 Immigration Act, Yamamoto split her time between attending the University of California, Los Angeles, and running the hog farm in San Bernardino. In Los Angeles, she enjoyed a vibrant urban youth culture that rebelled against reformers' approach to racial exclusion. In San Bernardino, she expanded her fortunes in a predominately male trade. Young women like Yamamoto embodied and flourished under the newest incarnation of the New Woman: the modern girl or the flapper.

The flapper was a global cultural movement connected to rapid changes to the economy, national goals of modernization, and a rebellious youth culture. In the United States, compared to her earlier more political counterparts such as the suffragette or the social worker, the flapper was criticized as apolitical. Historian Einav Rabinovitch-Fox argues the flapper represented the culmination of women's movements after World War I, including the right to vote and women's entrances to higher education and the workplace. She embodied new moral values associated with the expansion of women's freedoms, such as sexual liberation, independence, and individuality.[30] As the flapper emerged in the United States, so too did the modan gāru (lit. modern girl) burst onto Japanese metropolitan cities. Historians Gail Bernstein, Margit Nagy, Barbara Molony, and Miriam Silverburg show that the Japanese modern girl was interpreted as either the model of a modernity or the epitome of moral decadence. The modern girl challenged age-old definitions of female likeness through an open sexuality, public flirtatiousness, and independence from her family. Her very existence rebelled against the "traditional family."[31]

By the 1920s, the Japanese American flapper was a modern take on femininity to suit the realities of a nascent, working-class urban youth culture in downtown Los Angeles. Young women were exposed to urban changes of city living, took charge of youth-led organizations, and participated in an abundance of leisure. At the same time, Japanese American women had to negotiate their parents' stances on gender norms and occupational expectations. The Japanese American flapper can be defined by her entrance into the workplace, independence from her family, and unabashedly selfish participation in leisure. Young women worked for or developed immigrant business franchises, attended college only for a time or vocational school or refused to attend altogether, chose their own mates or their careers over marriage, and attended dances and movies with boys at the great risk of community gossip. Some varied in their political commitment to racial uplift and carved out their own definitions of respectability separate from the urban middle-class female reformer.

Rebellious youths diverged from elder reformers in multiple ways. Urban youths repurposed the racial uplift efforts of Japanese imperialists and Americanization incentives of white progressives to provide the opposite: urban leisure. While Japanese elders and white Christians built church facilities and expanded their youth programs to morally discipline, religiously evangelize, and train youths, youths converted the facilities of the ethnic church to provide spaces for socializing, companionship, and dating. For instance, youths utilized the church basement at the Japanese Union Church as their gym where they might host sports events, drama performances, or even dances. Other youths formed clubs through relationships with white progressive mentors who offered the Y or a school building to use as a meeting place for social events and dances. These gathering places became hubs for youths to socialize, dance, and sometimes ditch to instead go to the beach or a cinema. Youths unabashedly enjoyed each other's company, chatted about cars or movies rather than learn about Christianity or be concerned with reformers' definitions of respectability.

The ethnic press is another example of how youths repurposed an immigrant institution to advance their ideas of progress—particularly those of the New Women. Once a press that primarily aimed at an immigrant readership, the *Los Angeles Japanese American Daily News*, also known as the *Rafu Shimpo*, created a new section run by and for the second-generation youths in 1926. For the first time, a section aimed at youth readers was published in English and its new, young editor-in-chief was a departure from the primarily male editorial board. Louise Suski had grown up in Los Angeles, raised by well-to-do parents (her father was a doctor), and had a lifelong dream of being a physical education teacher, but was instead directed by her mother to study general education.[32] Under Suski's direction, the English section featured news of the various club meetings and a large sports section. Her sister, Julia Suski, contributed illustrations on the modern woman and is long suspected to have written columns such as "What Shall I Wear" and "Judie" on fashion.[33] Aside from her sister's columns, Suski also reprinted popular or controversial articles about the modern girl from other news streams. For example, an article reprinted in the *Rafu Shimpo*, "The Girl of Today," rallied women to be brave and strong and to not be discouraged by men, noting that progress has made the women more athletic and self-sufficient.[34] These depictions of the modern girl sent a message: no longer should women be docile and win the approval of men, but they should be independent, self-sufficient, and healthy enough to not need the assistance of a man. Suski herself never married.

Modern girls found a haven in youth leisure culture and felt resigned to the business opportunities of the ethnic economy. Unlike reformers who encouraged youths to racially uplift themselves through higher education, many youths felt that a university degree was a waste of time. Young women could easily find work as secretaries in Japanese-run businesses or companies. For instance, Teru Miyamoto took a commercial course at Los Angeles High School and, through her father's connections, went on to work for a Japanese grocer, Nippon Dry Goods. Like many other youths, Miyamoto did not enter college because she did not think it would ultimately pay off because of workplace racial discrimination. Rather, she wanted to become a businesswoman in the ethnic economy, to which her parents did not object. They did, however, object to her evenings out dancing at the Oliver Club and playing basketball at the Japanese Union Church. But Miyamoto unabashedly took the time for her leisure after a long day's work.[35]

Since some youths could not access respectability through professional status, many subscribed to trendy US definitions of beauty, fashion, and social activities as a way to access modernity. In fact, many spent their money on their looks, leisure, and material goods in order to access modern lifestyles. Some young women exchanged their long hair, lace, and pearls for short bobs and silk clothing. Some young women bought a new dress to wear to a dance. Wearing modern hair and fashion symbolized women's independence, agency in sexuality or marriage, and masculine power in the workplace.[36] This drastically departed from the logic of racial uplift, where women served the Japanese immigrant family and their community and did not spend money on themselves. Reformers understood buying a new piece of clothing for oneself as selfish. However, flappers unapologetically spent money on their personal extravagance.

Modern girls also brought forth a new set of social norms around dating and marriage. Unlike their parents' generation of family matchmaking, young people set out to decide their own marriage partners. New leisure created opportunities for mingling between the sexes in the form of courtship. Young women and men might walk to church together, sit next to one another in church, go automobile riding together, and go to the cinema. Daughters received the brunt of criticism and became the subject of scandal if they were seen in public with boys. However, many continued to socialize, ignoring elderly gossip. Many were less concerned with protecting their chastity before marriage and enjoyed a new social norm. Moreover, with more young women entering into the workforce, women tended to put off marriage and child-rearing.

Esther Bartlett, the assistant executive secretary of the YWCA International Institute, noticed the growing trend of Japanese American flappers: "There is [a] certain group of 'society girls' among the Japanese who are supposed to be quite social leaders, and they are regular little 'flappers' too." The group had formed among themselves and required some money to join. Bartlett explained: "A girl has to earn a certain amount of money to belong to it and they meet at regular intervals and have dinners at some café. It is always at one of their own cafes, of course, because they would not be admitted to one of the 'uptown' cafes or cabarets and fortunately, they are not allowed in the dance halls." But this group was not popular among the Japanese American elites who were invested in high culture: "those who consider themselves the best Japanese, not the society leaders, but the conservative, well-bred class, look much askance upon this group and there is much consternation if one of their daughters is ever seen with it."[37]

The YWCA attempted to provide new social services for young single women working or attending college in the city. Although in the early 1910s and 1920s the YWCA largely focused its services on the immigrant community, the new generation of Japanese American youths prompted the YWCA to expand services to teen women in the latter part of the 1920s. YWCA leaders attempted to create girls' clubs to promote health and exercise while also expanding Christian values, but its limited facilities did not meet the expanding population of young women. In fact, the YWCA International Institute considered purchasing the property at 2616 East Third Street for the purpose of a facility specifically for the Japanese American community—a Japanese YWCA.[38] This became the Japanese dormitory, where thirty girls lived in 1923.[39] The Japanese dormitory also served as a community center for the uptown Japanese American community, holding classes, clubs, and social gatherings.[40]

Yamamoto embraced many aspects of the life of the modern girl in Los Angeles. She enjoyed going to the movies, riding in automobiles and attending church socials. She mingled with girls and boys in public and did so in spite of the gossip of Japanese elders. Yamamoto did not join a YWCA girls' club but used the Japanese dormitory for housing and parties.[41] Unlike other downtown youths who could care less about entering university, Yamamoto had moved to the city primarily to study. However, her education served more as a status symbol than it did a vehicle for occupational mobility. She remained tied to her family business and often returned to San Bernardino to run the hog farm.

San Bernardino was part of what historian Matt Garcia calls the citrus suburbs outside of Los Angeles: an agricultural economy from San Gabriel to San Bernardino Valleys centered on citrus trees. In his study of citrus farming, Garcia argues that the agrarian myth and westward expansion was deeply embedded in social stratification, invisible migrant labor, and a reinterpretation of technology as part of nature. White settlers profited off of the erasure and displacement of Native communities as well as the labor pool of Chinese, Japanese, Sikh, Mexican migrant and white workers. San Bernardino had a community of about 150 Japanese immigrant residents. They ran local grocery stores, laundries, and restaurants.[42] As a result, communities throughout the citrus belt enjoyed a higher standard of living following the city beautiful movement but stood in stark contrast to the state of agriculture. Country lifers, such as city officials in the Department of Agriculture, organized a movement that attempted to forestall the flow of small "best of rural populations" farming families to overcrowded cities. A growing US eugenics movement expressed concern about rural-to-city migration and its effect on the US "racial stock." Adherents began to call for a return to farms or a reverse migration. This standpoint meant not an abandonment of modern technology but a harmonization of agriculture and industry to create more productive farms.[43]

By the 1920s, public health officials harmonized modern agriculture and industry by enforcing new initiatives in response to racialized fears around disease outbreaks. President of the San Bernardino City Board of Health George H. Stephens racially targeted immigrant communities and businesses for public health reform. In 1924, for fear of the potential spread of the pneumonic plague, Stephens began cleanup measures in what was known as the Mexican district. Although no case of pneumonic plague had been reported, Stephens announced that "all Mexican homes and outhouses are being white washed, lime is being spread in damp and unsanitary places, and war is being waged against rats."[44] Later, the spread of foot-and-mouth disease resulted in a city quarantine, which raised resident concerns about the disruption to their regular garbage collection.[45] The following year, Stephens cited the Yamamotos and threatened to bring them to court, complaining that garbage had been picked up late and there weren't enough vehicles to provide full service. Settling out of court with Stephens, Yamamoto increased the number to four wagons and implemented a rotating schedule to pick up garbage from businesses and apartment homes.[46] She had to develop the infrastructure to meet the new requirements: She purchased more hogs. She hired Japanese laborers to live and work on the hog farm.[47] She purchased garbage trucks. She hired Mexican immigrants as truck drivers.[48] As Yamamoto expanded her hog farming empire, local journalists found their new poster child for harmonizing New Woman values and reverse migration.

The main editor of the *San Bernardino Daily Sun* since 1896, Robert C. Harbison ran for Congress in 1916, espousing values of US industries, rights of labor, and a dry policy.[49] During the national debates over immigration, he advocated for exclusion. He even refused any proposed appeals for Japanese naturalization, but he recognized children of immigrants born in the United States as citizens by birth. By the 1910s, the newspaper tried to appeal to female readers by incorporating sections on the New Women. He hired Winifred Martin to oversee the "News for Society and Interest of Women" section. Around the 1920s, the *Sun* printed or reprinted profiles of young women doing remarkable, curious things in small towns across the United States, perhaps speaking to a particular anxiety about the best of rural women leaving for large cities. Profiles featured a college graduate receiving degrees from two colleges simultaneously in Raleigh, North Carolina; a judge pointing out gendered bias toward women's vagrancy charges in the courtroom in Kansas City, Missouri; an aspiring pilot flying across the Pacific Ocean in Oakland, California; and a YWCA director organizing a new diet system in Detroit.[50]

Editors of the *Sun* profiled Yamamoto as the perfect model that integrated the values of the urban New Woman to her agrarian community. With a circulation of over ten thousand, the *Sun* featured Yamamoto as a New Woman farmer and emphasized her return narrative. They highlighted her local origins as a student who graduated from San Bernardino High School who had earned enough money on her father's farm near San Bernardino to pay tuition at the University of California. After completing her college course, the article highlighted, she "chose" hog farming as her profession. Editors highlighted her "executive ability" as a New Woman effortlessly in charge of many employees. Yamamoto was quoted: "Women are just as successful as men in business when they think they can be."[51]

Through a focus on a return narrative, the *Sun* painted a distinctly new character of race progress, in stark contrast to the yellow peril. Emphasizing the fact that she was "American-born" helped to insulate her from anti-immigrant sentiment and the perpetual foreignness associated with the excludable Asian immigrant. Moreover, it endorsed the eugenics position that Americanization will improve children of immigrants. In addition, contrasting Yamamoto with Japanese farmers who were portrayed as ignorant of scientific methods by the anti-Japanese movement, editors highlighted that she had scientifically studied hog farming and related the importance of feeding garbage to hogs at just the right time. They highlighted her ambition to become renowned for finding an odor-proof garbage collection to feed to hogs. Finally, the *Sun* emphasized business rather than labor. Unlike the anti-Japanese movements' manipulation of women's work as a sign of bringing down the white man's standard of living, editors highlighted Yamamoto as a businesswoman who cleaned up the city's garbage and raised the standard of living.

Yamamoto's photo especially offered a new kind of media portrayal of Japanese American women to rural towns. Previous anti-Japanese campaign photos had typically portrayed Japanese American women clad in farmer clothing and working in the fields. Such photos attempted to rally the racialized fears of white men to vote for stricter land and immigration laws, in addition to justify the rationale to progressives. However, reformers captured Yamamoto sitting at her desk in crisp New Woman fashion (fig. 1.2). Her marcel waves and elegant silk attire represent the trendy practices of the latest American consumerism and female empowerment. Her education and executive abilities are brought to the fore, pencil poised over paper and a typewriter on her left and a telephone to her right. This new image embodied a modern take on middle-class respectability and race progress. Such a photo aimed to model a Japanese American New Women to young white women on how they, too, might become New Women and return to their hometowns.

Not only was Yamamoto's story published in the *San Bernardino Sun*, but her photo and story ran in at least a dozen newspapers in small and rural towns across the United States and Canada, including the *New Castle News* in Pennsylvania, *Sarasota Herald* in Florida, and *Winters Enterprise* in Texas.[52] Yamamoto's photo ran in syndication most likely because newspapers utilized her modern beauty to attract readers to a new model of rural womanhood that served the greater agenda of country reformers nationwide. The reprinting of Yamamoto's story suggests that although the country life reform movement was particular to Southern California, reform movements were occurring in agrarian communities experiencing similar migration shifts and eugenics anxieties nationwide.

1.2 Susie Yamamoto poses for her profile featured in the *San Bernardino Daily Sun*, 1927.

By 1928, Yamamoto had signed a ten-year contract for exclusive rights to garbage collection with the city of San Bernardino. Her hog farm had grown to forty thousand hogs, and Yamamoto was overseeing fifty employees.[53] Unlike other cities where the city levied a tax on residents to haul away their garbage, Yamamoto paid the city to pick up its garbage. Yamamoto agreed to a payment of $50 a month, providing the equipment and paying for truck drivers to pick up 5,200 garbage stops. By the late 1920s, Yamamoto had established a hog farming empire across Southern California, including the cities of San Bernardino, Long Beach, and Bellflower.[54]

MAKING A NEW DEAL, 1929 TO 1933

In the latter part of the 1920s, Yamamoto joined the rise of the modern girl in Los Angeles and the country life reformers endorsed Yamamoto's return as a savvy businesswoman in San Bernardino; subsequently, the Great Depression reversed this shift in gender roles and led to the reassignment of New Women to domestic or auxiliary roles.

In 1929, Yamamoto became engaged to John Ando, a law student at the University of Southern California with an extensive farming background.[55] They had in common growing up with a single parent and having ties to farming. Ando was born in Hawai'i, his mother died when he was four years old, and his father worked on various farms. Just as Yamamoto was active in urban youth circles, Ando had joined the first Japanese American boys' club, the Oliver Club. Ando and Yamamoto married at the Los Angeles Japanese Methodist Episcopal Church, in a ceremony officiated by Reverend Kawashima. Their wedding banquet was the social event of the season: with about 250 guests, they had a dinner party at Tomio Hotel in Los Angeles. In addition to friends, Yamamoto's colleagues also attended, including her Long Beach and San Bernardino attorneys, as well as social progressives such as Nellie Oliver, the head of the Oliver Club.[56] Ando's interest in law was to "be of service to the second generation in helping this group make adjustments to American life."[57] Ando worked alongside Yamamoto to manage their hog farming empire. (Although Yamamoto took Ando's last name, for clarity, I continue to refer to her as Yamamoto.)

The Great Depression affected Japanese American communities in and around Los Angeles in a variety of ways. First, the impressive growth of ethnic economies during the 1920s stalled. Historian Lon Kurashige argues that immigrant entrepreneurs in Los Angeles had to reimagine the patrons of Little Tokyo, who were at once the immigrant community, and sought to market Nisei Week Festival in order to build a new consumer body of young people.[58] Second, in agrarian communities, John Modell argues that the productivity of Japanese American farms peaked in 1930 and then tapered off, with many farmers becoming more cautious about their business model.[59] The economic uncertainty and instability for the immigrant ethnic economy led to the mobilization of young people's political organizing.

While the 1930s is usually defined as an era of labor organizing, Japanese American political organizations organized around citizenship eligibility. A new young people's movement partially took up the mantle from Japanese pioneers. Clarence T. Arai, a young lawyer who spearheaded the Japanese American Citizens League (JACL) in Seattle, believed it was young peoples' duty to "bring a closer relationship between the Japanese and Americans."[60] They aimed to utilize their collective voting power to put people in office who would enact favorable legislation toward all Japanese Americans.[61] Young people believed that their voting power must also incorporate the interests of the immigrant generation, who held no voting power. They created a representative system across immigrant elites and young people, where a central committee was made of a tripartite system: an advisory board of noncitizens who held key roles in civic and occupational organizations, an inner council of citizens over the age of twenty-one, and a junior council of citizens between the ages of eighteen and twenty-one.[62]

In its first full year of operation, the JACL carried on the political imperatives begun by immigrant elites, but now with the status that young people's citizenship afforded. At the national level, the JACL had two main goals: amend the Cable Act so that Japanese American women would not lose their citizenship if they married Japanese immigrant men, and assure that Japanese American veterans of World War I received their citizenship as promised by the US government.[63] Suma Sugi, a young single woman, traveled to Washington, DC, as a representative to advocate for an amendment to the Cable Act, which passed in 1932. Tokutaro Slocum, a war veteran who was denied citizenship, worked with the JACL to support the Nye-Lea Act, which was signed into law in 1935 and enabled Japanese immigrant war veterans to apply for US citizenship.

Moreover, the JACL continued on the mission to build young people as cultural bridges between the United States and Japan. Concerned that young people would become too Americanized, parents had often sent their children to Japan for schooling or trips. Young people also agreed that they would like to learn about Japan. The JACL sponsored a summer educational tour of Japan, where they met with prominent residents and officials, enjoyed the scenery of Japan, and viewed the daily living conditions of the poorer parts of Japan.[64]

The political organizing of JACL, however, relegated married women to supportive roles. For instance, in the election of cabinets, women were often selected for the role of vice presidency and rarely for the presidency. In 1930, Clarence Yamagata—a UCLA graduate, USC law school graduate, president of the Japanese fraternity at USC, the Gakusei-Kai, and practicing lawyer—served as the Los Angeles chapter's first president.[65] Yamamoto, a businesswoman, was the first vice president. Moreover, when it came to organizing events, women were often assigned to fund-raising. For instance, in its first year, the LA JACL held a number of events. It sponsored forums that brought city candidates to speak to the local Japanese American community, fought against a proposed segregation bill that would allow local school districts to segregate schoolchildren, and held meetings in which members engaged with the local body politic, such as the councilman of the Ninth District, which included Japanese businesses.[66] Still, Yamamoto was put in charge only of social fund-raisers, such as planning a dance.[67] Finally, married women often took a backseat to their husband's political participation. After Yamamoto stepped down as vice president, her husband John was elected president for the following year and held much more active roles in the JACL.[68]

The relegation of Yamamoto to a secondary status in Japanese American political organizing also paralleled the US federal government's approach to married women's relief during the New Deal. While New Deal programs were often aimed at increasing men's employment, often women were either not included or included at a much lower priority. Married women, especially, were discouraged from working because of the stance that men should serve as the main providers. The Economy Act of 1933 forced federally employed women to resign if they were married to another federal worker. However, when women worked in the home, they were unpaid and thus did not receive the benefits of social security. At the labor level, domestic workers who were majority women of color had to advocate for themselves, by forming unions or leagues in order to shape new legislation to be inclusive of women's work in the home. At the managerial level, Yamamoto also advocated for her workplace entitlement to relief, but she found her entitlement had diminished as a result of a return to anti-immigrant sentiment and conservative gender roles. When discussing business relations, local newspapers often printed her name as "Mrs. Susie Yamamoto Ando" to signal her marital status, which purposely worked against her. Many people believed that women should step aside (or return to the home) so that men could work to provide for their families.

Japanese American hog farmers suffered a devastating loss in 1932 due to the county's handling of the tenth outbreak of foot-and-mouth disease in California. Inspectors investigated and slaughtered over 18,000 hogs on four ranches in Orange County, three ranches in Los Angeles County, and one in San Bernardino County. Half of these were Japanese American farms. At Yamamoto's farm, when the state found a few infected hogs, it took drastic measures. Inspectors slaughtered 2,386 hogs on Yamamoto's ranch, promising to repay the losses of the destroyed swine, which were valued at nearly $24,000.[69] The state quarantined Yamamoto's farm for sixty days and told the sheriff to position eighteen guards around Yamamoto's ranch. A debate quickly arose over whether the state or the county would pay for the guards.[70] Other Japanese-owned ranches that faced massive slaughters were owned by Tom Kitahata (2,920), K. Sakoda (2,209), and George Kitihata (1,547)—all in Los Angeles County.[71]

After the loss of her hogs, Yamamoto advocated for herself in negotiating with the city to provide relief and a more equitable business partnership. Although they had lost over two thousand hogs, Yamamoto was still responsible for garbage disposal without a feeding outlet. In May 1932, Yamamoto went to the city to ask to be released from the contract or that the city provide relief. The city initially released Yamamoto from the $50 monthly contract for garbage collection for about six months.[72] By January 1933, however the city decided to enforce the contract, demanding that Yamamoto incur all the losses. Yamamoto considered opting out of their remaining six-year contract and take the $1,000 bond loss. However, the city attorney, William Guthrie, warned that the loss of bond would only be the beginning of their troubles, since they would then have to pay for some alternate garbage plan during the unexpired years of their contract.[73] Yamamoto had offered to continue her operations under a levy of fifteen cents a month against each place given garbage service, but the city council vetoed any move to impose a special tax for garbage service. If Yamamoto had to continue under the current conditions of the contract, she would have to forfeit her entire enterprise.[74]

The acting mayor, Ormonde Seccumb, considered several alternatives but ultimately supported a plan that prioritized the relief of white male workers and US citizens. Seccumb contemplated a plan to hire unemployed white men from the Citizen's Emergency Relief committee to take over the fleet of garbage trucks. Because a large number of workers were unemployed, this would help offset the loss of crew workers so they could pick up garbage when required. Yamamoto's hogs would still dispose of the garbage and she would also be released from the $50 monthly garbage disposal fee to the city.[75] This compromise would provide an equitable partnership, offering relief to Yamamoto while also providing employment to the unemployed white men of the city, but Yamamoto's current employees, who were Japanese and Mexican immigrants, would be without jobs. Yamamoto may not have agreed with that plan. However, Mayor Seccumb also entertained negotiations with other potential contractors, like the Municipal Contracting Company of Los Angeles. The president of the company, L. A. Sarkisian, proposed to levy a city fee of twenty cents per water meter to cover the cost of two collections each week in the residential district and daily service in the business district. The offer provided "water-tight truck bodies with canvas covers, in the collection of garbage." But most importantly, unlike Yamamoto, Sarkisian agreed that "only white American citizens would be employed, with San Bernardino men making up at least 90 per cent of the payroll."[76]

The city council saw Yamamoto's losses as an opportunity to prioritize the hiring of unemployed white men during the Great Depression. The mayor and city attorney waited for Yamamoto to give notice that she would forfeit her contract before they drafted an emergency ordinance to receive new bids.[77] Under the new ordinance submitted, the city could impose a levy of fifty cents a month to all private residences.[78] Bids opened on July 17, 1933, and despite Yamamoto making a bid, the council unanimously voted to contract with Phil Farrington.[79] Under the new contract, only "American citizens" would be employed by the contractor, a clause that excluded Japanese immigrants, who were ineligible for citizenship, in addition to Mexican immigrants recruited in the aftermath of 1924, and they would be given an eight-hour maximum day and a minimum wage of $2 per day.[80] Farrington planned to dispose of the garbage in a similar manner to Yamamoto and even established his hog ranch next to theirs on Mill Street.[81] After having been the city's garbage contractor for over ten years, Yamamoto officially surrendered her contract on August 1, 1933.[82]

Yamamoto's case exemplifies multiple concrete ways in which patriarchal gender roles and racial discrimination flourished in a period of economic decline. The city of San Bernardino saw Yamamoto's loss as an opportunity to push out a married Japanese American woman and nonwhite immigrant garbage men and instead, contract with a white corporation and reserve jobs for unemployed white men. This reflected the larger inequitable distribution of city, state, and government relief during the New Deal legislation, which pushed out immigrants and nonwhites in order to provide relief to white men first. Moreover, ideals of patriarchal gender roles played a factor in relief administration. Many people submitted to the nuclear family model where men were the main providers and women performed unpaid domestic labor. Yamamoto's status as a businesswoman was no longer a valuable model for immigrant populations and women in rural countryside; rather, she was seen as a selfish married woman who had no place in a relief economy reserved for white men.

In the interwar period, anti-immigrant legislation, the country life movement, and the New Deal relief policies shaped the development of the rural New Woman. In the early 1920s, anti-Japanese unions rallied around protecting normative patriarchal gender roles to pass anti-Japanese legislation. Immigrant elites also reinforced their beliefs by promoting the sentiment that women belonged in the home. By the late 1920s, country life reformers utilized the rural New Woman to endorse their eugenic ideals around building a better race in agrarian towns and encourage young women to return to their small hometowns. Reformers touted a new model of rural womanhood as combining the best elements of city and country life, as well as the ideal characteristics of immigrant and American, and promoted the rural countryside as a place where New Women can flourish. However, in the 1930s, during the Great Depression, Japanese American political groups expected married women to fulfill auxiliary roles within their organizations. Moreover, the local and federal government relegated married women to traditional roles in the home so that men could be employed as the primary breadwinners.

Yamamoto gender-code-switched alongside each political group's gender expectations. In the early 1920s, although she was a farmer working in men's spheres, Yamamoto tried to disassociate from any signs of excludable immigrant-ness in the era of anti-immigrant legislation, including learning proper domesticity at a time when many women made strides away from the home. In the latter part of the 1920s, Yamamoto embraced a local rural public identity as the college-educated, flapper-trendy, entrepreneurial woman. By the 1930s, Yamamoto did her best to organize within her community for civil rights through auxiliary roles, but when pushed to the wall she advocated for herself to hold the city accountable for providing relief to her farming enterprise during the Great Depression. Ultimately, her gender-code-switching, or her adoption of multiple gender roles, could not protect her from an era that disenfranchised both married women and nonwhite peoples.

This chapter examines the perspective of the reformee, the farmer's daughter, the flapper. She was the subject of national and community debate between various political and social groups advancing white nativism, white liberalism, or Japanese imperialism. The reformee neither cared for projects of racial uplift but tried to pick up etiquette and language with which to move through them unafflicted. She found social niches among urban youths. Unlike the self-sacrificing reformer, she unapologetically enjoyed consumption and leisure. Others downplayed or highlighted her success when deemed fit for their political agenda. She was used when convenient. And she benefitted on occasion and lost a great deal. In the next two chapters, I take a closer look at the perspectives of the reformers. I examine the making of transnational masculinity and womanhood as it was closely tied to Japanese settler colonialism.

2

The Intelligentsia New Man

MASAO DODO, a sociology major at the University of Southern California, submitted eight sociological reports on the state of Japanese America in Los Angeles to the Survey of Race Relations in the 1920s. In one report, he observed the development of young men as told through a biography of his roommate, whom he gave the pseudonym "Mamoru Takada." He opened the biography with the tragic and shameful story of how Takada became an orphan. Dodo painted Takada's father as a successful grocer in Seattle who had fallen into bad luck. After losing his invested wealth, Takada's father could not stop gambling and drinking. Takada's mother was at last exasperated from "domestic misery" and committed suicide by drinking poison. She left a note telling her husband to stop gambling, get the clock back, and take care of the children. Afterward, his boss had to oversee the disbursal of his wages, knowing he would spend it all in one place. In fact, Takada felt embarrassed when he had to walk his drunk father home along a busy street. Takada's father eventually died from tuberculosis, leaving Takada and his brother in the dormitories of the Japanese Methodist Episcopal Mission, and his three sisters at the Jane Couch Home for Girls.

Without a father figure, Dodo took it upon himself to mentor Takada and Takada's brother. At first, Dodo often found Takada "destitute of childish vigor" and "disgusted by the careless utterances of people around him." When helping Takada face community shame around his father's ill repute, Dodo had to "assure the boys that their father was an honorable man despite his shortcomings." Dodo repeatedly raised Takada's spirits with biographies and writings of great men. He instilled in Takada the expectation that young men must face hardships in order to win the respect of adults. Dodo monitored Takada's scholastic development, including his performance at school debates and participation in sports. When Takada approached graduation, Dodo spoke with pride about how Takada had finally learned how to handle hardship like a courageous man. On the day of his graduation, when a fire burned down Takada's dormitory along with his regalia, Dodo exclaimed he "bore the misery with noble resignation" and concluded that "Mamoru was no longer a poor submissive orphan child but a man of valour."[1]

Dodo's report of Takada was an exercise in how to mentor young men to reinvest in Japanese settler colonialism in the aftermath of US racial exclusion. Historian Eiichiro Azuma argues that immigrant elites turned to history writing as a response to the crisis of racial subordination, recasting themselves as pioneering frontiersmen that fit neatly into both American frontier narratives and Japanese colonial stories.[2] Dodo's reconstruction of Takada's past reveals how young men utilized a similar revisionist approach when reinterpreting personal family histories to racially uplift young men. Dodo sought to save the pioneering legacy of Takada's father as it was brought to shame by his gambling and drinking. Focusing on select tender memories of Takada's father, and paired with global canonical writings of successful imperial masculinity, Dodo developed and motivated a young Takada toward a scholastic masculinity. This chapter argues that Dodo was part of a new generation of intelligentsia that shaped transnational new manhood toward a colonial settler masculinity that could rise out of the ashes of racial struggle and gendered shame.

Dodo's mentorship mirrored larger community conversations on how to develop young men in the United States after the racial emasculation of not being admitted into the body politic. The 1924 Immigration Act resulted in the restriction of young women to the domestic sphere, but it also signaled the foreclosure of colonial settler manhood in farming. Unlike young women like Yamamoto, who turned to Americanization as well as embraced flapper lifestyles, young men like Dodo reinvested in

Japanese settler colonialism and held tightly to conservative patriarchal values. After anti-Japanese legislation prevented Japanese immigrant men from farming, community leaders revised the measures of manhood to two new arenas: intellectualism and sports. Unrestricted by legal exclusion, Japanese reformers aimed to racially uplift young men into New Men by encouraging their advancement in scholarship and their athletic development.

This chapter focuses on the reformer, Dodo, and the remaking of settler colonial masculinity. Dodo underwent a period of several tumultuous changes from the Japanese modernization and expansion, the passage of the 1924 Immigration Act in the United States, and the rise of Japanese military imperialism in East Asia. This chapter examines how settler colonial ideologies of masculinity—men as colonizers, patriarchs, and equal if not superior to the West—evolved from the Meiji Restoration to the Sino-Japanese War. Throughout the shifting tides of westward expansion, racial exclusion, and military imperialism, Dodo claimed to embrace "radical" ideologies removed from the status quo. Emboldened through a moral high ground, Dodo's vision of racial uplift ultimately clashed with the expansion of women's roles. Dodo's own story reveals how Japanese expansion continued to shape masculinity in the US.

JAPANESE CHRISTIAN IMPERIALISM, 1910S TO 1924

Historian Brian Hayashi has examined how Dodo's advocacy of Christianity in the early twentieth century was not simply a sign of assimilation into the nation-state.[3] This chapter supports the premise that conversion to Christianity was not a sign of assimilation, but it then goes further to show that Christianity was seen as a radical act from the status quo (and a part of building a new empire) through the eyes of migrants like Dodo. After all, Christianity was a missionizing religious minority in Japan that had faced persecution and national exclusion. Across the Pacific, the majority of Japanese immigrant settlements were of Buddhist faith with pockets of Christian believers.[4] Moreover, Japanese immigrants were a racial minority in the United States that also faced exclusion and national rejection. Becoming a racial and religious minority, a Christian in a Buddhist Japanese America, set the path for Dodo to evolve alongside Japanese settler colonialism. Dodo had a penchant for advancing "radical" ideologies that preserved a militant transnational masculinity.

In the early twentieth century, many factors shaped the manhood of Dodo and other young men, including the Westernization of Japan, the introduction of Christian missions in Japan as well as in the United States, and the expansion of Japanese settler colonialism in the United States. Significant transformation during the Meiji Restoration resulted in social upheaval for many samurai-descended families, including Dodo's. Although in the final years of the feudal era samurai were already declining in wealth and status, Japanese modernization resulted in even further decline. Motivated by the threat of US and European colonization, Japan sought to modernize and industrialize in the latter 1800s. Japan restored the emperor to power, established a centralized and bureaucratic government, developed an industrial sector, and amassed an imperial army and navy. When Japan dissolved the previously governing system of feudal lords, the samurai who used to lord their status over merchants, farmers, and craftsmen lost their class privileges. Some historians believe that the samurai had already begun losing their status before modernization. The decline of the samurai class resulted in a tumultuous transition from warriors to farmers, merchants, and civil servants.[5]

Dodo's grandfather, formerly a samurai, found the conversion to an industrial system difficult—he became an alcoholic and traded the land he had received during the dissolution of the samurai system for liquor. About Dodo's own father, Dodo wrote that "the entire career of my father was constantly downward." A son of a samurai, he had inherited no wealth, lost the family's class privilege, grew up in a period of tumultuous change, and his father (Dodo's grandfather) was constantly drinking. At the same time, the Japanese government encouraged businessmen, scholars, and farmers to migrate to the United States and to nearby islands to expand Japanese colonial power. That Dodo was born in the town of Sapporo, in Hokkaido, suggests that Dodo's family may have been part of the wave of ethnic Japanese settlers to colonize Hokkaido, which resulted in the dispossession of Ainu people, who were also forced to assimilate. And like many Japanese males who migrated to the United States in search of economic opportunity and colonial endeavors, his father migrated in 1903 when Dodo was eight months old.

The settler colonialism of many men led to the phenomenon of transnational families, where men often worked and lived outside of Japan and sent some of their wages to their families in Japan. Women took care of the children and elderly grandparents and often labored as well. Dodo grew up never knowing his father. Rather, he was raised in a household of women. His mother, Some, raised Dodo and his two sisters, as well as cared for her aging and ill mother-in-law. Moreover, she worked as the principal of an all-girls' dormitory school. The transformations of the Meiji Restoration also impacted women's culture in the home, with tensions arising between Dodo's grandmother of shizoku descent (from the ruling class), and Some of heimin descent (from the ruled class). Dodo's grandmother alternately reminisced proudly of the days when she worked for a feudal lord and complained of Some's and her grandchildren's poor manners. As Japan underwent industrialization, many migrants moved from rural areas to urban cities. In 1908, the Dodo family moved to Tokyo, the leading center of modernization and industrialization. In the northwest outskirts of the city where the Dodo family resided, the standard of living was higher. Of the $110 Dodo's father earned each month, he sent to his family the equivalent of $50, but this was not enough to meet the rising standards of living. The costs included all three children's education, uniforms, instruments, textbooks, and cooking and etiquette lessons that required special fees. Some took in sewing to make ends meet.[6]

Christianity became central to Japan's imperial vision. When Matthew Perry forced Japan to trade with the United States, the Treaty of Amity and Commerce in 1858 also gave permission to US visitors to practice their religion and build houses of worship in the open ports of Japan, lifting a centuries-old ban on Christianity.[7] Western missionaries began to establish missions in Japan as well as along the Pacific Coast of the United States to convert Japanese peoples to Christianity. Historian Emily Anderson argues that Japanese Protestants envisioned Japan as a Christian empire. She posits that Japanese Protestants were deeply committed to transforming their nation and profoundly inspired by an historic Christian lineage and an international community, Christians confronted the Japan's changes with a distinctly religious vision.[8]

Dodo's family was part of the Protestant conversion that envisioned the Japanese empire as a Christian empire. Soon after his arrival in the United

States in 1903, Dodo's father converted to Christianity and he worked at the Japanese Methodist Episcopal Mission. A few years later, when Dodo's mother moved the family to Tokyo, she became a Christian. She enrolled Dodo in Sunday school and English-language Bible classes. Dodo sang in the choir and developed a strong commitment to moral sensibility. He admitted being fascinated by the history of how Christianity had faced opposition in Japan and being moved by stories of child martyrs. He carried the Bible with him and wrote red marks all over it. In fact, Dodo saw himself as a moral leader at his own school. On one occasion, after hearing rumors of his principal's hypocrisy, Dodo took it upon himself to coordinate a dinner between the principal and the students to address the rumors. However, Dodo was disciplined as being disrespectful for questioning his elders. His mother was brought to tears when the principal reprimanded her for Dodo's behavior. Dodo soon became depressed and disillusioned with Japan's educational system.

The possibility of building new Japanese societies outside of Japan attracted Dodo. During the Meiji Restoration, the Japanese government encouraged people to emigrate to establish Japanese settlements in a broader vision of a borderless Japanese empire. Three major facets that made up Japanese imperialism in the United States included the expansion of commercial power and trade, obtaining higher education and implementing Western thought, and personal striving and success.[9] Having been a lifelong and successful student, Dodo aimed to pursue Western thought and philosophy, which he found lacking in the Tokyo schools. Also an avid reader, Dodo was greatly influenced by the biographies of national leaders, including President Abraham Lincoln, British Prime minister Lloyd George, and Great Noble of the Meiji Transformation Saigo Takamori. Inspired by their visions of creating new societies, seeing himself as a leader in training, and frustrated with the politics of his scholastic leaders in Tokyo, Dodo was drawn to the prospect of building a new Japanese society in the United States.

In 1921, Dodo arrived at Angel Island to a California in the throes of anti-immigrant sentiment. By then, Angel Island in San Francisco Bay was the main immigration processing station for thousands of migrants seeking entry in the port of San Francisco.[10] Dodo was detained at Angel Island for a short period—he went through a health exam and spent the night in a jail cell with five others. He read on the walls the poems of Chinese migrants who were detained years earlier. Dodo, however, seemed to approach unjust treatment with indifference. He engaged the immigration officers in conversation, and when his cellmates were sad, he sang songs to lift their spirits. After his release, Dodo settled in as one of many Japanese schoolboys, or student-laborers, who worked in the Japanese markets in Los Angeles.[11] Dodo attended a class in Americanization, where teachers attempted to transform students from immigrant families into proper American citizens during a period of anti-immigrant legislation.[12]

Anti-Japanese crusaders and racial liberals alike saw Buddhism as a characteristic of Japanese old world customs and Christianity as a characteristic of Americanization. Religious studies scholars Duncan Ryūken Williams and Tomoe Moriya argue that an overwhelming majority of Japanese immigrants were Buddhists, which prompted the eastward movement of Buddhism from Japan across the Pacific.[13] Early Buddhist temples in the United States were more than just religious centers; they also offered social and cultural services for immigrants in a new organized society. Japanese immigrant communities outside of Japan posed a need for religious institutions where they could express their spirituality and bury their dead, as well as access networks to find work opportunities. But because Buddhism was largely Orientalized, Buddhist temples had to Americanize, or make themselves appear akin to a Western religion, to avoid racial harassment.

While Christian missions often promoted Americanization, the Japanese Methodist Episcopal Mission is an example of the adaptability of Western Christianity to the imperatives of Japanese imperialism. Dodo and his father embraced Christian conservative ideas of social reform and paternalist intervention. They employed a moral doctrine, such as fidelity and sobriety, as a solution to the social ills facing Japanese American communities caused by industrialization, immigration, and racism. Japanese immigrant pastors reinforced traditional gender roles and patriarchal values to marital grief. Several social factors configured into the marital strife between picture brides and immigrant men, including the vast age difference, men's deceitful portrayal of their ages and fortunes, and the imbalanced ratio of men to women. However, counseling services often focused on policing the women. In fact, Dodo's father claimed women's infidelity to be the most dangerous social ill facing the Japanese American community. In one case, the church sought to counsel a married woman who was having an affair with another man and to convince her to maintain fidelity and monogamy. However, when they "failed to reform" her, or she would not discontinue her affair, they declared her unfit as a parent, took her children from her custody, and put them under the care of the church.[14] This stood in contrast to the church's approach to men's immorality: when Takada's father would not stop drinking and gambling, the church did not take away his children.

For children they had removed from mothers, the Japanese Methodist Episcopal Mission operated orphanages where they instilled nuclear family values. While Dodo's father counseled immigrant couples, Dodo stepped in to mentor youths. Dodo had built such rapport with Jane Couch, the director of Methodist Episcopal Jane Couch Japanese Home for Girls, that he became a sort of right-hand man at the institution.[15] The Home for Girls provided social services to young Japanese American women, including housing, English classes, a Japanese-language school, food, piano lessons, and Bible study.[16] Dodo interacted with, and at times monitored, youths. At one point, when one of the girls was suspected of stealing fifteen dollars, Couch and a Japanese American social worker asked Dodo to investigate. The Home for Girls was often celebrated as a successful intervention in the raising of chaste women. In fact, in revisiting one case of having removed children because of the mother's infidelity, the ministry men boasted that their intervention directly resulted in the two daughters growing up to marry newspaper men and keeping a good home life as proper married women.[17]

Despite the efforts of Dodo and the Japanese Methodist Episcopal Mission to morally reform Japanese immigrants to prevent anti-Japanese sentiment, liberal white Christians and Japanese immigrant elites failed to prevent the passage of anti-Japanese legislation. The 1920 California Alien Land Law, the US Supreme Court case of Takao Ozawa, and the 1924 Immigration Act closed any pathway toward US citizenship and therefore any way for men to fulfill their masculinity as measured through settler colonialism. Since successful masculinity was based on land ownership, citizenship inclusion, and international recognition, the 1924 Immigration Act signaled not only the racial embarrassment of a people, but the failed masculinities of Japanese migrant men. Settler colonial masculinity was in crisis.

SELF-RESPECT AFTER JAPANESE EXCLUSION, 1924 TO 1929

After the implementation of the national policy of the 1924 Immigration Act, the Japanese Young Men's Association (JYMA) in Southern California convened to discuss how to move forward in the aftermath of citizenship ineligibility and "absolute exclusion from the farming interest." The JYMA was part of a broader network of Young Men's Associations in Japan, originating before the Meiji Restoration to train young men in the Samurai arts. After World War I, it evolved toward national and civil training of young men, especially regarding national characteristics and good citizenship, including loyalty to the emperor and to parents, character building, physical training, and general efficiency. Each association was led by men in positions of power: political leaders, teachers, civil servants, religious leaders, and others.[18] By 1924, twenty associations across Los Angeles participated in a conference to discuss how the organization should move forward in training young men to meet the current political climate in the United States. At their convening, JYMA wrestled with their rejection from US citizenship and decided that, if they would not be legally recognized as equal to whites in citizenry, they must define themselves and develop their self-worth in broader ways and on different terms. No longer able to build their identities around the self-made men of land acquisitions and citizenship, JYMA decided to foster a "spirit of self-respect" through the development of intellectual and physical education among young men.[19]

It was no coincidence, though, that these arenas provided some measure of equal footing and were not bound to US immigration exclusion laws. The Gentlemen's Agreement had ensured that Japanese American students would not be segregated but could attend all-white schools. In addition, sports, though segregated in the United States, could offer a competitive playing field. Scholastic and athletic achievements were not limited or determined by US border closures, nor was the citizenship of Japanese immigrants an issue. Japanese immigrant students could obtain higher education in the United States and study alongside their white counterparts, and US-born youths could migrate to Japan for schooling. Moreover, although the borders were closed to migrants, Japanese sports teams traveled to the United States for a series of tours and played against various teams in the United States, and vice versa: US athletic teams could travel and play against teams in Japan. The spirit of self-respect served as a measure of self-protection against the legalization of racism and aimed to prevent youths from internalizing a second-class citizenry. Rather, the spirit of self-respect encouraged youths to "strive to attain to a higher ideal" than the national parameters established by US citizenship, immigration, and land laws.[20]

The new brand of self-respect continued to advance the goals of Japanese Christian imperialism. The strive to attain a "higher ideal," rather than national or legal recognition, confirmed Dodo's spiritual commitment to the higher morals set under Christianity for reforming Japanese immigrant communities. Reframing terms of worthiness and judgment under religious guidelines, rather than racial or national, reset the scale to an equal footing for all peoples, white and Japanese alike. It also allowed Japanese immigrants to reject their national exclusion by elevating their personal, spiritual, communal, transnational regard above local or national approval. Moreover, this revision enabled men to rebuild their masculinity while at the same time conserving patriarchal Christian moral values. However, it also began to create a rift even within the Japanese Christian youth community: as the JYMA moved away from building its identity beyond the definitions exclusive to the nation-state and toward a strict moral doctrine, other young people and women's organizations continued to be concerned with the social and racial categories defined within the nation-state and moved away from a strict moral doctrine.

With the new vision of transnational masculinity, the JYMA provided a space to develop intellectualism and athletics. For instance, the Los Angeles association focused on athletics, publication, and speech and lecture. It held a program that focused on athletics where each night offered a different activity, including ju-jitsu, fencing, table tennis, and speech. The Compton association promoted mutual friendship, physical, social, and intellectual welfare alongside a relationship with the Agricultural Association of Compton. The San Gabriel Valley association hosted gatherings to discuss relevant topics, promoted Sunday school and night school, created a baseball team, as well as fund-raised for the organization by hosting a yearly motion picture. Each association varied in how it categorized the age range of "young men"—some accepted members between the ages of fifteen and thirty, and other associations accepted members of any age.[21] The JYMAs sometimes competed against one another. For instance, the Los Angeles association held a debate with the San Bernardino association on the subject of "would young men succeed in life in the city or in the country?"[22] The Los Angeles association argued for the city, while the San Bernardino association argued for the country.[23]

Influential elders in the community who were particularly invested in developing transnational masculinity among the young men formed the Federation of JYMAs. The Federation of JYMAs included Noriyuki Toyama; Kohey Shimano, president of the first Japanese Language School; Hiroshi Suzuki of the *Rafu Shimpo*; Jiro Ono, secretary of the Japanese Hotel Keepers Association; Gongoro Nakamura, a USC law graduate; Yoshiharu Mizobe, a pharmacist; Tenyo Yasaki, a writer; Shiro Nakahata, president of the Japanese Farmer's Association; and Masuo Hiratsuka, secretary of the Japanese Associations of America.[24] The Federation of JYMAs aimed to develop the intellectual and physical talents of young men through a weeklong series of events known as Young People's Week, though originally conceived as Boys' Week. In their attempt to "inspire" and "arouse the youthful spirit among the young people," they coordinated a weeklong series of events in connection with local Japanese newspapers and churches. The week's events began with an evening of Christian sermons aimed toward youths, an evening of entertainment with young women displaying their musical talents for the leisure of men, athletic matches of both American sports such as baseball and basketball as well as Japanese sports such as ju-jitsu and fencing, oratorical contests, mock session of the National Diet, and a parent-child social.[25]

Despite its lofty goals, however, the Young People's Week was less than a resounding success in their attempts to draw in young people, especially young women and the "American-born." The planning committee did not take into account the perspectives of the youths, and most importantly, it neglected women's input. The program reflected the older society's ideas of what they should pass onto youths. They planned a nostalgic theatrical production of the diet, which was a hit among the Japanese immigrant elders but not well-attended by youths. Rather, youths were staging their own renditions of plays and theater that were largely modeled after US themes. They planned a social with parents that yielded a decent crowd, but it was not well-attended like the more popular peer-to-peer socials. Notably, the entertainment event was a disaster because it did not secure the participation of young women trained and skilled in classical instruments. Furthermore, the printed program was in the Japanese language, which few of the young could read. As a result, although it was "young people's week," youths were in sparse attendance. The only event that drew a large crowd of youths was the athletics component.[26]

The Federation of JYMA had difficulty expanding membership for several reasons. Immigrant leaders as well as Japan-born young men had their own vision of how young people should develop and did not hold back in criticizing them. First, youths created and expanded new organizations like Japanese Student Christian Association (JSCA) and the Oliver Club, but members of the JYMA had spoken out against the creation and expansion of other new youth organizations and saw no reason for having separate clubs, especially when youths could join an existing local chapter of the JYMA. The Federation of JYMA tried to encourage youths to attend their meetings.[27] However, young people were creating other organizations that focused on Americanization. The Federation of JYMA aimed to promote a unified front under their imperatives while young people emphasized diversity and specialty. Second, the Federation of JYMA clung to conservative moral values in an age defined by a loosening of morals. The Federation of JYMA had grown concerned about a thriving urban youth culture that might lead to immoral behavior, such as stealing and gambling. However, young people embraced a rebellious lifestyle of skipping church, spending their evenings out and about, and other acts deemed to be mischievous.

Third, the Federation of JYMA believed that US-born youths, who were enfranchised, should use their political voice to address the imperatives of those who did not have voting rights. Some felt that young citizens were not using their political voice to advance their community and were not necessarily aligning themselves with their elders' imperatives. And finally, the Federation of JYMA hoped that youths and elders would work together to advance elders' imperatives, rather than to advance what elders saw as young people's personal satisfaction. Seeing a need to address these tensions, the Federation of JYMA ran a series of programs: a "forensic" meeting, or a debate, to "promote better understanding between the two generations"; a club night to gather all youth clubs for a social and a discussion; a meeting for those twenty-one years and older to discuss the issue of voting; and a meeting to gather the representatives of all clubs, bringing youth and elder leaders in one room.[28]

The Federation of JYMA found themselves ideologically at odds with other youth-led organizations. The JSCA as well as the Oliver Club had different motivations and purposes. While the Federation of JYMA promoted self-respect, nondelinquency, and Japanese culture, other young people's organizations stressed racial inclusion, a tolerance for modern morality, and US culture. In an urban culture increasingly defined by the expansion of women's roles and sexual freedom, the Federation of JYMA provided a place for those nostalgic for the conservative values of the past.

College fraternities offered another sphere where Dodo's conservative patriarchal values and imperial masculinity could thrive. Historian Nicholas Syrett argues that, by the 1910s, during the period of Jim Crow segregation and the admission of immigrants on campus, US white fraternity men increasingly defined their manliness through athletic success, wealth, and whiteness. Academic performance, however, began to lose its appeal for men. By the 1920s, when women began to enter college in higher numbers and expanded their equalities and freedoms, fraternity men responded by embracing a more virile masculinity based on the sexual exploitation of working-class women as well as a culture of homophobia.[29] Dodo entered the world of college fraternities in the United States when he joined and later became president of a Japanese American fraternity, Gakusei-Kai, at the University of Southern California.

The Gakusei-Kai, a Japanese American fraternity under the auspices of the Federation of JYMA, paralleled some of the trends of white fraternities but departed in some distinct ways. As Japanese immigrants began to enroll at USC in larger numbers and likely were excluded from whites-only

2.1 Yearbook photo of Gakusei-Kai fraternity at the University of Southern California, 1926. Courtesy of USC Digital Libraries.

fraternities, Gakusei-Kai developed in the 1910s and incorporated in 1920. It later established its home base at the University of Southern California, which also provided much-needed housing for migrant students (fig 2.1). While white fraternities tended to place less emphasis on academics by the early twentieth century, Gakusei-Kai focused on intellectualism. In fact, the purpose of the organization was to promote higher education among a youth that did not see the benefits of a college education. Gakusei-Kai generated interest among potential members by hosting Japanese University Night.[30] Moreover, Dodo spoke to various Christian youth organizations to share his experiences as a college student and facilitate the interests of potential future university students.[31] Although Gakusei-Kai did not identify with a particular religious affiliation, it followed the larger secularization of college fraternities. It mirrored other social trends, including athletics and a vibrant social scene. Gakusei-Kai had several departments, including a library, athletics, forensic (debate), and social relations.[32] It had its own sports team to compete against other teams.[33] And finally, Gakusei-Kai participated in the emerging dancing scene among Japanese American youths.

With a fraternal focus on intellectualism, Dodo believed in social science as a way to investigate the Japanese question in the aftermath of the 1924 Immigration Act. As a sociology major, he joined the Survey of Race Relations investigation team. Historian Sarah Griffith argues that the Survey of Race Relations blended socioreligious ideology with social scientific research and reflected the larger evolving liberal Protestant opposition to anti-Asian racism.[34] The Survey of Race Relations aimed to foster interracial understanding between white and Japanese Protestant churches and sought to promote solutions to the Japanese question through interracial cooperation. However, Dodo's participation reveals that liberal Protestant Christianity and social science enabled a range of ideologies from Americanization to Japanese imperialism. In fact, Dodo's involvement reveals the larger evolving Japanese imperialist response to anti-Asian racism. Unlike sociologists who aimed to measure the assimilation capabilities of Japanese immigrants, Dodo aimed to measure the progress of Japanese imperialism. Unlike his peers who took the survey, Dodo was not interested in showcasing Japanese immigrants as assimilable; rather, he was interested in closely examining their social ills and diasporic connections. Although the 1924 Immigration Act had signaled the failure of moral reform efforts, Japanese imperialists doubled down on imperial ideologies based on moral reform and patriarchal values.

In fact, Dodo's submissions reveal his evolving politics through sociological observations of the Los Angeles Japanese American community, of which he soon declared himself as part of the Japanese American intelligentsia—a new generation of scholars and experts who could influence the direction of national politics. Dodo was interested in the development of Japanese colonies outside of Japan and examined Los Angeles as his subject. His eight reports to the Survey of Race Relations included an estimated population of Japanese in California, a catalog of literature read by the Japanese community (bookstores that he had visited in person), and observations of the Methodist Mission.[35] As a result of his research, Dodo purported himself to be an expert on the Japanese question. He started speaking at various student clubs in colleges across Southern California, including Occidental College.[36] After graduating from the University of Southern California with a sociology degree, he carried his vision to a new platform as an editor for the Japanese language section of the Japanese American newspaper *Rafu Shimpo* in Los Angeles.

TOWARD A MODEL MILITANCY, 1929 TO 1934

After two years as editor in the Japanese-language section, Dodo moved to become the new editor for the English-language section of the *Rafu Shimpo* in 1929. From the moment he stepped in, it was a wrong fit. Up until then, Louise Suski, an education major at UCLA, a member of the Oliver Club and active in the YWCA, had served as the first editor in chief for the English-language section since its 1926 debut; she was also one of the first female youth editors. Under Suski's guidance, the English-language section mirrored the evolving politics of the transnational New Women and a vibrant urban youth culture. Each issue highlighted club activities, recreational sports, and comic strips. After three years, the senior editorial staff unceremoniously kicked Suski to the curb and breezily announced Dodo as a new editor with their full support: "It now deems the second-generation men and women have attained a sufficient degree of community-consciousness to deal with their own problems."[37] Japanese elders deemed the young people's progress only "sufficient" because, unlike Suski, Dodo's politics and vision fell in line with the Japanese elders at *Rafu Shimpo*. Elders supported his new vision: Dodo wanted to bring "radical change" away from modernism—the new morality, a focus on US citizenry, and New Women values—and move toward what he termed "high idealism," which entailed a return to strict morals, Japanese diasporic citizenry, and patriarchal values.

Departing from the New Women editorial staff that focused on local and domestic news, Dodo centered a diasporic approach. Whereas previous years' issues focused on the local activities of the Japanese American youths in Los Angeles, Dodo endorsed broader coverage of Japanese settler communities across the Pacific. He changed the cover page of the English section, which had focused solely on news from Japan, and instead reported news from settler communities in Hawai'i, settler communities in states other than California, and settler colonies of Japan.[38] This reflected his vision of developing an organized and united Japanese community that bridged the Pacific. Not only would he cover Japanese news in many different regions, Dodo inaugurated an editorial section to convey his opinions about how the Japanese overseas community should develop through self-respect and higher ideals. Dodo pieced together his vision for a Los Angeles identity that maintained good moral Christian values in the face of racism and saw itself as a part of a larger settler community.

Dodo was invested in cultural diplomacy. From his perspective, white prejudice would wane if Japanese Americans took up their duty to educate white America on Japanese American achievements and culture. For instance, he praised the Japanese Hotel Men's Association's Industrial Parties that were well-received by local whites and the JSCA annual bulletin that highlighted student achievements and was seen favorably by whites.[39] Furthermore, Dodo lauded local communities for displaying the cultural merits of the Los Angeles Japanese American community to white America. He praised the uptown Japanese American community (or Uptown Nippon) for planting cherry trees. He also lauded the Japanese Drama Association for bringing a Ken-Geki troupe from Japan.

In terms of social mores, Dodo advanced a key characteristic of the model minority: nondelinquency.[40] He believed that crime and dependency prevented the formation of a strong society. Dodo aimed to discipline readers if they did not present the community as free of crime and possessing the ability to uplift themselves, especially in direct comparison with other ethnic minority groups. For instance, he reported that Los Angeles police statistics revealed that the Japanese group no longer enjoyed the reputation for being more law-abiding than any other foreign group. Los Angeles police had cited that Japanese Americans were not singularly law-abiding; in fact, they had more arrests than Chinese and Filipinos. Most of the arrests were related to gambling, violating prohibition, drunkenness, and prostitution.[41] Dodo believed he held the recipe for dealing with juvenile delinquency: a systematic reinforcement of moral institutions—the home, schools, and religious organizations—and athletics.[42]

Dodo believed self-reliance was key to friendship building between the United States and Japan. As the United States and Japan plunged into the Great Depression, Dodo did not believe that Japanese Americans should rely on US resources. Japanese immigrant charity organizations had given

$10,000 in 1929 to the Los Angeles Community Chest but received twice as much. Dodo believed the Japanese American community should give the full amount of what they received, if not at least half.[43] He charged, "Are we to remain a burden upon the shoulders of the American people?"[44] Dodo's message might not have resonated with young people who felt that the state and federal governments should provide for communities in need, particularly during a period of economic decline.

Dodo frowned on women's agency and often reinforced patriarchal values. He lamented when there were more than four divorces in one week. He called one case "pathetic," alleging that the woman gave her suitor a "false report" about her parent's consent. Three days later, she asked for an annulment and argued the suitor coerced her into marriage. Dodo took the side of the suitor: "We pity the girl for her frivolous notion of love and marriage and we sympathize with the young man for his mistaken choice."[45] Second, he praised youths for reforming dances to meet elder-approved moral standards, noting that women at dances maintained a more decent dress code and that women's immodest approach to fashion, such as "flappers and boobies," had waned.[46] However, Dodo warned against young women's lying when going out and threatened to sniff out their immoral ways.[47]

Dodo envisioned ways that youths might contribute to Japanese expansion. He kept an eye out for commerce and industry that would particularly resolve the problem of limited job opportunities for youths. He often looked to Japanese industries as places where youths could thrive. For instance, he pointed out how the movie industry in Hollywood was attempting to shift the major portions of the Japanese movie industry across the Pacific to Southern California. This would provide youths with job opportunities.[48] He also encouraged the Japanese American community in Los Angeles to expand toward Mexico. A Japanese silk factory in Mexico escaped Mexico's new labor regulations against any industry using US capital.[49] In fact, because of the Japanese company's tax exemption, Japan began to build international relations with Mexico. In turn, Mexico would become a site of Japanese industrial interests and Los Angeles might become the logical point of trade, which would provide youths with job opportunities. With a prescient sense of the future, Dodo encouraged the youths to learn Spanish.[50]

At the front of Dodo's mind was a comparative and relational understanding of Japanese Americans to other Asian immigrant groups, but he had not yet embraced interethnic solidarity, instead opting for interethnic competition. As Dodo saw similar patterns of racial violence toward Filipino immigrants as Japanese immigrants, he utilized racial violence as "lessons" for the Japanese American community. In 1930, white and Mexican workers targeted and committed acts of violence against Filipinos through a series of riots across Central California. Five days of rioting broke out in the Watsonville area. White mobs of up to seven hundred people raided the taxi dance hall and local ranches that employed Filipino labor. Rioters chased Filipinos, forcing them to seek refuge in the city council room.[51] Dodo concluded that economic conflict could be adjusted and that "racial aversion," or in this case social integration and miscegenation, was highly "durable." Yet in a problematic and myopic comparison, Dodo held the Watsonville riots against Filipino immigrants as a measure of Japanese progress in continuing to go "undisturbed" in building their foothold in California without the nuisance of such "casual occurrences."[52]

By the end of his tenure at the English section of the *Rafu Shimpo*, Dodo became disillusioned by all the various forms of youthful rebellion, from acquaintance with communists to involvement in nonviolent crimes. Dodo disagreed with the radical Communist Party tactics in the 1930s. Japanese American youths participated in communist uprisings in Los Angeles. Four youths were arrested for "disturbing the peace" by printing communist ideologies.[53] Three Japanese immigrants were arrested in a communist march against city hall. It was reported that two were likely to be deported.[54] Although Dodo agreed that economic structures needed to be changed, Dodo did not approve of their methods. He believed that they should be allowed to march but should not be given any attention through police brutality and martyrdom.[55] Dodo often conflated the media attention around protesting with the negative reports of delinquency. In one of his last editorials, he publicly shamed three "American-born" boys for disgracing the rest of youths. One had committed a holdup, another had robbed two houses, and another forged eighteen checks.[56] Unable to believe that the Japanese youths were ethically worse than youths of other races, Dodo took a leave of absence in order to study youth problems.[57] After becoming disillusioned with Los Angeles urban youths, he ended his tenure at the English-language section and returned to the Japanese-language section of the *Rafu Shimpo*.

Dodo found a new home for his staunchly strict beliefs: Japanese military imperialism on the road to World War II. Elements of Dodo's transnational new manhood tracked with Japanese military imperialism for several reasons. First, his belief in cultural diplomacy between the United States and Japan found an end goal: their imperial alliance as the new center of power. In the first part of the 1930s, Japanese military imperialists saw the United States as a potential partner or ally in their drive for empire building. Dodo attempted to build bridges with white leaders in the United States as Japanese military imperialism turned aggressive toward China. Second, for Dodo, Japan and the Japanese diaspora served as the model for all Asian countries, and their diasporic communities, and later, all non-Western countries and people of color. In the latter part of the 1930s, Japanese military imperialists abandoned hope for an alliance with the United States and adopted and promoted the Greater East Asia Co-Prosperity Sphere, an ideology of a pan-Asianism in which Japan liberated Asian countries from Western imperialism by incorporating them into the Japanese empire. Dodo turned to interethnic solidarity, or building alliances with racial minorities, in the United States under the mantle of Japanese imperialism.

Dodo would have to first convince Japanese American youths to serve as cultural diplomats in a very unpopular move made by the Japanese imperial army. After blowing up a railroad in order to provide justification for its occupation, the Japanese army occupied Manchuria, in northeast China, in 1931. This event opened the Japanese government to considerable criticism for infringing on Chinese sovereignty. Still, Japanese newspapers argued that the Japanese army had acted only in defense. In the United States, widespread criticism against the Japanese military led local leaders to build a campaign of education among Japanese Americans as a self-protective measure against anti-Japanese sentiment, where young people served as cultural and transnational diplomats to educate and defend Japanese actions in China as a measure of bringing coalition and prosperity to Asia.[58]

Drawing on his experience in debates, Dodo served as a cultural diplomat to reinterpret Japanese aggression into China to audiences critical of

Japan's actions. In March 1932, Dodo participated in a very public debate with Dr. Samuel Phang, a Chinese instructor at the University of Southern California and member of the Chinese Defense League, at the Los Angeles Liberal Forum. Taking place at the Wilshire-Ebell Theater, with a seating capacity of 1,238 people, the forum offered a chance for Los Angelenos to learn from racial representatives, a Chinese immigrant and a Japanese immigrant, about the conflict in East Asia. They each answered this question: Is Japan justified in its policy toward China? Phang argued the negative and Dodo the affirmative. In his speech, Dodo offered an interpretation of the history of Japanese aggression into China as a "justice of necessity" and explained that the goal was peace and prosperity in Asia. Dodo's speech, but not Phang's, was later reprinted in the *Rafu Shimpo*.[59]

Dodo was among the young journalists contributing to the intellectual construction of the Pacific era as a racial project. Dodo wrote *The Era of the Pacific and the U.S.* in Japanese, which *Rafu Shimpo* published two thousand copies of to sell at local Japanese bookstores.[60] The Pacific era was a school of thought that interpreted a series of events around Japanese occupation of Manchuria and identified how Japan would lead the Asia-Pacific region to an era of peace and prosperity. The Pacific era built up the significant role of young men in developing an alliance between two great nations across the Pacific: United States and Japan. Many bookmarked the Manchurian Incident as the beginning of the Pacific Era. With the rise of the Pacific era, parents sought a Japanese education and believed that the Japanese language would be the language of the future. This would end the period of Americanization, in which Japanese parents refrained from teaching their children the Japanese language. The Pacific era reimagined the East-West divide and the Western colonization of the rest of the world. Instead of a Eurocentric grouping of nations, it seemed plausible that a powerful Western nation like the United States might build an alliance with a powerful Eastern nation like Japan. Whereas in the previous era the Atlantic had served as the center of commerce, Japanese military imperialism signaled the rise of the Pacific as the new center. This racial project provided young Japanese American men with a sense of pride and purpose during a period of national exclusion and global depression.

Although Dodo stated that he wrote his book to educate youths on their part in the Pacific era, it was written in the Japanese language, which

2.2 A Japanese bookstore in Los Angeles. Courtesy of United Methodist Church.

many US-born youths could not read. This assumption perhaps signaled the greater divergence between Japanese settler colonial masculinity and an urban LA youth culture enmeshed in Americanization. Although some youths did partake in public intellectual education in defense of Japanese military aggression through speech competitions, many turned away from Japanese imperialism once it digressed from an alliance between the United States and Japan. When Dodo realized that he could not convince Japanese American youths in Los Angeles to join the cause of Japanese military imperialism at the start of the Sino-Japanese War, he turned his efforts toward recruiting African Americans in Harlem to support Japan's vision during World War II. Dodo joined the Japanese-language newspaper *Tokyo Nichi Nichi* in New York and focused on recruiting a group of people based on shared histories of US racism and a common approach of militant opposition to their suppression.[61]

Dodo's evolution from a converted Christian schoolboy in favor of Americanization in the 1910s to a public intellectual in defense of Japanese military expansion in the 1930s did not seem like a radical turn of events but rather a consistent commitment to paternal and militant ideologies. What began as an investment in Christian morals in the period of Japanese expansion in the 1910s, evolved as self-respect through fraternal organizations in the aftermath of US exclusion of the 1920s, and turned into a public intellectualism foreseeing the rise of the Pacific Era in the 1930s. Dodo aligned with Christianity because of its intersection with imperial (and evangelical) aspirations, but more so its insistence on the preservation of the nuclear family and moral values that would resolve anti-immigrant sentiment. Dodo joined Japanese Young Men's Associations, which continued to preserve Japanese imperial masculinity in the face of US exclusion laws, but he found itself increasingly at odds with New Women and a rebellious urban youth culture in Los Angeles. Finally, he utilized his editorial platforms to discipline young people to return to socially conservative values, becoming a model to other ethnic minorities amid the Great Depression, which ultimately led to an alignment with Japanese military expansion in Asia.

Dodo's story reveals how ideals of masculinity under Japanese imperialism evolved in an era of tumultuous change. Japanese imperial masculinity shifted alongside the age of Japanese expansion and US immigration policies, while maintaining its reactionary opposition to expansion of women's roles and rights. Before 1924, Japanese imperialism motivated young men to build colonies abroad. However, in the aftermath of the 1924 Immigration Act, Japanese imperial masculinity shifted its parameters and young men instead built self-respect and racial equality through education. In the 1930s, the racial project of the Pacific era incorporated Japanese imperial masculinity by reinterpreting the advancement of racial equality through military aggression. Japanese imperial masculinity preserved its incredible staying power through old conservative institutions such as Christianity, academic elitism, and radical ideology. At the same time that Japanese imperial masculinity adapted and preserved itself, Japanese ideals of "good wife, wise mother" adapted and preserved itself against the hypersexual reputation of the flapper, as we see in chapter 3.

3

The Highbrow New Woman

In her interview for the Survey of Race Relations, Chiyoko Nina Otera confessed that she felt quite restricted at home. Her parents held onto "many old Japanese ideas about girls" and expected her to spend all of her time at home. However, the new youth ministry at her church hosted many attractive social affairs. Otera's father required convincing for each event that Otera wanted to attend, and he gave his consent only sparingly. If she wanted to attend a social gathering, her brother had to escort her, and both needed to return by their curfew. When she wanted to attend student conferences put on by the Christian Endeavor and the YWCA, her mother had to convince her father to allow her to attend. However, there was one social activity that the entire family ultimately agreed that she should not engage in: dancing. Dances posed a particular concern for parents who felt it was inappropriate for young women to be intermingling with boys so openly. In fact, Otera explained that abstinence from courting was a shared value among high-culture families: "Never was I permitted to go out with a boy, for my parents repeatedly stated that it was improper in Japan as well as the best American homes." Although at first Otera rebelled, she soon came to the same understanding: "My parents have always been opposed to dancing, and in this respect my brother sided with them because he did not want his little sister to dance. This idea became so deeply ingrained in me that I never cared much for dancing."[1]

Otera's inherited sentiments about dancing offer a window into the perspectives of Japanese modernists that shaped the US New Woman in Los Angeles. The Japanese imperial project was premised on molding modern women into domestic roles as "good wife, wise mother." When a flaming youth culture ushered forth new roles where women spent more time outside the home, danced at parties with boys, and even filed for divorce, modernists believed that the flaming youth culture and the US New Woman morally degraded their society. Japanese immigrant families aimed to preserve their race and their society amid the shifts and changes. As Otera's own family demonstrates, her parents relented and went along with some changes, but maintained complete opposition to others. Through this active negotiation between daughters and parents, immigrant families aligned their Japanese modern values with highbrow white culture. As young women embraced some US New Woman characteristics, the Japanese modern ideals of "good wife, wise mother" continued to play a significant role in shaping transnational new womanhood.

This chapter examines how Japanese modernists and "good wife, wise mother" trope shaped young women like Otera from the 1920s to the 1930s. Young women like Otera had to balance between her parents' modern Japanese understanding of women's roles and her peers' leap into flapper youth culture. Otera embraced moderation: the alignment of highbrow white culture with highbrow Japanese culture. This chapter argues that Otera found a measure of safety, privilege, and freedom through the modern adaptation of "good wife, wise mother." Otera's story demonstrates how the "good wife, wise mother role" persisted and changed in the Los Angeles Japanese American community.

THE DECLINE OF THE JAPANESE MODERN WOMAN, 1910S TO 1924

A small minority of Japanese elites set the tone in shaping modern womanhood in Los Angeles. They viewed the expansion of women's freedoms, such as participation in urban leisure and a right to divorce, as signs of imperial decline. Criticisms around women's roles and the flaming youths mirrored anxieties of white families in the United States over the influence of "bad" morals and changes to the nuclear family, but differed from white families precisely because of how Japanese immigrant critics assembled their vision for Japanese development in response to Japanese exclusion. Under Japanese development, Japanese immigrant communities aimed to maintain moral superiority in the United States, a country that appeared to be descending into immorality through divorce, dancing, and debauchery. Japanese imperialists believed and promoted the "good wife, wise mother" ideology. They believed that a woman's place was in the home, that she became an educated woman in the highest forms of arts, and that she must remain chaste. Although many Japanese immigrants believed in adopting certain Western values, including civic and democratic principles as well as capitalist values, Japanese elders wanted to steer clear of what they viewed as the "bad" parts of Americanization, such as changing women's roles, rising divorce rates, and young people's merrymaking.

By the 1920s, Japanese elites in Los Angeles believed that the expansion of women's freedoms led to a breakdown in the nuclear family and undermined national progress. Women filed for divorce for a variety of reasons, including not getting along with or being misled by their newly arranged husbands and being courted by other men. Japanese elites, however, grew concerned that rising divorce rates reflected their community's moral decline. Some elites attributed the rising divorce rates to "freedom of women, gay life, and merry-making." For instance, Masami Suzuki, a male medical student studying in the United States and an attendee of the Japanese Methodist Episcopal Church believed that "too much freedom" made women "valueless creatures." Suzuki lamented: "Women in this country are too free, and if such conditions keep up, moral deterioration will be hard to overcome."[2] Attributing divorce to the expansion of women's freedoms, elites like Suzuki believed the solution was that women should cultivate a peaceful home life and beautiful personalities.

The Otera family may have been one statistic that raised anxiety over national progress, since Otera's parents, Tsuru Anastasia Otera and Tsunekichi Alexander Otera, divorced in Los Angeles. In the late 1890s, Tsunekichi Alexander and Tsuru Anastasia Otera had lived in Shirakawa, Fukushima-ken, Japan. Tsunekichi was the fifth of ten children and the third son born to a wealthy farmer and water mill manager, Jinuemon Otera, in Shirakawa-machi, Japan. By 1904, the Oteras had four children, all born in Japan: Yakow

"Jacob" (son) born on April 29, 1894; Kimi (daughter), the first daughter, born May 23, 1896; Tetsuya Akira Allen Aquila (son), born January 26, 1901; and Chiyoko Nina (daughter), born February 24, 1904. Chiyoko Otera was the only child to migrate with her parents when she was two years old, in 1906 to Seattle. Her siblings migrated at a later time. The Oteras gave birth to their fifth child, Ada Otera, in 1911 and moved to Los Angeles. Tsunekichi ran a tailor shop, specializing in formal business attire for men, working on coats and pants. By 1921, Tsuru Anastasia divorced Tsunekichi Alexander. By 1923, Tsuru Anastasia was remarried, to Chuzaburo Yashima, former secretary of the Japanese Association of Southern California and later entrepreneur in the furniture business.

Japanese elites attributed such divorces like the Oteras to US moral decline, and moreover, many attributed children's lack of filiality to the breakdown of the nuclear family as well as the poor quality of public education. Doctor Nakaya, a well-respected physician within the Los Angeles Japanese American community, believed that children raised in the United States had too much freedom and independence compared to how he was raised and how children were raised in Japan. He attributed this to environment. He concluded that the ghettoization of Japanese American youths in the US public education system ultimately led to youths' adoption of the "bad parts" of American culture. Although not a Christian, he believed that the solution was to place children in Sunday schools. He believed that youths who attended Sunday School were better behaved. He wanted his own children to be God-fearing.[3]

Immigrant elders and parents alike put their hopes in the expansion of ethnic institutions, such as a Japanese church, to provide a wholesome influence for young people. On February 17, 1918, three congregations—the Los Angeles Presbyterian Church, the Los Angeles Congregational Church, and the Japanese Bethlehem Congregational Church of Los Angeles—merged into a single congregation as the Union Church in order to serve a burgeoning youth community.[4] The local community successfully fund-raised for a new building, and Reverend Giichi Tanaka became the first pastor. By 1924, the Union Church provided separate services for the older immigrant community in the Japanese language and for youths in the English language, a structure that attracted families like the Oteras. Sociologist Gretchen Tuthill noted that the English service began at eleven o'clock. The hymns, which were sung from English-language books published in the United States, were led by a choir of ten or fifteen young people, and the sermon and short prayer was adapted by the assistant pastor for the English-speaking youth audience.[5] Immediately following, Reverend Tanaka led the Japanese-language service. Chiyo Otera played an integral role in the English language services, serving as the main organist for the Union Church.

Union Church organized its own Christian Endeavor, a ministry for young people, in hopes of promoting moral values through youth-centered programs and events.[6] Founded on the values of developing international friendship, the Christian Endeavor quickly became a space for white Christian mentors to build close relationships to Japanese American youth. Leadership expanded to hire white social workers to lead Young People's Societies.[7] The Christian Endeavor was progressive in its vision for leadership, allowing women to serve in leadership capacities. For instance, Leela Leech served as the Young People's Society director at the Union Church. White social workers often provided spaces for youths to hold important political, spiritual, and personal discussions. They asked them to discuss the Japanese question as it related to them, including tensions and misunderstandings at home with their parents and their national identity. At the same time, they also learned singing and debating skills. Social workers also encouraged Japanese American youths to think about how they could serve their communities. Chiyo Otera, for instance, served as assistant superintendent in the Intermediate Christian Endeavor, a ministry dedicated to young people of high school age.

The Union Church not only served as a spiritual gathering but quickly became the center of recreational and leisure life for Japanese American youths. The church's facilities offered a place for recreation and after-church events, such as basketball games, concerts, play performances, and other youth gatherings. Young people organized recreational events to fill their social calendars outside of the regularly scheduled church services and youth group devotions. However, as more and more young women became involved in the Union Church, youth groups, and athletics, parents raised concerns about their daughters' extracurricular lives. Many young women who served on planning committees or played sports often faced opposition from their parents.

One member of the Union Church, Hida Watanabe, became very involved with the activities and came home to parents who were weary of her absences. Watanabe had been assigned to be on different committees at the church, like the decorating committee, and after she and two other boys decorated the Union Church gym until midnight for three consecutive nights, her parents disapproved of her coming home so late. Her father said that he knew where she was, but the Japanese American community might not be so understanding. Her mother told her that "in Japan girls don't go out in the evening" and that "we must think of appearances a little." Watanabe did not think her parents were being unreasonable, and in fact, her parents wanted youths to have a good time but not to be "conspicuous."[8] Parents began to question the influence of the church and wanted to limit their daughters' participation.

Teru Miyamoto's parents said that she was "getting worse all the time" since she joined the Union Church. Miyamoto, who was never active in athletics while she was at Los Angeles High School, liked to go play basketball in the evenings at the Union Church after a long day at the Nippon Dry Goods company. However, her mother rationalized, "Japanese girls don't do that." Miyamoto reasoned, "But we are in America and we ought to have the American ideas and do as Americans do." She also reminded them that she was eighteen years old, the age that the US recognized youth as adults. Miyamoto suspected her mother did not like her conversion to Christianity because her mother was Buddhist. Miyamoto's father, however, was concerned about what Japanese elites in Los Angeles might say. He explained, "It is all right with me, I know where you are going. But other people don't know, they can't stop you and ask where you are going."[9]

Parents and daughters found and negotiated ways for young women to engage in social leisure. Kyo Inouye, another eighteen-year-old living in Los Angeles who attended the Union Church, explained that some daughters often bent the truth in order to attend a social affair. Inouye pointed out that because the system left young women with little agency, as a result, they found ways to get around the system. She explained, "I think it is bad because the children get to lying and get smart." Inouye admitted that her father did not let her go out much in the evenings, but she found that she could use chaperonage as a bargaining chip.[10] She explained, "My father isn't that strict, I beg him real hard and he lets me go. Sometimes when I want to go someplace my brother takes me and that is alright. My brother-in-law helps me, too." She believed that the older members of the Union Church did not mind it if young people went in groups or with chaperones. Despite the assurances that chaperonage provided, they could not act "too free" at social events. As Inouye put it, "we have to be awfully careful because Japanese people love to gossip and anything spreads so quickly."[11]

In an ironic twist, parents began to warn one another not to allow their kids to go to church. Parents wrote about their concerns in the ethnic newspapers. Chiyoe Sumi, a Union Church attendee, recalled: "Just a little while ago someone published an article in the paper warning the parents not to let the young people go there. This man said that they would say they were going to the church and then they would go someplace else."[12] But Sumi believed that the church needed to bear the responsibility of keeping the youths interested by providing church activities in the afternoon, between the English-language service in the morning and the Christian Endeavor at night. Sumi's critique pointed to the larger issue that ethnic institutions built by the immigrant generation did not change to meet the needs of the youths, which factored into behavior like ditching a church service to go to the beach. In the end, Japanese elites' plans for the ethnic church to control the behavior of the youth backfired. They wanted to inculcate them with moral values but had not predicted that youth might repurpose the moral institutions.

Still, few young women like Chiyo Otera embodied the kind of female progress that Japanese elites had envisioned. Otera admitted that she did not have much in common with her peers. Otera was an outlier compared to the majority of urban youths, whose highest education was a high school degree or who had even dropped out of high school to earn money. Rather, Otera was part of a small fraction of youths heading to the University of California, Los Angeles. She lamented that most young people did not take their futures seriously and attended church only so that they could meet other young folks. She explained, "I do not fit in with the young people there because so many of them do not seem to have very high ideals; they seem to be chiefly interested in having a good time." As a youth ministry leader, she found it nearly impossible to lead a rigorous discussion on Christianity; young people would rather discuss baseball, go on auto parties (activities centered on going out in cars, which had become affordable and available to the middle class and provided opportunities to travel anywhere and some amount of privacy without a chaperone), or do nothing for Sunday observance. She even considered leaving: "I would rather go to one of the other Japanese churches where they carry on more live discussions, but I am staying from a sense of duty because of what I may be able to do to help some of the others." Although Otera did not share the same ideals as her peers, she stayed out of her sense of obligation to serve as a model to the youths.[13]

MODERATION OF THE US NEW WOMAN, 1925 TO 1930

Her first semester at UCLA, Otera immersed herself in the cultural world of white highbrow women by joining the YWCA and the Women's Athletic Union. Otera began to mediate between Japanese elites' ideas about the modern Japanese woman and the US New Woman role espoused by the YWCA. Otera embraced moderation when it came to Americanization, following what Japanese elites considered to be high-class US values and rejecting what they deemed unrespectable. A majority of Japanese American families were often more open than restrictive, but they were quite mindful of a few Japanese elite thinkers whose opinions about what made one "modern" that would cast judgment on them. At the same time, they kept an eye on the popular and acceptable trends among the educated white class. As a result, they embraced high-class aspects of white high culture, including higher education, hairstyle and dress, and women's clubs, but rejected what they perceived to be lowbrow qualities, such as dancing. Otera incorporated the high-class values of both US and Japanese modernity, creating a highbrow transnational New Woman that assumed leadership roles in respectable ways. By participating in the YWCA Girl Reserves, Otera was able to access independence while maintaining her respectability.

Japanese elite women led the way in advocating for moderation. Minnie Inui, a literati elite who graduated from Stanford and was married to a professor of East Asian history, best exemplified this approach. In the immigration hearings over anti-Japanese legislation in the 1920s, she testified that she embraced Americanization.[14] Having taught American ideals at a Japanese school and Christian teachings, she believed in Japanese adoption of US practices. However, in the aftermath of the 1924 Immigration Act and the ushering-in of modernization through changing gender roles, consumerism, and leisure, Inui began to retreat from Americanization.[15] Having returned to the United States in 1926 after a year of living in Japan, she reflected on her observations of the youths in an editorial. Inui argued that youths were so obsessed with becoming Americanized that they acquired both positive and detrimental characteristics of US culture. In an attempt to restrain second-generation youths, she recommended investing in respectability, since even white people of refinement, "high brows," were tempered by judgment and moderation. Inui pleaded for youths to listen to their parents because, she declared, "Who can be a better teacher?" Inui advised the youths to embrace moderation by modeling themselves after the "well-bred Americans"—incidentally, the white highbrows who did not dance. And she argued for a remembrance of Japanese history and culture.[16] Such a call for moderation set the tone for young women like Otera and her negotiations between Japanese modernists and the Girl Reserves movement.

Japanese modernists did value some aspects or incarnations of the US New Woman, particularly the progressive women who entered higher education. LA organizations invested in the educational advancement of youths at a time when many were disillusioned with higher education and racial discrimination. Organizations such as the Japanese Citizens Educational Aid Society in Los Angeles developed scholarship funds to encourage youths to enter college. Scholarship funds aimed at youths from immigrant families as a part of racial uplift. For many immigrant families, education was expensive. In 1919, the annual college tuition cost $6 for a resident, $26 for a nonresident, and $495 in housing and supplies. In fact, many youths did not go to college after high school for a variety of reasons. Some had to help their family businesses, while others did not think that college would lead to more job opportunities. Few women were able to attend college because of a lack of scholarships. Otera was a perfect candidate: she was a Japanese citizen, spoke Japanese at home, and served as a stenographer for the Japanese Consulate in 1924.[17] Otera was part of a select group of Japanese American youths that received a scholarship.

Women were expected to obtain higher education to contribute to the expansion of the Japanese empire. Women were expected to learn from

Western institutions and return to Japan to train others in Western education. Women were expected to serve as educators and were not expected to move into other professions. For instance, when Otera first decided to attend college, she had wanted to become a doctor. She wanted to help the community. Her father, however, thought her aspiration impractical, since he believed no one would hire a female doctor. Although Japanese immigrant women had a long history of serving as midwives to their communities, their profession experienced a downturn.[18] Instead, Otera planned to enter into two fields where women's entrance had increasingly become the norm: sociology and home economics. After her education, because her status as a non-US citizen precluded her from teaching in US schools, she planned to teach in Japan.

While they embraced higher education for women, Japanese proponents of the modern Japanese woman rejected the most recent trendy Western beauty sensations, particularly bobbed hair. Modernists opposed such a rebellious and masculine trait that threated the gendered social order. Others believed it was a Western trend that would be merely a fad among few but would not change the national landscape. One journalist opined that, while bobbing was fashionable in the United States and Europe, the large majority of Japanese women did not bob their hair and it would not gain a foothold in Japan. The reasonings behind this prediction were that bobbing necessarily followed a change in clothing, but Japanese women would never shed the kimono, and, second, the bobbed hair would not add beauty to the body type of the Japanese race.[19]

However, in Los Angeles, a majority of college-aged Japanese American women challenged elders' assumptions about the hairstyle by bobbing their hair. By the mid-1920s, many young Japanese American women embraced the move toward the gender-bending androgynous look. Largely fashionable among both white and Japanese American women in college, bobbed hair quickly became associated with the educated class. By her second semester at UCLA, Otera described herself as the only Japanese woman at the university without bobbed hair. Otera had to convince her father that bobbed hair was a sign of modernity and collegiality, not of masculinity or rebellion. Otera adopted bobbed hair as a means of embracing the US New Woman and showing her belonging to a new class of white and Japanese American educated elite. By the following year, Otera joined the other young collegiate Japanese American women in bobbing her hair in marcel waves (fig. 3.1). The bobbed look also began to trend among high-schoolers. This new generation of high-class, bobbed-haired, college-educated modern women redefined elder ideas of modernity.

But much like how they felt about bobbed hair, Japanese proponents of the modern woman also subscribed women to auxiliary roles in the ethnic church. This felt limiting to a New Woman whose higher education qualified her for leadership roles. Otera outgrew the limits of women's auxiliary roles in the ethnic church. After Otera surrendered her position as an organist at her church, church leaders asked Otera to take it on again when they had difficulty finding a replacement. However, she explained, "But I think two years is long enough for one person to have the honor."[20] Otera moved to leadership roles in youth-driven organizations that emerged from white Christian movements. Otera was elected president of the senior group of Christian Endeavor at the Union Church.[21] The following year she was reelected and served as part of an all-women cabinet.[22] Otera participated in public debates, featuring college students versus high school students, in teams consisting of mixed genders of young women and men.[23]

Historian Valerie Matsumoto conducted a plethora of oral histories to uncover the world of female-led youth organizations in Los Angeles during the 1920s and 1930s. She argues that girls' clubs served as a bulwark against racial discrimination and as a bridge between the immigrant community's expectations of young women and the lure of popular culture.[24] While young women believed that clubs helped to maintain their respectability, strict moralists believed that clubs led to a lack of respectability. In one scathing editorial, Akatsuki Sakano believed that clubs encouraged unchristian, immoral behavior. Although the clubs were led by Sunday school teachers or leaders of the Young People's Societies, he believed the proliferation of clubs were simply rendezvous for males and females.[25] Youth leaders often felt these criticisms were unwarranted and superficial.[26] Other women emphasized the value of such clubs, noting the facts that clubs were part of nationally recognized institutions and provided one of the only means of organizing youths.[27]

Otera was a strong advocate for girls' clubs—particularly those that emphasized wholesome Christian values alongside collegiate affiliation. In fact, Otera began joining college-aged clubs while at UCLA. Otera was

3.1 By the time of this family portrait (1925 or 1926), Chiyo Otera had bobbed marcel waves. Top row: Tetsuya Akira Allen Aquila Otera, Yakow Jacob Otera, Nozomu Paul Otera. Bottom row: Chiyoko Nina Otera, Tsunekichi Alexander Otera, Ada Hiwa Otera. Courtesy of Roger Endo.

an original member of the inaugural Japanese YWCA Girl Reserves club, called "The More The Merrier Girls."[28] Otera helped to cultivate a collegiate urban youth high culture that would lend itself to more serious conversations as well as leadership roles for women. This created a large gap between women. Non-college-attending women at the Union Church saw Otera as stuck-up because she did not attend their socials, while Otera viewed the non-college-attending women as stunted or immature because all they cared about were socials.

The mixed gender social activities of young people became the subject of a community town hall. In the spring of 1927, ministers, delegates from Japanese-language schools, businessmen, members of the Japanese Associations of America, evangelists, and newspaper editors, the YWCA, the Women's Federation, and the Women's Club, gathered for the meeting. Foremost in the discussion was the social life of youths, such as "friendship between boys and girls; dates; joy rides; movies; dancing; the whole gamut of social life problems." The conservative subset believed that "the Flaming Youth took too many joyrides, saw too many movies depicting the gay life, and in short made the existence of the older folk dwindle into obscure shadows in comparison."[29] Eight men voted to abstain their daughters from dancing. But the majority of the community members present were more liberal to the question. Many resolved that it was the responsibility of the parents to oversee adequate chaperonage and that the youths must be taught the "happy medium of life."

In fact, the student clubs, in partnership with the Japanese Associations of America, newspapers, and doctors, sponsored a series of lectures on "social hygiene." While immigrant elites and youth clubs broke the silence and encouraged open discussion about sex, social hygiene was a conservative movement that preached abstinence. Concerned about their society's moral standards, venereal disease, and family life, the Japanese Student Christian Association funded a series of lectures given by Dr. Edith Hale Swift, a physician of women and children, of the American Social Hygiene Association. Swift's lectures were twofold: remedial, which encouraged the elimination of factors that weakened or destroyed the home, and constructive, designed to foster the correct attitudes, ideals, and behavior.[30] Swift was a part of the social hygiene movement that often pushed for conservative moral approaches to controlling disease because of limited public health options. Social hygiene lecturers promoted sex education as a key tool to create healthy and moral young people, families, and communities. Sex education encouraged abstinence, emphasized the seriousness of venereal disease, and discouraged masturbation. Sex education also encouraged dating practices that were considered moral, such as socializing in groups and introducing dates to parents.[31]

Japanese elites used the US sex education movement to discourage divorce in young couples and prevent sex outside of marriage. Proponents of the Japanese modern woman remained concerned with high divorce rates across the Japanese empire. Newspapers reported that the divorce rates in Tokyo "show[ed] enormous increase."[32] Moreover, many in the United States were troubled by the public display of affection and by sex outside of marriage; they were also concerned that "unfit" people might have babies. The social hygiene movement intersected with the eugenics movement, which promoted ideas that only people with desirable and honorable characteristics to reproduce. The eugenics movement discouraged those deemed undesirables, those with illnesses or disabilities, low-brow characteristics, or of the poor or working class, from reproducing. Many blamed the emergence of the New Woman whose frivolous sensibilities encouraged young women to enter quickly into marriages and then hastily seek divorce, or that they might have babies outside of marriage, making them unfit parents.[33] Sex education provided a method to prevent divorce and conceiving babies out of wedlock.

Japanese modernists celebrated youth engagements that took the sanctioned steps. *Rafu Shimpo* adopted the tradition of making high-society engagement announcements that emphasized the public approval of parents or paternal figures. These public announcements featured young women from Girl Reserves and often mentioned lengthy engagements. By 1926, Otera announced her engagement to Thomas Tozaburo Sashihara at a club dinner and in the *Rafu Shimpo*. Sashihara was a pharmacy student at USC and a member of the Japanese Christian Institute. Their engagement was approved and facilitated by Otera's father and by Tokuzo Iwaki, the owner of a drugstore where Sashihara worked as the manager.[34] They married at Union Church in front of five hundred guests (for clarity I continue to refer to Chiyo Otera as Otera and Thomas Tozaburo Sashihara as Sashihara), and became a power couple among youths (fig. 3.2).

3.2 Wedding portrait of Chiyo Nina Otera and Thomas Tozaburo Sashihara, June 16, 1927. Courtesy of Roger Endo.

GOOD WIFE, WISE MOTHER, 1930S

While young women had experienced new forms of independence in college, many entered higher education to prepare for a domestic life in the private sphere as newly married women. This was certainly the case for Otera, who professionally trained in home economics to prepare for life in the private sphere as a suburban housewife. Otera and Sashihara became part of a new transnational middle class that was part and parcel to the regeneration of the Little Tokyo business district and the expansion of urban youth culture. The new transnational middle class enjoyed several changes during the Great Depression: nuclear family households, entrance into white suburbs, commercial expansion in the downtown ethnic economy, and most of all, a vibrant leisure and social life that revolved around parties and dancing. In this new middle class, Otera was designated a homemaker as a counterpart to the transnational new businessman, and she played an active role in the community as a steward of transnational high youth culture.

Otera and Sashihara became part of a transnational middle class that arose alongside urban industrial growth and suburban expansion. Increasing automobile accessibility and freeway building led to the suburban sprawl so central to the making of Los Angeles. Los Angeles had a mix of middle-class and working-class suburbs. Bell Gardens, South Gate, El Monte, and Azusa were working-class suburbs where from the 1920s to the 1940s residents labored in the expanding economy; their goal for nurturing families was less aesthetic and more economic than their middle-class suburban counterparts.[35] Parts of the San Gabriel Valley, including Alhambra, South Pasadena, Monterey Park, and San Gabriel, were white enclaves within Los Angeles's "white spot" prior to the 1940s. Waves of nonwhite settlement and white flight ended de jure residential segregation.[36] Otera and Sashihara was part of one wave of nonwhite settlement that moved from the urban metropolis of downtown Los Angeles to the suburban neighborhoods of the San Gabriel Valley.[37] By 1930, the Otera and Sashihara moved to Alhambra, a streetcar suburb, one of the fringe cities that expanded the suburban sprawl and Victorian ideals, located ten miles east of downtown and functioned as the gateway to the San Gabriel Valley.[38] Set apart from multigenerational households where couples lived with elders, the couple became part of a small community of Japanese American nuclear families residing in Alhambra.

As part of the new suburban middle class, Otera became a full-time homemaker. The 1930 US Census lists Otera as a "homemaker," which it defined as "the woman member of the family who was responsible for the care of the home and family."[39] Otera fit neatly into the new meaning assigned to the US homemaker by the early twentieth century. Historians explain the field of "home economics" revalued household chores as a "science" to be studied and mastered while advertisers portrayed homemaking as a profession to court female consumers.[40]

With Otera's role firmly identified as the homemaker, the family met the status quo of New Deal policies that endorsed a return to normative gender roles during a time of economic crisis. The US government issued new policies and relief programs that prioritized white men's employment, bolstered by the belief that men were the household breadwinners. Otera's strategic decision to move away from professional fields often reserved for men, and towards social work fields predominately occupied by women, was sanctioned through the established gendered social order and shielded her from the tumultuous changes many working women experienced and the labor activism they had to advocate for during the Great Depression and the New Deal.

At the same time, Otera embodied the vision of Japanese imperialists who believed that women should be trained in proper domesticity in order to become good housewives and wise mothers. Similar to earlier Japanese women who obtained Western educations so they could return to Japan to educate a new generation of Japanese women, Otera wanted to study home economics and teach in Japan. After her engagement, however, Otera majored in home economics at the University of California, Los Angeles, so she could apply it to her own role as a homemaker.[41] Otera learned about child development, food and nutrition, home management, hospitality, and hygiene in the home.[42] She received one-on-one counseling from Dr. Smith, who taught not only sex education but also how to rear children.[43] Within the span of four years, Otera gave birth to three children: Thomas Fujio (1929), Diane (1931), and Maureen (1933). Otera was fully occupied between upkeeping the home, preparing meals, and taking care of the children.

Still, as part of her high-society domestic role, she played community hostess and practiced her hospitality skills by bringing colleagues and friends into her newly domesticated suburban life. For example, Otera threw a surprise birthday party for Sashihara at their new Alhambra home.[44] Inviting their closest friends, she served two huge cakes and offered games. On another occasion, Otera threw a small party for her friend, Kimi Mukaye, who had recently returned from Japan.[45] Because they shared a common youthful past, Otera decided the theme would be an "old fashioned party," where they used to play games from the "old days" and ended up dancing the Virginia reel. Otera served salad, sandwiches, and tea. Through social gatherings of friends and colleagues, Otera created a vibrant leisure scene that thrived on middle-class consumption of trendy foods, music, and dress.

Otera held influential positions in community organizations like the YWCA and Chi Alpha Delta, which helped to develop young women as cultural ambassadors. She remained on the YWCA board overseeing the activities of the Girl Reserves. After all, she was one of the first members of the original Japanese American Girl Reserves. Although she was not an original member of the all-Japanese American sorority, Chi Alpha Delta, she received honorary alumni status.[46] Otera had served in an advisory capacity to the sorority, whose main purpose was to establish a campus home for Japanese American women and to build friendly relations with white organizations. She allowed her home to be used by her alma mater for their sorority events.[47]

While Otera was advising girls' clubs from the comfort of her suburban home, parents and youths in downtown Los Angeles organized another town hall to discuss the "problems of dancing and sex matters." Two dozen parents met to discuss dancing at a community forum at the YMCA, this time less determined about individual policing and instead turning to community standardization. In 1930, fathers gathered at the Japanese Association Hall and complained about the frequency of dancing.[48] They expressed concern that daughters were lying in order to attend dances and spending too much money on dresses. Parents and youths discussed some terms of agreement at a conflict resolution meeting, but they ultimately disagreed on the number of dances youths could put on.[49] Elders and youths were at an impasse.

Then, an exchange of editorials between an old-time anti-flamer and a flaming youth rehashed the debate but agreed that dances put on by clubs were the only respectable venues for dancing. An editorial writer frowned on the excess of dances and made serious accusations encompassed in his title, "Our Dance Mad Daughters."[50] He offered an exaggerated depiction of a girl's low morality and obscene demands from the family—the writer feared women were becoming too materialistic and expected too much from their family. The writer laid out a hierarchy of the preferred venues for girls to dance, at the top clubs and friends' homes, and at the bottom dancing halls. In fact, community members had protested against the opening of a Filipino dancing hall three years earlier.[51] The elder pleaded with girls' organizations to restrict dancing among young women. However, young women defended their perspective on dancing. One UCLA student justified the amount and variety of dances put on by many different organizations to meet and serve the recreational desires of an ever-growing youth population. She did not believe that dancing degraded one's morals, stating instead that "the results of evils from dancing is a matter of the degradation of personal ideals or a lack of training at home." Girls' club dances provided a respectable outlet in comparison to the dance halls or beach resorts.[52]

By the 1930s, couples like Otera and Sashihara had a vested interest in sponsoring a transnational high youth culture. Clubs often held dances to fund-raise for their yearly organized events. For instance, Otera's alma mater, UCLA Bruin Club, held semiformal dances. Otera and Sashihara were invited as patrons.[53] They were in the company of other patrons and patronesses, such as doctors, classical performers, and consuls. These dances fund-raised from the alumni attendees and funds would go toward Bruin events that year, generating a rich club scene for Japanese American student life at UCLA. In another example, they also played their part in building US-Japanese friendship through fund-raisers. In 1932, the year the Olympics were held in Los Angeles, Otera and Sashihara attended a dance fund-raiser for Japan's Olympic team.[54] The funds offered a "goodwill gesture" on the part of the young people who hosted two hundred athletes. Otera and Sashihara were among the fourteen prominent young couples, in addition to white patrons. The couple's public appearance at these dances marked their support of a competitive Japanese athletic showing an urban youth community's endeavors to build recreational transnational relations. In fact, couples like Otera and Sashihara became a major source of financial support to fund social affairs.

While Otera labored and entertained in the home, Sashihara took on a more visible role in Little Tokyo development. Sashihara served as treasurer to the Japanese Chamber of Commerce, a group that oversaw the interests and development of Japanese-owned businesses.[55] As treasurer, Sashihara had a say in the development of resources. For instance, he served on a social welfare committee that proposed to utilize the funds received from the emperor and the princes of Japan to build a community center building (a library).[56] That same year, Sashihara was elected chairman of the Japanese YMCA board of management, which oversaw the YMCA boys' clubs and programs.[57] Through overseeing organizations like the YMCA and the Japanese Chamber of Commerce, they enabled a vibrant youth culture to ensure the replenishment of their ethnic economy, neighborhoods, and businesses.

Moreover, Otera's status as a homemaker was a direct reflection of Sashihara's professional occupation and public reputation as a successful businessman. Sashihara followed in the footsteps of Tokuzo Iwaki, who had opened the Iwaki Drug Company at the intersection of First and Los Angeles Streets in the heart of downtown Little Tokyo in 1923.[58] By then, Little Tokyo had transformed from small mom-and-pop shops to larger commercial businesses. First Street was lined with department stores like the Asia Company, large hotels, and big pharmacies run by "young people" who were now managing immigrant-owned businesses, like Iwaki Drug and Tenshodo.[59] Iwaki Drugs catered to Japanese immigrant communities and ran English-language ads in the Japanese-language section of the *Nichibei Shinbun*. By 1931, Iwaki Drug Store expanded to two stores, the new location just a block from the original store.[60] In 1933, the Iwaki Drug Store was one of five in Little Tokyo, including Tenshodo, Kyosai Drug, Taiyo Drug, and Eagle Pharmacy.[61] By 1934, the Iwaki Drug Company was part of a conglomerate of department stores and pharmacies in downtown Little Tokyo, including the Asahi Shoe Company, the Asia Company, the Chu-O Shoe Store, the Empire Trading Company, the Hori Brothers, the Kyosai Drug Company, the Kimura Brothers, the Mitsuba Trading Company, the Tensho-Do Drug Company, Tokyo Dry Goods Company, and the

Tomio Company. That same year, the original Iwaki Drugstore expanded from prescription and nonprescription drugs to general bargain retail next door.[62] They observed the popular and successful emergence of five-and-dime stores across the United States, and expanded by opening their own five-and-dime in Little Tokyo to appeal to a growing transnational Japanese American middle class.

The original Iwaki Drug Store became a hub for socializing, a place of employment for young people, and a gateway to consumer goods associated with the New Woman. Like most US drug companies of the day, the Iwaki Drug Store had a soda fountain and lunch counter. Young people made up a large portion of the customers. They often socialized with their fellow community members while shopping at the store, eating at the fountain, or having a cup of coffee.[63] Moreover, the Iwaki Drug Store became a hub for sports audiences. Men would meet at the fountain to weigh in about a sports match.[64] The Iwaki Drug Store also employed many young people. For instance, Carol Tokunaga had worked at the Iwaki Drug Store and later opened up her own drug store in San Jose with her brother.[65] During special sales, the Nisei Employment Bureau placed young people to do temp work at Iwaki Drug Store.[66] When the Iwaki Five and Ten Cent Store opened, Sashihara hired three young women, Hana Sakuda, Teru Ito, and Molly Oyama. Oyama had previously worked at her father's cosmetic company, so it was likely that she and the other girls sold cosmetics at the Five and Ten Cent Store, expanding their clientele to young women interested in the latest makeup trends.[67]

Sashihara was able to leverage his commercial power and civic advocacy to expand civil rights for a small group of middle-class professionals and commercial business. Sashihara was unable to obtain a pharmaceutical license because he was designated as an "alien." In 1935, Sashihara, along with other aspiring pharmacists, Ray Fukushima and Fred Sakuda, appealed to the California Court of Appeals.[68] Sashihara argued that the state's pharmacy act conflicted with the terms and provisions of the Treaty of Commerce and Navigation between the United States and Japan, creating "an abuse of police power and an arbitrary and discriminatory classification and deny to such aliens the equal protection of the laws." The courts came to the conclusion that the pharmacy act did not prohibit aliens from "operating or owning drug stores or working as clerks therein," meaning that Japanese immigrants could still own drug stores or work as clerks without a pharmacy license but could not be pharmacists themselves. Further, the pharmacy act had the right to exclude "aliens" to protect public health, safety, and general welfare, mirroring yellow peril sentiments that legitimized the exclusion of Japanese immigrants for the safeguarding of the white population. More broadly, it reveals how the California courts interpreted racial exclusion at the judicial level, using a language of public safety to maintain discriminatory practices.

Shortly after their appeal failed in the California courts, the appellants of the Iwaki Drug Company reached out to the California Druggist Association. This time their argument aligned with selective inclusion defined by recent immigration laws. They proposed a bill to amend the state pharmacy act from restricting aliens, arguing that it would not have much effect in light of the Immigration Exclusion Act of 1924. Except for a few immigrants, the number of US citizens who were Japanese American outweighed the number of Japanese immigrants who would require such an amendment.[69] The rationalization to make an exception for a few, while resting on racial exclusion for the rest, succeeded.[70]

From the 1920s to the 1930s, Japanese modernists had utilized US institutions and movements to cultivate a transnational highbrow culture that molded Japanese American women under the modernist ideology of "good wife, wise mother." At first, Japanese modernists looked askance at the emerging flaming youths who danced at parties, participated in courting, and turned to divorce. They built ethnic institutions like the ethnic church and the Japanese-language school to counter what they saw as a moral degradation ushered in by US culture. However, modernists began to adopt moderation and encouraged youths to absorb only highbrow white culture that matched their values. Young women like Otera attended UCLA, joined the YWCA, and bobbed their hair. Youth clubs worked with elders to hire white doctors from the sex education movement in order to discourage the spread of disease and divorce. By the 1930s, a transnational highbrow community emerged that would meet both US gender norm conventions during the Great Depression as well as the Japanese empire's goals for modernity. Consisting of traditional nuclear families living in the suburbs, and away from the downtown morally loose youth community, highbrow elite enjoyed a high standard of living while expanding the ethnic economy around urban youth culture in downtown Los Angeles.

Otera's story reveals how Japanese imperialism, and its emphasis on "good wives, wise mothers," played a significant role in shaping the US New Woman. New Women proponents in the United States encouraged more women to move into the public sphere and largely considered a homemaker a traditional or outdated role. However, Japanese modernists understood a "good wife, wise mother" as a modern gender role. This approach aligned with US institutions that responded with moderation to the New Woman. Japanese modernists utilized US-based academic movements such as home economics and sex education, as well as social service institutions such as the YWCA Girl Reserves, to become professionally trained as homemakers as well as encourage their homemaking sensibilities. As a result, the homemaker played an active role in generating a vibrant social and leisure culture among the transnational middle class. From the mid-1920s through the 1930s, Japanese ideologies of the "good wife, wise mother" continued to shape young Japanese American women. The next two chapters examine how Japanese American New Men and New Women were shaped by the progressive movements of US imperialism.

4

The Muscular New Man

IN HIS INTERVIEW with William C. Smith in 1924, Gene Sakamoto, a graduate of the Los Angeles Polytechnic High School and a member of the Young People's Society at the Japanese Christian Institute, talked about his dream of going to college and becoming a social worker. He wanted to attend college immediately after graduating from high school in 1921, but instead he had to enter the workforce because of his "home conditions." His father was "feeble and unable to do any work," a condition that Sakamoto attributed to his father's past. His father had a fairly good education in Japan, but Sakamoto observed that "after coming here he has dissipated a great deal and caused a lot of trouble in the family," including taking up smoking, drinking, and other vices.[1] Sakamoto's necessity to work was also compounded by the effects of the 1920 California Alien Land Law, which permitted white lessors to charge higher rents to Japanese immigrant families. Sakamoto's family incurred debt from a three-year lease on the rooming house they ran. Because his father could not work, Sakamoto assumed a primary role in the financial responsibilities of his family by entering into the ethnic grocery market business.

Although Sakamoto had to pursue a career as a market man, he found other ways to contribute to the expansion of Christian progressive values in the Japanese American community, particularly in an advisory capacity. Sakamoto became a Sunday school teacher and youth leader at the Japanese

Christian Institute. He led young boys on nature hikes and discussed the relationship of recreation and spirituality at a Bible study. Moreover, Sakamoto also became affiliated with the Pasadena Japanese YMCA, by playing on their basketball team. He helped the YMCA to welcome visiting baseball and wrestling teams from Japan. Finally, Sakamoto also became a leader in the Oliver Club, the first Japanese American boys' club in Los Angeles that offered socializing and recreational activities. As the club expanded, he volunteered his time as basketball and baseball coach for the Oliver Juniors, which became the team to beat in the newly formed Japanese American basketball and baseball leagues in southern California.

Sakamoto's one foot in the ethnic market and other foot in youth recreation expands our understanding of the making of transnational manhood as developed by the progressive movement in the United States. Sakamoto moved between two worlds. He inherited a segregated immigrant economy centered around the ethnic market: a formal network of Japanese-owned or -run businesses, housing, and farming that supplied its community members with the majority of their needs and consumption. At the same time, Sakamoto apprenticed under white progressives who introduced him to Americanization and muscular Christianity through social support networks like the Oliver Club and the YMCA. Bridging these two worlds, young men like Sakamoto developed a transnational muscular Christianity: a philosophy of masculinity built around health, sportsmanship, American internationalism, and ethnic attachment in the interwar period.

This chapter explores the second main way that young Japanese American men rebuilt masculinity in the period of racial exclusion: athletics. While intelligentsia rebuilt transnational new manhood that was more closely aligned with militant Japanese imperialism, Sakamoto and other recreational social workers rebuilt a transnational new manhood that was more closely aligned with American internationalism. This chapter explores how organizers like Sakamoto created and expanded recreation and ethnic sports leagues as part of training youths to serve as cultural bridges between the United States and Japan. Boys Clubs and J-Leagues created an infrastructure to maintain transnational ties, serving the double function of Americanization as well as maintaining ties to one's ethnicity.

RECREATION AS AMERICANIZATION IN THE EARLY 1920S

By the 1910s, Japanese elites criticized Christian white middle-class progressives for their hypocrisy when it came to race: they publicly supported US naturalization of Japanese elites, but the organizations they led were complicit in segregation policies. In 1913, when California passed the Alien Land Law, Dr. John R. Mott, secretary of the International Committee of the YMCA, believed a just recourse to the Alien Land Law would be to allow Japanese immigrants currently residing in the United States to become naturalized citizens while restricting future immigration. In response, Kiyoshi Kawakami wrote an editorial published in the *New York Times*, calling out Christian hypocrisy in refusing to admit Japanese elites into the YMCA. YMCAs in cities across the Pacific Coast, including Honolulu, San Francisco, and Los Angeles, had rejected nearly all membership applications from Japanese elites. In Los Angeles, the YMCA conceded to allow one Japanese American applicant to become a member if he did not use the swimming pool. Kawakami pointed out that Japanese elites shared many of the middle-class values of white elite men, including the fact that they had a reputation for "cleanly habits," attended prestigious universities, and were respected professionals such as an employee of a US bank. Kawakami called out the hypocrisy of YMCA leaders who called for the naturalization of Japanese immigrants into the nation-state while upholding exclusionary policies within their own local YMCA organizations.[2]

By the 1920s, in Los Angeles, Kawakami found an audience among white female progressives of the Americanization and kindergarten movements. White progressives criticized that Los Angeles municipalities had provided little recreation for Japanese Americans. In 1924, for instance, the Girls' Secretary of Church for All Nations Catherine Lee Wahlstrom observed that recreational facilities were meagerly provided for the fifteen thousand Japanese American residents within the Los Angeles city limits. There was no designated playground and no library specifically designated for Japanese Americans. When some Japanese aristocrats tried to access public or private golf courses and tennis courts, city officials passed ordinances prohibiting their play. Wahlstrom identified one hall where Japanese immigrants could put on plays or other entertainment, but its expense limited the number of events. Rather, she observed, "there are numerous billiard rooms and pool halls which are crowded with Japanese." Wahlstrom concluded that the recreational facilities were meager compared to the amount of libraries, playgrounds, theaters, dance halls, and auditoriums provided for the same number of white people in Los Angeles.[3]

Tuthill argued that Los Angeles County maintained a tenuous balance around these segregated city policies by forcing Japanese American communities to be primarily responsible for their own recreational opportunities. For instance, the Union Church provided the main facilities for recreation for youths, including a small auditorium for plays, a gymnasium where they held basketball games, ju-jitsu exhibitions, and wrestling matches. Additionally, the Japanese Young Men's Associations believed in cultivating athletics among young men for the purposes of developing self-respect. On one occasion, they were able to reserve the YMCA in Boyle Heights (then also called the Hollenbeck Heights) to hold a "Field Day" in 1923. Field Day was a full day of athletic competition, including baseball games, tennis tournaments, wrestling and ju-jitsu exhibitions, races, and basketball games. Six hundred participants came from all over Southern California, San Diego, Imperial Valley, and even San Francisco. Over five thousand spectators attended the games.[4]

While a majority of recreational services were spearheaded by Japanese American institutions, Nellie Grace Oliver, a progressive leading the kindergarten movement, helped to oversee boys' athletics as a form of Americanization. Interdisciplinary studies scholar Hillary Jenks argues that, while Oliver believed in Americanization, that did not mean she believed in doing away with Japanese culture.[5] In fact, Americanization was one of two parts in developing youths as cultural bridges between the United States and Japan. As a kindergarten teacher at the Hewitt Street School, she worked primarily with children of Japanese, Chinese, and Mexican immigrants. In 1920, Oliver taught between eighteen and twenty-five Japanese American kindergarteners. Oliver also served as the superintendent of the Stimson Lafayette Industrial Institute, a school on Lafayette Street for children ages nine to fourteen, which offered Americanization classes such as cooking and sewing, in addition to "physical and moral training." Her Americanization efforts were part of a larger plan for youths to learn

American culture alongside Japanese culture. In fact, Oliver shared the building with Rafu Daiichi Gakuen, where Koehi Shimano taught youths the Japanese language. Shimano had hoped that Japanese American youths might become "bridges of understanding" between the United States and Japan. Aside from teaching, Oliver was a public advocate of the Japanese American community. She testified before the congressional immigration hearings that Japanese immigrants were assimilable and patriotic. Although she advocated for an immigration quota from Japan, she also advocated for equal restrictions across all groups. She felt that she could only make real change with a small group.[6] Oliver also traveled to Japan, where she spent two months learning about Japanese culture.

Oliver offered to sponsor the Japanese American Boys Club, which became the venue for teaching middle-class masculinity around order and discipline. Oliver testified at the immigration hearings that she invited young boys to her home in the evenings to socialize, and from there they began the Japanese Boys Club as well as the girls club.[7] At a time when it was difficult to procure space for young Japanese American men, Oliver made the Stimson Institute available to the Japanese Boys Club of Los Angeles in 1917. While the boys met at the Stimson Industrial School on Friday evenings, Oliver met with the boys once a month and with the girls twice a month. Oliver instituted Robert's Rules of Order, brought in a singing teacher, and initiated quizzes and activities such as round-robin storytelling. In their meetings, they learned civic ideology, such as electing their club representatives, which would help them to become voting members of society.[8] The Japanese Boys Club was later renamed the Oliver Club in honor of Oliver.[9] Under the direction of Oliver, the club was spearheaded by young men of working-class immigrant families who lived in the Japanese parts of downtown Los Angeles, like Gene Sakamoto.

The Oliver Club was a welcome change to Sakamoto's experience in public school. Between 1917 and 1921, Sakamoto attended the Los Angeles Polytechnic High School, a high school with predominantly white faculty and students. At Polytechnic High, he admitted he felt awkward around his white peers and got along more with the other Japanese American students. In Sakamoto's senior year in 1921, his graduating class of 274 students had only six Japanese American students, including Sakamoto. The white residents of that area had polled strong support for the passage of the California Alien Land Law of 1920.[10] In fact, anti-Japanese advocate Senator Phelan came to Polytechnic High School on October 15, 1920, in his reelection campaign. His slogan "Keep California White" clearly promoted the yellow peril ideology and called for Japanese exclusion. Among the anti-Japanese political atmosphere, racial tokenization coexisted among youths. Sakamoto was the only nonwhite player on the high school football team. Attendees cheered on the only Japanese American football player on the team—and his team took home the city championship that year.[11]

The California Alien Land Law impacted immigrant families like Sakamoto's, which prevented him from attending college and pushed him into a career in an ethnic market. A son of immigrants, Sakamato's father, Hisamato Sakamoto, was born in 1870, and his mother, Kume, was born in 1881 or 1883 in Japan; they married around 1900 and immigrated together to the United States in 1902. After residing in Napa, they moved to Los Angeles, where they started operating a rooming house in 1922. Rooming houses were often located in densely populated areas, in walking distance to restaurants where lodgers could take their meals. Japanese laborers who worked seasonally, migrated alone, and women in low-income jobs often took rooms. While managing a rooming house gave the Sakamoto family a sense of social and economic distinction among the Japanese American community, many of Sakamoto's friends did not know the family was actually in debt, because they had to sign a lease for three years (April 1922 to 1925). Due to the parameters of the California Alien Land Law, white lessors could charge higher rents to Japanese immigrant tenants. The Sakamotos hoped to come out even when the lease ended and were unsure whether they would be able to renew the lease. Sakamoto's mother, Kume, had her hands full with two younger children, Chiyoko, born in 1912, and Kiyoshi (Richard), born in 1919. As a result, Sakamoto went into the market business right out of high school to support the family business.

During the years of the lease, Sakamoto found his outlet and spent his free time playing basketball through the Oliver Club. By 1924, Sakamoto captained the Oliver Club to the basketball championship in Japanese American sports circles in the state of California. The team in 1924 included Mas Igasaki, Walter Hamamoto, Charles Kamayatsu, Beach Morita, Jiro Kamayatsu, Min Watanabe, David Hamamoto, and Fred Shimizu.[12] These young men were aged between sixteen and twenty-four; some had been born in California and others in Hawaiʻi. Because of the scarce basketball scene among Japanese American youths in Los Angeles, the Oliver Club traveled to play against teams in Northern California, which had been organized through universities and churches. They defeated the Blazing Arrows in San Francisco to win the state title for the Japanese American basketball league of California.

Japanese immigrant elites believed that boys clubs provided a service to working-class youths like Sakamoto, especially as a form of moral uplift through organized sports. Japanese moral leaders had grown increasingly concerned over how to keep youths off the streets and away from vices associated with the immigrant working class and poor. In fact, Frank Nakamura, a student at Occidental College and youth leader at the Japanese Union Church, observed that young men tended to crowd the streets and become involved with gambling, a recreation criminalized and seen as morally depraved by progressives and imperialists alike. Nakamura explained that one strategy was to give more responsibility to the youths so they would spend less time on the streets. He provided a success story: "Two years ago there was a great run on playing cards among the boys. Three of these boys were baptized and were put to work when they changed and became dependable in the church."[13] Nakamura aligned with Americanization teachers who believed that boys clubs would help to organize young men into respectable members of society.

The Oliver Club helped boys cultivate a transnational identity that blended US democratic principles and a passionate attachment to their Japanese heritage and community. One member, Leo Toyama, best exemplified this transnational vision for the role of youths. He firmly believed that youths' greatest mission was to bring white and Japanese peoples closer together "so that they will understand each other in a friendlier manner than in the past." He testified that young people had become more familiar with American ways, but he believed that they bore a responsibility to carry on Japanese culture, despite the fact that it was difficult to learn the Japanese language while also getting an American education. Every year, some young people took tours to visit Japan. Still, even as young people became Americanized, Toyama believed that they still felt proud to be Japanese: "the American-born Japanese is an American by birth, but Japanese at heart."[14] Despite recognizing a loss of Japanese culture because of Americanization practices, Toyama still felt passionately attached to his ethnicity.

By the 1920s, although young men were increasingly joining sports teams through their churches, they still were denied entrance to YMCA facilities. Seiichi Nobe, for instance, explained that San Francisco had a separate Japanese YMCA, while in Los Angeles they had yet to build a separate Japanese facility by the early 1920s. Once, Nobe played basketball with his white Sunday school team at the local YMCA. He could tell he was not welcomed there, but because he was on the team they did not deny him any privileges. In fact, his friends had proposed that he apply for membership at the main YMCA and thought his last name could pass as European. But when he went in person to the office, he was denied. He could see that nothing had changed since his older brother's denial to use the YMCA in the late 1910s. His brother, who had served in the US Army in World War I, had been given passes to the YMCA along with other soldiers, but when he went to exercise, he was denied use of the shower room and the pool.[15] Since he could not use the Y, Nobe commented that he also did not feel free to go to the beaches. He clarified that, although he had not been outright forbidden to go into the surf, he felt that he was not wanted there, so he never tried. Nobe's experiences between the YMCA and youth sports teams reveal the gaps between older Y exclusionary policies and a new generation of Christian youth sports organizations that made exceptions for Japanese American athletes via Americanization.

TRANSNATIONAL MUSCULAR CHRISTIANITY IN THE LATE 1920S

By the late 1920s, ethnic sports teams like the Oliver Club participated in organized mainstream sports leagues in the city of Los Angeles. By 1926, various Japanese American basketball teams played against non-Japanese teams in municipal leagues across Southern California. In Los Angeles, the Japanese Pasadena YMCA basketball team played in the Pasadena city leagues. The Oliver Juniors played in the Hi-Y leagues, the high-school leagues under the YMCA. Spurred by competitiveness with other Japanese diasporic communities outside of Japan, recreational organizers held a vision for an organized league solely within the Los Angeles Japanese

American community that would compete against other teams across the state, nationally, and internationally. The converging interests of three groups—YMCA organizers who believed in expanding muscular Christianity to Japanese American youths, merchants who had their own economic interests in ensuring that youths buy in to the ethnic community, and Japanese youths who wanted access to recreation—ultimately led to the creation of the J-Leagues. An all-Japanese American basketball league provided a platform for coaches and players to build youth sports and competitive play within Japanese America, a new kind of masculinity around physical fitness, discipline, and Christianity, and transnational ties with teams from universities in Japan.

The organization of the J-Leagues began with the installation of the Japanese YMCA in Los Angeles. A YMCA rally was held at the Japanese Los Angeles Reform Church to discuss how to establish a Japanese department of the YMCA.[16] Japanese American youths were increasingly interested in building a Y facility dedicated to the recreational needs of young men, particularly because many were denied access to mainstream Y facilities. Some had felt their ostracization was a constant reminder that they were racially inferior, so organizers proposed a dedicated building to Japanese American youths as the solution. Various Japanese American organizations supported the building of a separate Y, including the Japanese YMCA of Pasadena, a group of Japanese American civic leaders affiliated with the Pasadena YMCA; the Hi-Y, a group of high school students; and the Japanese Student Christian Association (JSCA), an organization of college students. The club known as the Japanese Pasadena YMCA members included President Jiro Morita, a leader who believed in cultivating peaceful and friendly relations between the United States and Japan.[17] Morita had migrated to San Francisco as a young boy to receive an education and later moved to Pasadena, where his uncle resided. He became a member of the Pasadena Japanese Union Church and served in the US Army during the Great War.[18] Members of the JSCA included college students such as Paul Hirohata, president and later teacher at the First Gakuen of Montebello; Tadahito Shisuoka; and George Takahashi, who had given a speech to a Hi-Y boys meeting on why he favored the Hi-Y and YMCA work and an editor of the *Chapterometer*, the official bulletin for JSCA; and Paul Takeda.[19]

While youths expressed a desire for a facility all their own, white secretaries of the YMCA sought to expand the Y mission to young Japanese American boys as a response to the anti-Japanese movement of the 1920s. Historian Sarah Griffith argues that, by the 1920s, because of the anti-Japanese movement in the United States, missionaries in Japan were forced to redefine their own understandings of imperialism, republicanism, and the responsibilities of Christians to promote social equality at home and abroad. Ultimately, they created a new language of advocacy rooted in antiracism and Christian internationalism. For instance, George Gleason, the former secretary of the YMCA in Osaka, Japan, and the current director of the Los Angeles YMCA, had studied and published on the debates over Japanese immigration, criticizing some leading anti-Japanese opponents and acknowledging that Japan was justified in demanding that Japanese immigrants in the United States receive full racial equality on par with white Americans. He believed that it did not make sense to carry on with Americanization while simultaneously segregating Japanese American youths in public schools and he believed in creating dialogue between white and Japanese American populations in Los Angeles.[20] No doubt he promoted cooperation and friendship when he gave a talk at a Young People's Union Service.[21]

Members of the local YMCAs began to encourage the building of a separate Japanese department in their new mission of building world brotherhood. With their emphasis on boys work by the 1920s, some YMCA secretaries had begun Y outreach to young high school boys. For instance, Adrian H. Maxwell, secretary of the Hollenbeck branch of the YMCA, worked with Japanese American boys in Boyle Heights. Known for his inspiring talks that instilled community spirit and cooperation, he helped to create a separate YMCA boys club, the Hi-Y Club, which aimed at expanding the Y mission among young Japanese American high-school aged boys.[22] The Hi-Y Club organized in the fall of 1925 after a group of Japanese boys of the Union Church and Maxwell and Luther Hoobyar returned from summer camp in the Little Green Valley in the San Bernardino Mountains.[23] With the support of the Hi-Y, Ralph Cole, state secretary for boys' work, gave the main speech for the evening of the YMCA rally, arguing that the work of the Y helped to develop the physical, mental, social, and devotional sides of boys' character.

In the end, the alliance between the YMCA and Japanese American youths helped to convince the immigrant generation, who donated $3,500 toward establishing its own department.[24] Although some churches already provided recreational sports facilities and the Japanese immigrant community had created their own sports leagues, elders were likely convinced by the message of building cultural bridges and unification. Further, some of them had expressed concern over Japanese American youths picking up vices when left out in the streets. A Japanese Y would help to instill good Christian values that might prevent delinquency.

The newly built Japanese YMCA provided recreational opportunities to expand muscular Christianity and to build transnational ties. For instance, Fred Shimizu, the first secretary of the Japanese YMCA in Los Angeles, and Maxwell chaperoned a camping trip to Bear Lake. About fifty boys attended, swimming, fishing, enjoying music, and engaging in Bible study.[25] These camping trips were recruitment sites to encourage interest in the Y and in organizing clubs. The YMCA also approached camping as an integral opportunity to promote Christian education, interaction with nature, and mentorship. In addition to camping, the Japanese YMCA hosted an annual track-and-field day. The one-day competition held contests in 100-yard dash, pole vault, shot put, and so on. Japanese American boys came from Los Angeles, San Diego, Hollywood, and San Pedro to compete.[26] Finally, the YMCA also provided occasions of meeting with Japanese youths visiting from Japan. For instance, the Japanese YMCA organized a banquet at the Union Church, where members of the YMCA organizations met Japanese student wrestlers.[27] About fifty students sat down for dinner and sang songs.[28]

YMCA organizers began to build a network of basketball teams organized through boys' clubs. Established Japanese American teams played in city leagues and against non-Japanese opponents. For instance, the Japanese Pasadena YMCA basketball team, composed of post–college aged players, had played in city leagues, such as the Young Men's Division League of Pasadena. Desiring competitive play with Japanese American teams, they often put out calls in the newspaper with an open challenge to any Japanese American basketball team that would like to play them for the Southern California basketball championship to no avail.[29] Among high-school age basketball players, the Hi-Y entered the Y leagues and played against non-Japanese basketball teams, such as the Black Hi-Y team at the "Colored YMCA."[30] Los Angeles Japanese YMCA secretary Shimizu started to develop interest among young boys by hosting basketball practices and tryouts. Many boys had expressed interest in forming a team, but they would have to find coaches to train and manage their team.[31] Coaches needed to become familiar with the rules, attend league meetings, and surrender their evenings to practices and games. But more importantly, they needed to be invested in muscular Christianity.

Sakamoto stepped into the role of mentor to mold the next generation in muscular Christianity. In fact, at the Japanese Christian Church, Sakamoto had led bible study on the topic "Christ's Standards for Our Recreational Life."[32] Sakamoto and Jiro Kamayatsu began training for a new Oliver Juniors basketball team. They ran the first practice of the season using the Union Church gym.[33] The Oliver Juniors used the Union Church gym for many of their individually arranged scrimmage basketball games against non-Japanese teams. They had a heated rivalry against the Pasadena Union Church.[34] Other opponents included the Red Shirts, a white team; Black Shirts, a Japanese American team; the Ninth Street, a white team; and the Hi-Y Second Team, a Japanese American team.[35]

While YMCA leaders were able to generate interest, form teams, and organize games, Japanese American merchants took the step to formalize an all-Japanese American basketball league. In fact, the *Rafu Shimpo* Sports editors, like Ken Tashiro of Sumida Sporting Goods Store, had a vested interest in organizing a league.[36] As historian Lon Kurashige documents, immigrant businessmen had to appeal to youths as their next consumer base. Merchants wanted to create an ethnic consciousness among youths and encouraged them to shop in Little Tokyo.[37] A sports league would expand the clientele at Sumida Sporting Goods Store around young people's leisure and recreation. The store sold musical instruments, sporting goods and clothing, and toys. An organized basketball league would generate more demand for athletic uniforms and equipment.

Tashiro attempted to standardize organized basketball by creating the Southern California Japanese American Basketball Association, which streamlined the fees, scheduling, scorekeepers, and trophies.[38] He organized the municipal league with the Los Angeles Department of Recreation, which required that athletes be members of their organizations. All games were played at Lincoln High School on Thursday evenings, where one could see three games sequentially in a row. Game admission fees cost fifty cents per game, and one-fourth of the money went to the club that sold the ticket and another fourth went to the Basketball Association fund.[39] Organizers decided to create two divisions: Class A and Class B. Class A would round up the older organizations—the Young Men's Division, Hongwanji, and Pasadena YMCA—while Class B would round up a younger set of boys in high school and college—including the Hi-Y, Gakusei-Kai, Bruins, and Nakashima's All-Stars.[40]

Tashiro envisioned creating a Los Angeles–based readership, consumption, and fandom around Japanese American athletic games, where Japanese American Los Angelenos could take pride in their diasporic community. Sports editors believed that an all-Japanese American league could unify the Japanese American community, especially across age, immigration status, class status, and the Pacific. Tashiro's vision mirrored several other league organizers along the Pacific Northwest. Historian Samuel Regalado researches how a boxer-turned journalist like James Sakamoto developed an ethnic baseball league in Seattle to galvanize Japanese Americans and strengthen the Nikkei network from Seattle to Portland. Young men played the role as "bridge of understanding" to the wishes of Japanese elders and they successfully positioned themselves to win favor as bona fide Americans to white observers.[41]

By 1928, Los Angeles recreational leaders organized the J-League for baseball. Although individual baseball games had been long organized by elders within the community, the J-League expanded baseball to a new generation of young players and formally organized a board made up of representatives from the teams, newspaper men, and immigrant elders invested in baseball like C. Sumida, owner of the Sumida Sport Store and later president of the Baseball Association.[42] That year, they hosted a summer league, divided into the A and B classes. Class A included the L.A. Nippon, Grand Central, Nishi Hongwanji, Hollywood J.B.C., Old Timers, L.A. Asahi, Hollywood Hi-Y, and Long Beach Nippons. Class B included South Pasadena, Long Beach Y.M.A., Santa Monica, Oliver Juniors, Compton, and Gardena.[43] *Rafu Shimpo* sponsored the trophies.[44] Winners of the A League played against visiting teams from Japan. For instance, the L.A. Nippons, winners of 1928, played against Keio University.[45] The J-League

4.1 Coach Gene Akira Sakamoto (top row, far left) and the Oliver Juniors Baseball Team, 1929. Courtesy of Dennis Suski.

enabled young men who already competed in the A Leagues to also become mentors for the B league, for instance, Sakamoto played for Sun Produce in the A League, while coaching the Oliver Juniors in the B League.

The J-Leagues were successful largely because of boys' club leaders and coaches like Sakamoto who operated in the nexus between Japanese immigrant merchants, white YMCA organizers, and a new generation of boys' clubs. Sakamoto was in the market business, and though he may not have sold athletic goods, he had a vested interest in appealing to the younger community so that the ethnic market—and his business dealings—would continue to thrive. At the same time, he was a product of muscular Christianity and believed in expanding recreational values. His life revolved around this nexus between managing an ethnic market and leading the Oliver Club. In any typical given week in 1927, Sakamoto moved between his market, his club, and sports. He worked in the market business most mornings and days.[46] On Thursday evenings, he coached the Oliver Juniors basketball team in the Japanese Basketball B Leagues at Lincoln High

4.2 By 1929, Gene Sakamoto was president of the Oliver Club, which hosted many celebrations and parties. Courtesy of Dennis Suski.

School. Sometimes, he also played in the Japanese Basketball A Leagues for the Japanese YMCA. On Friday nights, he led the Community Sing at the Oliver Club.[47] On Sundays, he attended the Christian Endeavor service or Sunday school. He even helped to manage the rooming house that his family leased. And in his spare time, he coached the Junior Olivers basketball and baseball teams' practices.

Coaches helped to raise a new generation of male youths in muscular Christianity as well as provide a world of connections to their ethnicity. Coaches like Sakamoto passed on muscular Christian values such as discipline, teamwork, health, and exercise. At the same time, coaches encouraged youths to buy into their ethnic community and connections to Japan through consumption and fraternalism. As their bridge between communities, the younger community often looked at their coaches as role models. In fact, the Oliver Seniors, Juniors, and Midgets celebrated their basketball coach by throwing him a stag party at the Oliver Club. There, the captain of the Juniors basketball team, Eiichi Kito, gave a short speech of thanks and appreciation to Sakamoto.[48]

In 1930, Sakamoto was injured while playing for Sun Produce, a semi-professional baseball team that also played in the J-Leagues. He needed stitches and took ten days off of work as the manager for a new grocery store owned by Ushijima in Beverly Hills.[49] Reporters lamented this stroke of bad luck, since Sakamoto had just come off of coaching a game for the Oliver Juniors baseball team.[50] A year later, he retired from playing and coaching competitively and returned to playing recreationally. Sakamoto began to focus his attention toward the development of the Southern California Japanese American Savings Association, a fraternal organization where young men were able to borrow when necessary and pay back with interest. The organization aimed to establish a self-supporting business unit among young Japanese American men in Los Angeles, where they pooled the savings among a group of dependable fellows, sought advice from good advisors, helped members get a start on their business career, and invest their money wisely. Business-minded men bonded together largely through recreational sport and leisure, which solidified kinship and cultivated shared economic and political interests. By 1934, the *Rafu Shimpo* praised the organization, remarking that the membership was powerful enough to become a Junior Chamber of Commerce.

Sakamoto and other young men began to grow out of the boys' clubs and found themselves in need of an organization for young professionals. Sakamoto and his peers utilized their social networks around sports and service clubs to create a new organization around business and savings. In 1928, Sakamoto was among the twenty-five young men who created the Japanese American Savings Association. This savings association had a three-fold purpose: to encourage saving, to support the financial businesses of young entrepreneurs, and to create a social network among young men who graduated from high school or college and outgrew boys' clubs. Seeking to build their reputation among the older generation of businessmen, the association aimed to encourage thrift among young Japanese American men. The club wanted to lay the foundation for a financial superstructure through a mutual benefit scheme particularly for young businessmen aiming to prove themselves to elder businessmen.[51]

Sociologist Fumiko Fukuoka argues that the Japanese immigrant community had a long history of utilizing mutual aid in order to practice social and economic self-sufficiency. From the 1900s to the 1930s, Japanese immigrants held a number of associations, such as Kenjinkai, Japanese farmers' associations, and religious organizations. Japanese immigrants organized their savings associations similar to Kenjinkai—a prefectural association where one's membership was based on their shared roots from the same prefecture in Japan. Members could deposit their savings and also take out loans. These associations were significant to developing Japanese immigrant economy around commerce, farming, and fishing, especially as US banks did not extend credit to Japanese immigrants. However, when the Great Depression struck, these associations could no longer offer loans.[52]

In contrast, Fukuoka argues, youths were becoming more individualistic and tended to utilize American models. She points out that youths did not carry on the traditions of mutual aid among Japanese and Japanese immigrant societies. However, the Japanese American Savings Association was one of the few young people's organizations that carried on in the tradition of group savings and loans, combining self-help with muscular Christianity. The association organized around a common sociality: raised by immigrant parents, attending or having finished schooling (high school or college), and participating or having participated in ethnic service clubs and muscular Christianity.

The club nominated its first officers, all of whom had run in similar circles of sports league and a service club.[53] The president was Dr. Tetsuya Ishimaru, an optometrist. He had attended Los Angeles High School, played sports as part of the Berkeley team, became a coach of the Bruin basketball team in the A League, and served as an advisor to the Occidental Hi-Y organizations.[54] The vice president was Clarence Arima, once president of the Salt Lake Nisei Club, graduate of the University of Utah, and currently a manager for a produce truck company.[55] The secretary was Ernest Iwasaki, a graduate of Occidental College, president of the Young People's Society at Union Church, and bookkeeper of Okuhira Produce Company of Los Angeles.[56] The treasurer, Sakamoto, was in the market business and continued operating the rooming house; he also became president of the Oliver Club. The financial and membership committee included Seiichi Nobe, an insurance and real estate agent at Rivers and Elliott, graduate of Polytechnic High School and UCLA, member of the Young Men's Division, president of the Bruin Club, and tennis player.[57] Born in Hawai'i, Edward Tanaka was a graduate of Polytechnic High and USC, dentist, golf player, married to Yoshiko Oishi, and also served on the financial and membership committee.[58] Robert Kuwahara, a graduate of Polytechnic High School and Otis Art Institute, tennis player, and cartoonist, was the third member of the financial and membership committee.[59]

About a year later, by April 1929, the members numbered thirty-five young men—including college students, college graduates, and young businessmen. Many were US citizens or born in Hawai'i, born to Japanese immigrant families, and college graduates, and in their twenties. In fact, initially, members of the Young Men's Division, which included all high school graduates or working boys, overlapped and dissolved into the Japanese American Savings Association. The association hosted informal and formal get-togethers or meetings at a local café or at the YMCA. The members were allowed to submit any amount they wished to the treasury.[60] The savings association was an exclusive organization. The association held a discussion and voted on whether to accept each prospective member, generally excluding women from membership.

Young men in the savings association contributed to the thriving economy of Little Tokyo as new businesses opened and a rooming house like the one the Sakamoto family ran supplied housing for laborers. The 1930 US Census reveals that the Sakamoto family continued to operate the rooming house. Residing on 182 East First Street, in the heart of a burgeoning Little Tokyo, the Sakamoto family of four (his father had died sometime between 1924 and 1930) lived with thirteen lodgers in their rooming house. Although the census labeled them as "guests" of the Sakamoto family, they likely worked at the grocery store that Sakamoto managed and either paid for their rooms or lived at the rooming house as part of their salary. The lodgers included a majority of Japanese immigrants as well as a small number of Mexican immigrants and white men. The lodgers were all male, mostly single, and ranged in age from the twenties to the sixties. They worked in various labor sectors, including as a truck driver, gardener, fry cook, carpenter, and odd jobs. Several of the Japanese immigrant lodgers (in their twenties and thirties and having migrated between 1918 and

1922) worked in grocery sales. Their neighbors on East First Street consisted of a majority of Japanese immigrants and other white working-class residents.[61]

The savings association sought mentorship from Japanese elders who were prominent public figures. For instance, Dr. Yamato Ichihashi, professor of Japanese history at Stanford University, spoke at one association meeting. An outspoken intellectual funded by the Japanese government during the debates over the Japanese question, Ichihashi encouraged youths to serve as cultural bridges. In fact, his new book at the time focused on Japanese immigrants and their children.[62] The association also invited speakers such as Kumai of the Sun Produce Company to relate the origins of their association.[63] The Sun Produce Company was founded by three young Japanese immigrant men with separate produce stalls at the Los Angeles market who combined their resources in the 1910s, becoming the largest Japanese produce wholesale company in Los Angeles by the 1930s, boasting fifty employees.[64] Since the Sun Produce Company had built a successful company out of the coalition of a few immigrants, its history suggested that young men build partnerships with one another and cultivate new successful enterprises in Los Angeles. Later, the Japanese American Savings Association also served in a mentorship capacity to the young college students and businessmen of the Young Men's Division of the Japanese YMCA.[65]

At its heart, the savings association organized around men's recreational sports and leisure to build fraternalism and their club identity. Organizational meetings took place at members' homes or at the Japanese YMCA. Often at these meetings they held a sports matches. At one meeting, they played a basketball game between the college graduates and the college students.[66] They got together to play volleyball and other indoor sports.[67] They also held a horseshoe pitching contest among themselves.[68] In addition to playing recreationally among themselves, they played matches against other clubs. They formed teams to play in the table tennis league. They played tennis matches with the Bruin Club as well as the Commercial Club.[69] At other meetings, they enjoyed leisurely consumption symbolizing middle-class masculinity. On one occasion, Sakamoto held an organizational meeting at his home on 3492 East Fourth Street, near Boyle Heights, at which they smoked pipes.[70]

By 1931, Clarence Arima, then president of the Japanese American Savings Association, boasted the organization's success. Their savings accumulated into the second thousand, having enjoyed a prosperous year in 1930. The membership held strong at twenty. At each meeting, they invited an authority to speak on some phase of investment or another topic of interest to young Japanese American men.[71] Their annual anniversary meeting was the social event of the season. Fifty couples attended the association's exclusive semiformal dinner-dance to celebrate its third-year anniversary.[72] The association began to groom the organization to follow in the footsteps of a Chamber of Commerce, inviting the president of the Los Angeles Junior Chamber of Commerce to speak on their outlay and foundation.[73]

While the first few years of the organization focused on building fraternalism, the association adopted a more public role as cultural bridges as tensions brewed between China and Japan. The savings association began to act as a translator between international politics and the local community. It sponsored select public education events that helped to maintain diplomacy between the United States and Japan. For instance, as the Japanese military became more aggressive toward China, the savings association sponsored educational films about Manchuria and Japan in order to allay a public surge in anti-Japanese hostility. It hosted T. Nakagawa, secretary of the YMCA at Dairen, Manchuria, to speak on the economical and political situation in Manchuria.[74] The association also sponsored a meeting at the Japanese YMCA hall, where Consul T. Sato of the local Japanese Consulate and Ken Nakazawa, as English translator, spoke on the Manchurian situation. This event was open to the general public, particularly to the Japanese American community who could themselves be informed and combat the rise of another yellow peril wave.[75]

The savings association participated in charity drives that benefitted the Japanese war effort as well as local ethnic businesses. It ran a Japanese canned food drive through a benefit dance. Benefit dances were gaining even more popularity in the 1930s, likely because young people's organizations were able to combine their experience of fund-raising, their history of youth dancing, and their commitment to serving. The savings association asked each attendee to donate three cans of Japanese food as their admission fee. Purchase of Japanese-based goods would profit the ongoing

Japanese war efforts in China. They secured the Japanese YWCA gymnasium, invited Frank Watanabe and Honorable Archie of KNX radio station, a comedic duo of a stereotypical Japanese American houseboy and his housemaster, and hired the KFI station's dance orchestra to provide the entertainment. They sent invitations to young people's organizations and furnished the trucks to transport the cans of Japanese food.[76] Their goal was to collect a thousand cans and give them to 150 needy Japanese American families across Los Angeles. The savings association worked with the Japanese Chamber of Commerce and the Japanese YWCA. Various stores in Little Tokyo donated sacks of rice. Churches also made preparations to supply many families with food and clothing.[77]

However, their efforts did not go without class critique. A Bruin columnist pointed out that three cans of Japanese foods could run quite high, especially since the high tariff necessitated a heavy duty on Japanese foods.[78] To the columnist's point, only society's elite could afford three cans of Japanese food to attend a benefit dance. Moreover, the dance would benefit major stores such as Tokai, Tozaiya, Asia, and the Nippon Company. In fact, by September 1933, *Rafu Shimpo* featured a "where are they now" column that identified a host of athletes who turned into businessmen in produce, hotel, insurance, and law—society's elite.[79]

While many members had aged out of boys' clubs, J-Leagues, and even retired from coaching, many of them continued to endorse muscular Christianity through a scholarship fund. By the 1930s, recreational organizers had established the Japanese Athletic Union (JAU), which hosted leagues in basketball, football, baseball, and other sports. Members of the community saw that what the JACL did for the community politically, the JAU did for the community athletically: "through the unification of athletes into one body, they could gain benefits for themselves they could not individually."[80] Some of the benefits included a Japanese athletic center, privileges at fieldhouses, playgrounds, gymnasiums, gridirons, baseball diamonds, and the recognition of sporting authorities and bodies.[81] In 1936, the savings association sponsored Outstanding Athlete of the Year and sportsmanship awards in the JAU.[82] Because of unprecedented access to nicer playgrounds and facilities, J-Leagues expanded as clubs grew in size and generation. And this directly benefited local businesses and the ethnic economy.

Although the savings association had sponsored events that contributed to the spread of Japanese wartime propaganda, their history of muscular Christianity reveals a unique adaptation of Japanese imperialism. The association largely aimed to educate the Japanese American community on the political state of affairs in Japan in order to prevent anti-Japanese sentiment, as well as maintain cordial ties with the general US public, but their Americanization through clubs and recreation ultimately separated them from Japanese imperialism in the 1930s. Their organizational values rested on democratic election and US patriotism. They had built a sense of fraternalism through ethnic sports matches and leagues based on the values of muscular Christianity. Moreover, their relations with Japan largely relied on an ethnic connectedness to Japanese culture and economic incentive around replenishing the ethnic economy, not necessarily imperial ambitions.

Sakamoto developed a transnational new manhood that bridged muscular Christianity with the ethnic economy. Sakamoto inherited his family's debts through the family rooming house business, which marked his necessary entrance into the ethnic market. His real passion, however, lay in recreation and sports, where Sakamoto became an apprentice of Americanization teachers like Nellie Oliver and Sunday school teachers at the Japanese Christian Institute. The first of its kind, the Oliver Club taught young men Americanization and middle-class manliness such as how to organize democratic elections, how to run a meeting, and how to be a gentleman. By the late 1920s, business leaders merged their interests with YMCA organizers to build a dedicated YMCA facility and sports league to the Japanese American community. As a coach, Sakamoto facilitated muscular Christianity among the next generation through sports teams as well as maintained an ethnic connectedness by playing in the J-Leagues. By the 1930s, business leaders created the Japanese American Savings Associations that advanced the business interests of young men while collaborating with a centralized network of ethnic sports leagues under the JAU. As a member of the savings association, Sakamoto enjoyed fraternalism and the economic benefits of the replenishment of the ethnic economy around muscular Christianity.

Sakamoto's story reveals how young men navigated US and Japanese imperialism through the development of muscular Christianity, ethnic fraternalism, and community-based capitalism in the interwar period. Sakamoto rebuilt a transnational masculinity that was more closely aligned with US imperialism. In particular, he believed in advancing transnational muscular Christianity, which cultivated racial uplift among young men through organized sport. His masculinity mirrored the business elite that managed major business entities, held membership in influential governing bodies, and participated in charitable services to the community. At the same time, he negotiated Japanese imperialism by participating in diplomacy and public relations but did not seek to advance Japanese imperial ambitions. Although recreational organizers never discouraged women from participating in athletics, they did not focus on building a market around young women's athletics as they had with young men—which often sidelined them. The next and final chapter examines how young Japanese American women built their own support services through the Japanese American Girl Reserves movement.

5

The Progressive New Woman

In her life history written to her confidant, Dr. William C. Smith of the Survey of Race Relations, Satow admitted that on the outside she looked like the perfect daughter. However, Satow confessed that she struggled to fulfill her mother's greatest desire for her. Satow's mother decided that Satow would train to become a pianist so that Satow could earn a living. Satow initially consented to majoring in music at the University of Southern California, though she was still unsure of what fields she liked and what she wanted to be. By the end of her first year, Satow realized she had no musical talent and could never be happy in the music profession but was scared to tell her mother she wanted to quit piano. Satow felt tremendously guilty in addition to feeling indebted to her mother. Noting that her mother made handkerchiefs all day and her father worked as a day laborer to provide an education for Satow and her brother, she confided, "If my parents should die, their blood would be upon my head."[1] As a result, Satow continued to train at the piano, where her mother insisted that Satow spend three hours of practice at the piano every day, in addition to studying the Japanese language.

Satow, however, dreamed of becoming a social worker. Satow's approach to education diverged from her mother's. Since her earliest days as a child, she loved to read. She devoured adventure tales such as *David Copperfield* and *Les Misérables*. In high school, she avidly read biographies of missionaries in Japan, Egypt, and Spain, as well as social reformers in the United States, such as Booker T. Washington and Jacob Riis. She became interested in current affairs and internationalism, the idea that US investment and trade abroad would bring freedom to other people. She was often invited to speak at various white churches on the Japanese question. She believed in the solution of uplift: "in order to eliminate prejudice, the standards of the Japanese must be raised and their conditions improved." She attended a YWCA Student Conference and, as she put it, she was "possessed by an intense longing to serve." However, she hesitated to ask for her mother's consent, expecting her mother to be disappointed and angry.[2]

Satow's inner turmoil with her mother reflected some of the larger tensions and shifts between generations of women. Satow's struggle to come to terms with playing the piano as her life's endeavor didn't simply reflect a personal conflict; in fact it represented competing projects of gender and imperialism. Satow's mother promoted the Japanese imperial project of highbrow modern womanhood. Central to the project of Japanese imperialism were women who served as educators of Westernization and symbols of national elite. Japanese American women studied and trained in Western institutions to become the next great pianist. However, Satow's interest in becoming a social worker resembled the newfound US imperial project of progressive new womanhood. The YWCA became newly interested in cultural plurality and began to include Japanese American women into social work so they could spread progressive values to daughters of immigrants. Japanese American women entered new roles as secretaries and expanded New Woman values through the Girl Reserves.

This chapter explores how Satow navigated the competing projects of gender and imperialism to construct a progressive new womanhood. First, this chapter examines the Japanese imperial project of women's musical education through a history of the piano and its changing context within the institution of the immigrant family and community in the 1920s. In contrast to Japanese imperialism and a cultural shift toward modern womanhood, the YWCA built a Girl Reserves movement that developed New Women in a period of American internationalism and recruited nonwhite women as their new leaders. Navigating between these projects, Satow trained young women to serve as cultural ambassadors through the Japanese American Girl Reserves movement. Although Satow had felt entirely at odds with her mother, and indeed the Girl Reserves was altogether different from the classically trained pianist in gender roles, when examined more closely, these competing projects shared some common values of imperial endeavors, urbanity, and status narrowness.

MODERN MUSICAL WOMEN IN JAPANESE EXPANSION, 1910S TO 1920S

Satow's mother, Kiyose, who hailed from Tokyo, experienced the modernization and urbanization of gender roles and the introduction of Western music to Japan in the early twentieth century. Historian Mari Yoshihara posits that both Western imperialism and the Japanese pursuit for Westernization shaped Western-style music in East Asia. She argues that in addition to Western music playing an influential role in advancing Western-style militarization and Christianity, the Japanese government considered music to be an important element of modern education and implemented Western music into the school curricula as well as established institutions for advanced musical training.[3] Japanese elite's pursuit of the piano was both the result of Western imperialism and Japanese imperial endeavors.

Historian Sandra Weiland Howe argues that women played a central role in the introduction of Western music to Japan during the Meiji Restoration. Concerned that other nations might not see Japan as a modern nation, they implemented a practical education for women under the motto "good wife, wise mother," emphasizing the roles of women in the management of the home and the education of children. This concept of gender roles relieved the state from responsibility for the old, young, and the ill and could be achieved only by elite and middle-class families. Japanese women learned Western music from Christian missionaries as well as under the compulsory education system. From an early age, women received musical training at the Tokyo Women's Normal School, founded in 1874. Girls studied liberal arts subjects, sewing, etiquette, and domestic economy. Women often trained to become teachers. Women also received musical training in the Tokyo Music School.[4] Western musical training was linked to notions of Japanese femininity, management of the home, and women's role in modernizing education.

Historian Sidney Lu has examined how the Japanese imperialists shaped women to be "good women" when expanding empires abroad to the United States and Asia. In the age of empires, the status of women became a measurement of civilization. After the Gentlemen's Agreement enabled the migration of picture brides, Japanese imperialists quickly trained women to be proper representatives before they migrated abroad. Lu has argued that reformers ran a series of domestic education programs to discipline picture brides in California who brought shame to Japanese imperialism.[5] Reformers like Michi Kawai of the Japanese YWCA trained picture brides in proper US home life in order to showcase these women as the best, most civilized of Japan. Kawai first saw a need for reform during her visit to the Pan-American Exposition in 1915. She visited the detention station at Angel Island where Japanese immigrant women were detained and spoke to them about "American home life and moral standards and the Japanese people's responsibility to the land they had come to live."[6] Kawai implemented women's training programs in Japan prior to their immigration to the United States. She started classes in the Yokohama Association for girls and women emigrating to the United States and created leaflets. Kawai believed her training program was necessary to build international friendship and lessen international friction prior to the 1924 Exclusion Act.

Although imperialists imagined that women would be exemplars of modern womanhood, the harsh reality of rural working-class life brought their imperial intentions to a crisis. Imperialists believed that a strong urban elite based on the foundations of modern womanhood would showcase the imperial strength of the Japanese empire. Indeed, many women who migrated to the United States and agreed to marry men abroad believed they were migrating to a better life. However, when they arrived in the United States, they experienced downward mobility. The domestic reforms did little to prepare them for the harsh living conditions of their new husbands' farm lives. Life was difficult for many Japanese immigrant women, who performed farm labor alongside their husbands as well as the domestic labor at home. In fact, the rising number of women's deaths caught the attention of Japanese imperialists. One *Shin Sekai* editorial asked why there were so many deaths of women around age twenty. Some women died because they contracted diseases or they committed suicide or, as one newspaper put it, they "became hysterical." The editorial lamented: "They probably thought that if they came to America, they would live in a civilized city, in a fine house with a piano."[7] Without educated women in the home, Japanese imperialists worried about the state of Japanese development.

Kiyose Satow's migration reflects the difficult shift from an urban city life in Japan to a rural farm life in the United States. She entered into a marriage with a prosperous Japanese immigrant farmer in California. When she moved to California, they lived in a rural district outside of San Mateo. She experienced terrible loneliness, unable to associate with white residents because they did not have a common language. Moreover, she felt she had very little in common with other Japanese immigrant neighbors because they did not share her status as a refined Tokiojin who descended from samurai. However, the family suffered a devastating loss after a friend defrauded their enterprise, leaving them to start over financially. The situation was so dire that the Satows had to temporarily place Lily and her brother Masao in the Ellen Stark Ford Home in San Francisco until they could again care of their children.[8] After they moved to Los Angeles, rebuilt their home, and could financially care for them, the Satows retrieved their children from the orphanage and brought them to live in an uptown white neighborhood away from the Japanese Americans who congregated downtown.

Urban elite of the educated classes often distinguished themselves from farmers. This paralleled an urban/rural hierarchy between the immigrants, where those pursuing Western education set themselves above the average working classes. In one case, one couple, the Fs, had immigrated to the United States with the "sole motive of becoming scholars," distinguishing themselves from the working class, whom they believed had come to the United States only for work and money. At that time, though, there was much excitement over growing strawberries in Gardena. At first, "they objected that they had come to this country not for wealth but for learning," but they finally gave into the booming business of strawberries. Unfortunately, they came out of the business in debt and with the loss of a child. Moving back to Los Angeles, F entered the auto business and took his family to live in a "comfortable little rented house" where "the living room was small but contained a piano."[9] F explained that they were finally "prosperous" but could never return to Japan for their "shame in not becoming scholars." In fact, it was not a matter of economics that gave F cultural capital of empire, but that of educational attainment of the genteel class. The piano became a sign of educational aspirations that distinguished the literati elite from the uncultured working laborers.

Japanese American modern womanhood, as displayed through the ownership of a piano, could also convince white racial liberals of their civility during the rise of anti-Japanese sentiment. In an era when the anti-Japanese movement complained about the unfair work ethic of the Japanese farmers and their low standard of living, the piano represented an immigrant's investment in the moral institution of high culture. White sociologists observed Japanese immigrant homes to investigate anti-Japanese claims. For example, Constance Ricketts observed Japanese American families in the Gardena farming area and concluded that the father of what she called the "Manchida" family worked hard to build "a good home" for his family: "The Manchida family own their own home and little truck farm. The house is of fair size, and extremely neat. The furnishing is very good, and they are the proud possessors of a piano." Ricketts praised the aspirations of one particular woman: "A young lady friend of the Manchidas is a very accomplished pianist. The pianist expressed, 'It took long time, hard work and many hours to learn to play.' But she is earnest in her desire to become a figure in the musical world, and she is willing to give up other things for that end." This convinced Ricketts that Japanese immigrants were not racially inferior and should not be legally excluded from land access or migration, reasoning, "Honesty, industry, appreciation, and desire to be Americanized seem to be the great elements of good in these people."[10]

The piano became an instrument of respectability and class, linked to urbanity and modernity, and reflected a status hierarchy within the Japanese American communities in California as well as a door to white liberal friendship. One white female sociologist, El Koempel, submitted observations of a growing gap between her Japanese female friends while growing up in Hermosa Beach. She observed a distinction between Yoshiko, a respectable young lady, and Rhea Nakimura, her friend, a field worker:

"Yoshiko was a distinct type. The fact that she was preparing herself to teach in Japan set her above the average, ordinary, truck-gardener. She studied music, both the piano and the violin and even gave lessons in piano to aid in paying for her violin study." In fact, Koempel and her peers discussed the Japanese question in class in front of Yoshiko, believing that she would share their perspective; however, their discussion resulted in Yoshiko feeling ostracized. On the other hand, her friend did not share the characteristics that Koempel and her friends considered to be part of the educated class. According to Koempel, "Rhea worked in her father's fields and was rather noisy and boisterous. Her English was not as careful as Yoshiko's. There was a lack of something which prevented any friendship between the two girls." Rhea never made it past the first year of high school.[11]

By the 1920s, immigrant parents invested in their daughters' musical education as a response to racial discrimination and market patterns. For example, Dr. Peter Suski, a prominent children's physician, planned to give his children the best US education. Living in Boyle Heights among European immigrants and Mexican Americans, Suski observed: "There seems to be a general tendency among the Japanese parents to educate their children, it will appear that the Japanese children in America will surpass many other groups in this respect." Departing from working-class families where children contributed to the family income through their labor, well-to-do families like Suski's expected return investments through his children's high performance in education. Suski explained: "I am going to give my children every opportunity for a good education." About the future of youths, Suski believed that "they will compare favorably with the average of Americans, but, nevertheless, when they seek employment they will be handicapped, on account of the discriminations against them because of race." Parents turned inward to equip their children with preprofessional skills to overcome a racist job market. Suski observed: "If the American-born Japanese are to win a place for themselves, they will have to excel in a special line, and that idea is quite largely responsible for the encouragement which Japanese parents give their children in school."[12] His daughters, including Julia, Louise, Clara, and Flora, all learned to play the piano.[13] Julia went on to become a piano teacher.[14]

Moreover, parents invested in their daughters' Western musical education as part of maintaining a transnational connection or nostalgia to dignified Japanese culture and modernism. Elders were concerned that young people were becoming too Americanized, creating a gulf between generations. A critic signing off as "Mrs. Grundy" wrote an editorial that dunned young people as "spoiled" in comparison to the racial discrimination and economic hardship their parents had faced years earlier. Grundy explained that youths of the day were born with privileges such as citizenship and tended to "take new fads readily." Moreover, the critic compared the youths to "refined Japanese from Japan" and noted that the young people "lack modesty, restraint, and politeness." Grundy believed that the youths lacked character and resilience, charging that, "despite the fact that they possess innumerable advantages, they "complain."[15] As a result of youths' disappointing development, parents enrolled their children in cultural institutions such as Japanese language schools and music schools in order to foster nostalgic Japanese characteristics within their children, maintain their children's transnational connections to Japan, and even improve their relationship with their children.

By the 1920s, playing the piano or violin was a distinctly Japanese American phenomenon. White educators tapped into a clear market for piano lessons by creating the Cosmopolitan School of Music in Los Angeles, where Japanese American children were the main clientele. Music teachers included young single white women, including Miss Myrtle M. Winnie, who had studied at Rector Institute of Music and was once affiliated with the piano department at Pasadena University as well as with the Los Angeles Conservatory of Music.[16] The music school taught students to play the piano or violin, or receive vocal lessons. Parents could enroll children as young as the age of eight, although most pupils were eleven or twelve years old.[17] In 1928, the Cosmopolitan School of Music enrolled fifteen Japanese American pupils in piano lessons. The following year, the enrollment nearly doubled. The Cosmopolitan School of Music granted diplomas, certificates of promotion, and teacher certificates. For instance, at the 1928 commencement, Chitosey Nagao, a fifteen-year-old student at Jefferson High School, received a diploma after completing music school.[18] Fuji Fujino, a graduate of Roosevelt High School, earned a teaching certificate at the age of nineteen and began teaching piano in her home in Boyle

Heights.[19] The Cosmopolitan School of Music gave graduation recitals where students showcased their mastery of European and US children's classics.[20]

Piano was a form of educational investment shared by urban elites and working classes alike. Japanese American parents who enrolled their children into music school came from a range of occupations, including a broker, a barber, a janitor, a rancher, a salesman in produce, and a retailer from a dry-goods store.[21] Some immigrant families supplemented their income by also becoming managers of a rooming house, which gave those families some status within the community. While Japanese immigrant families rented a large place from landowners, they also rented out rooms to lodgers, including other Japanese American families, white married couples, or single Japanese male laborers, or single white women. For instance, Shigizo Yamane, father of Mikiko Yamane, an eleven-year-old pupil at the music school, managed a rooming house with fifteen lodgers ranging from single women in their sixties to Japanese male laborers in their twenties, in addition to his family of four.[22]

Few students of music went on to become successful pianists, but many more became piano teachers. Fumi Iwasaki was one budding young pianist.[23] Iwasaki was a student of Cora Bowler, a private piano teacher.[24] Iwasaki had lived with six other girls in an orphanage run by Margaret Fries.[25] It is unclear whether Iwasaki was an orphan, but it was common for Japanese parents to place their children in orphanages when parents could not afford to care for them; young women also rented rooms in orphanages. As a pupil of Bowler, Iwasaki put on piano recitals at the Japanese Home for Girls.[26] Iwasaki also played in organized programs run through the Commerce Club, Filipino Club, and Cosmopolitan Club at Polytechnic High School.[27] Iwasaki went on to major in music at the University of California, Los Angeles.[28] She accompanied soprano singers at their concerts.[29] Iwasaki began to teach piano to younger Japanese American women, who held their own recitals at local churches.[30]

Satow's mother decided that Satow be trained in piano so that she could earn a living. While Satow took music courses at the University of Southern California, Satow's father performed laundry work and other domestic services for families.[31] Satow's mother stayed at home as a full-time mother, but when Satow entered college she took on "homework"

5.1 Satow family portrait, early 1920s. Seated: Peter Shuzo Satow, Kiyose Satow. Standing: Roy Satow, Lily Yuriko Satow, Masao William Satow. Courtesy of Ron Fujiyoshi.

by making and selling handkerchiefs.[32] Satow witnessed her mother toiling "incessantly from early morning to late at night." Satow felt guilty. Although becoming a music teacher provided promising job stability, the pursuit of the piano created a debt that Satow did not want to co-sign. Satow even offered to quit school and work in order to pay for her own education.[33] When Satow realized that she "had no musical talent and could never be happy in the music profession," she could not bring herself to approach her mother. Satow was scared of her mother's temper but more so of her mother's tendency to gossip openly about her trials and tribulations as a mother, which violated Satow's trust. Even as Satow "yearned for a mother's sympathy, for someone, with breadth of vision and depth of understanding," Satow circled back to her indebtedness: "Be that as it may, I am under eternal obligations to her for all the planning, work, and sacrifice which she has done for me."[34]

NEW PROGRESSIVE WOMEN IN AMERICAN INTERNATIONALISM, 1924 TO 1928

While the Meiji Restoration and Japanese expansion shaped Satow's mother's ideas of the modern woman, Satow's ideas of the New Woman were shaped by racial progressives in the United States in the aftermath of World War I. International and domestic events reshaped how social progressives thought about race and international relations. President Woodrow Wilson entered into World War I based on the public moral cause of ensuring that self-determination be given and assured for all nations. However, despite espousing self-determination, Wilson often imposed moral imperialism and military intervention in countries that the US government believed needed lessons in democracy. A similar paradox undergirded progressive organizations that rallied to Wilson's support, believing that the United States could disseminate progressive values abroad. Scholars have argued that progressive organizations like the YWCA aimed to build a global fellowship of women, but their attempts bolstered or perpetuated existing race, class, and national hierarchies.[35] At home, the YWCA made a concerted attempt to attract communities of color and advanced a pluralist model of fellowship. While espousing cultural pluralism, however, the YWCA continued to impose

Americanization and did not dispose of its white middle-class norms. The YWCA advanced the New Woman through the Girl Reserves movement, in which interracial justice became a central characteristic.[36] With a new focus on interracial work, the YWCA educated white women and encouraged select elite young women of color to enter into social work and join their progressive movement. They reached out to young Japanese American women through their universities, their churches, in the YWCA International Institute, clubs, and conferences.

Satow fundamentally disagreed with her mother and other Japanese elders on modern womanhood, which gestured to a larger critique of ageism and ethnocentrism. She did not believe in studying only Japanese culture and shaping her womanhood into the refined domesticity attached to "good wife, wise mother." She had grown up as a tomboy and preferred to be out in the public sphere, speaking to church groups or leading youth groups. She loved reading and played basketball. While she could not face her mother in her own home, Satow was outspoken in the community. In response to the Grundy editorial that scathingly criticized youths' lack of Japanese refinement, Satow submitted her own letter to the editor. Young people were unfairly ridiculed as ignorant of things Japanese because this was beyond their own control. Satow protested, noting that these young people were not Nipponese, but American. Satow believed that youths needed to be equipped with tools to navigate US society. The older immigrant community provided not guidance but rather a flurry of criticism. Satow asked: "How many Japanese parents are teaching their American-born children to become good citizens of the United States? How many of the first generation are inspiring the second-generation with high ideals?" She pointed to the church as a place that signaled young people's true character and their capability of leadership: "It is the much criticized young people who are the Sunday School teachers, the pianists, the ushers, the choir members, the hard workers."[37]

Although Satow advocated for the leadership of young people, she did not entirely mesh with the young people of downtown. When Satow began to attend the Japanese American Union Church downtown, she felt out of place, which she attributed to a difference of "mental, moral, and social conceptions." She lived in an upscale neighborhood and attended a comparatively more resource-rich high school with students coming largely from well-to-do white families. This led to her declaration that she felt educationally superior to them in their studies. She was initially not a part of the YWCA "The More The Merrier Girls" club that all of the Japanese American girls at the Union Church had joined. But she did try to embed herself in their leisure culture. Still, her perceived moral superiority framed how she viewed her peers. She felt they were drifting without a definite aim and that they lacked a comprehensive outlook on life. She turned to self-improvement and desperately searched for a noble purpose.[38]

The YWCA Asilomar Student Conferences were designed to help college women from well-to-do families prepare for a vocation as social workers. In 1913, the National Board of the YWCA established the Asilomar campgrounds in Pacific Grove, about two hours south of San Francisco. Asilomar hosted student conferences in collaboration with YWCA organizations on college campuses that might recruit women into the mission of the YWCA. Student conferences promised to "give them a clearer sense of the world in which they lived" and aimed to inspire women to contribute to "rebuilding" the world. Student conferences invited young women to "create a deeper understanding with God that may bear the responsibilities of leadership commensurate to their opportunities." The student conferences included Bible study, lectures on the essentials of Christian faith, mission and community study, technical councils that could direct women into YWCA work, missionary addresses, and recreation.[39] These student conferences particularly targeted college students in the western United States, especially California, Arizona, Nevada, and Utah. A majority of conference attendees were well-to-do white women.

The Asilomar Student Conferences made a concerted effort for the 1926 conference to reflect the YWCA's newfound imperative toward interracial work. A number of national and international events shifted the direction of the 1926 student conference. After the Great War, YWCA programs abroad became increasingly under the administrative purview of the World YWCA. This shift reflected larger trends to move away from nationalism and imperialism, the main causes of the Great War, and toward democracy and self-determination. The 1930 International Survey of the

YWCA stated that the aim of the North America YWCAs in launching "foreign work" was to assist in founding "self-supporting, self-directing and self-propagating national movements." The transition began in 1923–24, when the national association began to rethink its expansion of programs abroad, recognizing that former colonies of the British Empire viewed themselves as equals of other nations. This was in direct contrast to the US government's rejection of Japan's racial equality proposal in the Treaty of Versailles. YWCAs in India, Japan, and China shifted more into the hands of national leaders rather than secretaries sent by the YWCA of the United States.[40]

The transition to supporting national movements abroad mirrored a domestic movement at home for racial equality in the United States. Given the climate of the passage of the 1924 Immigration Act and the resurgence of the Ku Klux Klan in the Midwest, the student conferences began to call for interracial work as well as world fellowship. The student conference at Asilomar incorporated world relations as a theme and diversified both its conference planners and student attendees. However, attempts at racial inclusion were limited in two respects. First, the conference still primarily catered to a white middle-class female population. Speakers of color were brought in to educate white women about racism and to broaden their understanding of the world. Second, organizers only selected highly educated, urban elites of color that advanced a politics of respectability. These organizers aligned YWCA progressivism with their own politics: Japanese American cultural ambassadorship and Black uplift.

One conference planner that greatly influenced the direction of the 1926 Asilomar Student Conference was Miya Sannomiya, a young Japanese American woman who approached the YWCA student movement as an opportunity for cultural ambassadorship. A daughter to a farming family, Sannomiya had served as an interpreter for legal cases in the aftermath of the passage of the California Alien Land Law. Later, she attended the University of California, Berkeley, to study German. In 1926, she was selected for a three-month tour of Japan, with the purpose of cultivating young people as cultural ambassadors between Japan and the United States.[41] The tour exposed young people to the history and beauty of Japan as well as allowed them to interact with important officials. During her trip, Sannomiya also explained the role of the YWCA and student movement to students in Japan.[42] Her time in Japan shaped her approach to planning the student conference at Asilomar. As chair of the YWCA Asilomar Student Conference Division of World Relations, she developed the theme of group living into two divisions: "Principles in Connection with Service" and "Leadership in the World or International Relations." Sannomiya endeavored to build bridges between the United States and Japan, guided by her motto that "successful world fellowship . . . comes from intimate living, playing, and thinking together." She emphasized that a large delegation of "foreign and first generation American students" needed to be encouraged to attend the Asilomar conference. For the first time, ten Japanese American students were in attendance.[43]

That same year, Ida Jackson, one of the first Black teachers in California, was in charge of the theme of "inter-racial work."[44] Jackson was born in Mississippi and her father was a farmer, storekeeper, and minister. Her father stressed the importance of obtaining an education. She attended New Orleans University and received a normal teaching diploma and a certificate in home economics, but when her family moved to California, she was denied a teaching position in Oakland. She then went to the University of California, Berkeley, where she helped to create an all-Black sorority, the Alpha Kappa Alpha. She earned her master's degree at UC-Berkeley. In 1926, Jackson became the first certified African American high school teacher in Oakland public schools. She taught history at the elementary and high school levels. Jackson recalls that "there were no Blacks at the YWCA when I was at Cal." When she and her friends were sent to the Oakland Y for swimming classes, they were told they could not use the pool, refusing even after they asked to use it just before the water was changed on Friday night. Later, Jackson helped to organize a YWCA in Oakland for a group of girls. They were permitted to hold meetings and form a basketball team, but they could still not use the swimming pool. She befriended Lillie Margaret Sherman, an executive director at the YWCA at the University of California, Berkeley, and was eventually asked to take charge of a seminar on race relations at the Asilomar conference. Having grown up with a strong emphasis placed on education, Jackson also promoted other women of color to cultivate a range of skills, including education, and to be open to moving east, where there might be more opportunities for Black teachers.[45] At the conference, she offered a presentation on the conditions of Black people in the United States and called for "inter-racial justice."

Ichihashi, a scholar of Japanese history and cultural ambassador between the United States and Japan, gave a "World Education" keynote address at the 1926 Asilomar Student Conference. He gave a speech titled "Facts Around the Pacific." He spoke about the immigration laws, cultural background of immigrant groups, philosophy and religion in Asia, and the current economic and social conditions of Asia.[46] Historian Yuji Ichioka has uncovered the motives behind Ichihashi's writings and speeches on Japanese immigration.[47] Ichihashi's appointment at Stanford University was partially funded by the Japanese Consulate, as well as by private donations from Japanese businessmen in California as a response to the passage of the California Alien Land Law. Ichihashi was hired to partake in a "campaign of education" to change opinions around Japanese immigration and ultimately prevent anti-Japanese legislation. Ichihashi's writings included a pamphlet, *Japanese Immigration: Its Status in California* which directly counteracted false statements spread by anti-Japanese leaders. Ichihashi had previously spoken to the Japanese agricultural associations, particularly to farmers and laborers, about creating friendlier relations between the tenant and the landlord, as a means to dissuade Californians from renewing the Alien Land Law in 1920. Although he had privately held a low opinion of his fellow Japanese immigrants, he publicly defended them and advocated for naturalization. After the 1924 Immigration Act, he published another book in 1932 and advocated for a revision of the 1924 Immigration Act.

When it came to "the second generation problem," Ichihashi also came to the defense of Japanese immigrant parents. It was a personal and a scholarly endeavor for Ichihashi to study second-generation youths (he was one of the first scholars to use the term "second generation") as he was raising his own six-year-old son. Like many other parents, he wanted to prepare his children for economic self-sufficiency. He stressed: "I am planning to give him the best of advantages educationally in America, but I am also going to encourage him to learn the Japanese language so that he can go to Japan if he meets too many obstacles here." From his perspective, the rift between the parents and the youths was not just a matter of language: the youths did not pay respect to their elders. He explained: "I believe that I have been able to get Americans to appreciate this culture without learning the language, and so that ought to be possible as well with the Japanese young people. An appreciation of this sort would avoid many difficulties."[48] Ichihashi held a paternalistic view toward the young people, believing that they did not pay respect to the immigrant generation. At the student conference, he gave a series of five lectures and was chauffeured by Kazuo Kawai, a student and president of the new Northern California Institute of Pacific Relations. Ichihashi had met with the Japanese American student conference attendees for one discussion group and "urged them not to preserve the attitude of challenge toward their parents but to start the advances toward co-operation with the first generation."[49]

Of the four hundred college students from California, Arizona, Nevada, and Utah who attended the Student Conference at Asilomar in 1926, a small cohort of ten Japanese American women represented their respective college campuses (fig. 5.2). The cohort included Mine Harada of Riverside, known as a "Stuck-Up," a once derogatory but reclaimed term given and worn by girls who stayed for the entire duration of summer at Asilomar because they could afford to do so. In addition, a group of women from Northern California included Carol Tokunaga, treasurer of the San Jose College YWCA, Yuri Negi, secretary of the San Francisco Japanese Students Christian Association, and Sumile Morishita, president of the Berkeley Fellowship. From the Southern California JSCA, Julia Suski, Kimi Mukaye, Lily Satow, Ruth Aiso, Louise Matsuyama, and Ruth Wakayama boarded the train to attend the ten-day conference.[50] When the students broke out into discussion groups, the young Japanese American women often formed their own group, most likely due to the YWCA's segregation practices. Aside from lectures and discussions, the girls went on hikes, played in athletic tournaments, roasted marshmallows, and snacked at midnight. They were also able to visit the Monterey Japanese Church and eat Japanese food.[51]

Although the 1926 conference had primarily targeted the racial justice education work toward white women, it gave young Japanese American women like Satow the noble and beautiful purpose she was looking for: to advance respectability through a platform of self-determination and

5.2 Lily Satow (see detail on facing page) and a small cohort of Japanese American young women attend the YWCA Student Conference at Asilomar, 1926. Courtesy of California State Parks.

internationalism. While white college students learned from educated and respectable people of color about racism and the world, Satow wanted to become one of those respectable people of color who would educate others. Satow recalled that the conference activities had served a twofold purpose: "To give each girl a better understanding of herself and her fellowmen and to bring her into closer fellowship with that universal driving force which we call God." The world relations approach of the Asilomar Student Conference provided Satow with an education on the wider state of race relations in the United States as well as international relations between the United States and Japan, the United States and Mexico, and so on. She had experienced a spiritual racial utopia at Asilomar that she did not find in her circles in Los Angeles. By bringing in different speakers on US-Japanese relations, on Mexico, and the Black experience in the United States, the Asilomar conference offered a vision of cross-racial solidarity in uplifting different minority groups in the United States, as well as a global fellowship of encouraging self-determination in other countries. Satow found friendship and sisterhood with the other nine Japanese American women from across California. Satow felt a calling to be a part

of the YWCA project of self-determination and progressivism within her own community. After Asilomar, Satow returned to Los Angeles determined to become a YWCA secretary so that she could work with young Japanese American women across Los Angeles.

After making her decision to become a social worker, Satow hesitated asking her mother's permission. It was not until she overheard her mother telling a neighbor that "my life is bound up in the life of my children" that she finally revealed to her mother her wishes to quit playing the piano. To her surprise, her mother consented, answering, "Do as you please, just so you are happy." Satow's new vocation as a YWCA social worker still fell in line with her mother's wishes for Satow to obtain a modern education. Although Satow intended to advance US ideals, the two projects shared an imperial imperative attached to racial uplift and national status. With her mother's blessing, Satow switched her major to sociology at the University of Southern California. Through social work, she would repay her debts to her parents.[52]

THE JAPANESE AMERICAN GIRL RESERVES MOVEMENT, 1928 TO 1934

When Satow became a social worker, she entered into a world dominated by well-meaning but racist middle-class white women. Much of the objectives of white progressives like Esther Bartlett of the YWCA International Institute had been to Americanize Asian immigrants and young women. Often, their vision was shortsighted in assuming nonwhites to be naturally inferior. As the new Los Angeles YWCA secretary, Satow believed in combining the best of Japan as well as the best of the United States, which encouraged select components of Americanization but also nurtured unique attachments to Japanese culture. As a result, Satow promoted an elite urban Japanese American girlhood culture that bolstered existing race, class, and gender hierarchies. By 1930, as Japanese YWCA secretary, Satow developed a Girl Reserves culture of cultural ambassadorship in training: presenting interracial friendship and racial uplift to white progressives, educating immigrant parents on American culture and Christianity, and promoting transnational New Woman Christian values in spaces of their own.

From the outset, the Los Angeles Japanese American Girl Reserves Movement was sponsored partly from the Los Angeles Community Chest movement, an organization of white progressives seeking to advance a progressive agenda, and partly from the Japanese American community. One of many other community chests that began shortly after the Great War ended, the Los Angeles Community Chest incorporated on May 29, 1924.[53] Community chests were collections of donated monies from well-off individuals, families, or businesses, used for the purposes of civic or nonprofit organizations to impress and build up social values. The Los Angeles Community Chest supported the mission of cultural ambassadorship promoted by social service institutions like the Japanese YWCA. For instance, in 1930, the Los Angeles Community Chest gave $20,000 to Little Tokyo service organizations.[54] The money went to Japanese Children's Home, the Maryknoll Home, the Japanese branches of the YMCA and YWCA, and the Salvation Army. However, a part of that money was initiated through the fund-raising by YWCA social workers within the Japanese American communities. Satow and other members of the Y raised $10,000 from the Japanese American community for the Los Angeles Community Chest. One weekend, about ten women established posts on the four corners of San Pedro and East First street, the heart of Little Tokyo business district, to ask passersby to purchase Community Chest badges.[55] Japanese American giving often depended on the fluctuation of the economy, ranging from giving $10,000 in 1930, whereas the number dwindled each year into the Depression, dipping to $5,000 in 1933.[56] Aside from the community chest, the Japanese YWCA often fund-raised on their own through concerts and dances for their programs.

The institutional structure of the Japanese American Girl Reserves reflected their unique positionality that already placed them as a go-between across white institutions and their Japanese counterparts. The Japanese American Girl Reserves was a tightly organized community segregated from the larger YWCA Girl Reserves movement and deeply embedded within Japanese American Christian institutions. By 1927, YWCA advisors of Japanese American Girl Reserves organized the Inter-Club Council, a council made up of presidents and vice presidents, to coordinate across all the clubs across Southern California.[57] By 1929, seven Japanese American Girl Reserves had sprouted up across Los Angeles, including SOF (service, opportunity, and friendship), SOF Juniors, Emba, LC, ST (later Triple S), All Around, and Loha-Tohela.[58] Each club, which consisted of eight or more girls, had formalized under a community institution, like an ethnic church.

Historian Valerie Matsumoto explores how young girls and women found in their clubs a haven from racial discrimination and parental pressures, as well as a place to gain skills. Within their clubs, young girls pushed the boundaries of gender behavior expected by their immigrant parents while also maintaining some parts of their parents' gender ideologies. Club activities facilitated young women's participation into cultural coalescence: the selection and adaptation of cultural forms from an array of models in multiethnic southern California. Because of their club activities, young women became very visible in their communities.[59]

In fact, Satow put on their annual Japanese American Girl Reserves Conference retreat where they hosted speakers and planned their annual programs that relayed their vision for young women to serve as cultural bridges. Camp leaders hosted speakers, including a YWCA social worker in Japan, a sociologist, and a high school vice principal.[60] Each speaker attempted to inspire transnational connections and encourage women to take on their role as cultural bridges between US institutions and Japanese immigrant communities. For instance, the second conference hosted a sociologist, Frances Lucas, who encouraged the women to be the "link between the past and present." She discussed family life in Japan and that youths could be the link between their family and American society "by association with girls through the Girl Reserves in friendship, fun, and development." Moreover, Lucas ended her speech by promoting progressive values and Americanization, with her main message preparing the youths for the future: "Train the G. R. for community service in the future and train them for citizenship. Live up to the code of the Girl Reserves and not worry of the future of America."[61] Afterward, the girls discussed the progress of each club and planned the program for the upcoming year.[62]

Within each Japanese American Girl Reserves club, their annual program instilled progressive values and reinforced building respectability among young women. For instance, Satow served as advisor to Loha-Tohela. In 1928, a group of younger girls at the Japanese Christian Institute organized the Loha-Tohela Girl Reserves.[63] The Loha-Tohela officers elected Charlotte Shimidzu as president, Teruo Miyako as vice president, Emy Odanaka as secretary, Hoshiko Kusudo as treasurer, Miyoko Mikariya as reporter, Toshiko Shinagawa as service chair, and Naoko Odanaka and Margaret Suzuki as the membership committee.[64] The girls' ages ranged from ten to fourteen. They lived various distances from the Japanese Christian Institute, in mixed neighborhoods, and attended different high schools. During their first year, the Loha-Tohelas studied the "Ideal Girl" and discussed fashion. They also attended a lecture on social hygiene at the YWCA International Institute.[65]

The Japanese American Girl Reserves also served as a training ground for cultural ambassadors in a variety of public spaces. Satow accompanied a small cohort of representatives of Japanese American Girl Reserves to regional conferences where they were racially tokenized to reinforce the pluralist vision of the Girl Reserves movements. The Mid-Winter and Summer Girl Reserves Conferences, for instance, were planned by national leaders in conjunction with local leadership, hosted representatives of Girl Reserves, and provided opportunities for inspiration to white

Girl Reserves.[66] These conferences provided the only opportunity where white Girl Reserves might intermingle with Girl Reserves of color, but these conferences were aimed at developing and enriching white young women. Often the work of interracial justice fell into the hands of the nonwhite YWCA secretaries, whether by representative inclusion or planning. For example, Satow accompanied six young Japanese American women to a student conference at Asilomar in 1931. Representatives included Fuji Sugahara and Mary Wakamatsu of All Arounds, Alice Sumida of Embas, Charlotte Shimidzu of Loha-Tohela, and Florence Suzuki and Ida Takeuchi of SOFs. The conference had a variety of speakers and topics, but often relegated the work of racial justice to YWCA workers of color. The conference held a predominately white lineup for speakers on topics seen and understood as universal: Dr. Fred H. Stolz, executive of Institute of Child Study of the University of California (girls' personality); Dr. John Burton, graduate of Oxford University (world peace); Dorothy Harvey, teacher at Berea College (religion); Rhoda Foster, national secretary for rural communities (job market); and Bartlett Head (marriage). But when it came to discussing race relations, they assigned it to one of the few Japanese American YWCA secretaries, Toyo Domoto, the secretary of the YWCA International Institute of Oakland.[67]

While Japanese American young women played the role of racial tokens at Girl Reserves conferences, they also preserved and promoted Japanese traditions among young people. No better example was the annual Japanese doll festival. The doll festival began out of an early form of cultural exchange between Japan and the United States. Hina dolls that represented the Japanese imperial court were put on display. Sweet drinks and various dishes were served. Schools and clubs across Southern California observed the Japanese custom. For instance, the Japanese Christian Church observed the doll festival, holding playlets, musical numbers, and speeches. For their program, the director of the language school invited the parents of the children who performed. It was a combined effort among the students of the language school, the kindergarten Sunday school children, and the Girl Reserves at the Christian church.[68] While that event was particularly for Japanese immigrant parents, the Japanese YWCA's participation in the doll festival was primarily targeted to encourage young women to maintain Japanese traditions. Various girls' clubs took charge of a specific duty for the festival, such as decoration, doll collection, refreshments, and program planning/performance, including a play, a skit, and a musical. All the Girl Reserves participated in selling admission tickets.[69] They advertised to clubs, public libraries, and churches.[70] At a time when Japanese imperialists were concerned that young people took too readily to Americanization, some understood and approved the success of doll festivals as young people finally taking interest in things Japanese.[71]

YWCA work also aimed to bridge generations in the home, primarily through annual mother-daughter banquets. The banquet served as an opportunity to educate their mothers on Girl Reserves culture and blended Japanese and US customs. The mother-daughter banquet was tailored to the Japanese American community first as a family tea in 1927. By the modern period, young women associated tea with bridal training, and older women took tea as a hobby.[72] A tea ceremony invited mothers to a familiar cultural ceremony, but the daughters could introduce a bridal training that aligned Japanese imperialism with US internationalism. Often held at the YWCA International Institute, young women "explained what a Girl Reserve is and what she does." The welcome and explanations were given in Japanese language, but the entertainment program was delivered in English, singing Girl Reserves songs and joining together in prayer. Some even played a piano solo. Each Girl Reserves offered a summary of their club's accomplishments that year. Girl Reserves held a candlelight ceremony and initiated new girls into clubs. Moreover, ceremonials honored a few select young women that received the coveted GR ring, the highest honor recognizing an active member of their club. Satow, for instance, was awarded the GR ring in 1929 for her service as club advisor.[73] Such an occasion provided an opportunity for mothers, like Satow's mother, who were more familiar with Japanese modern womanhood, to find legibility and put a value to the gender training of the Girl Reserves movement.

While Japanese American Girl Reserves engaged with popular Japanese traditions to reinterpret modern womanhood to immigrant mothers, Satow also helped to institute an annual children's camp, introducing the YWCA to young Japanese American girls (or potential future Girl

Reserves). The organizing leaders consisted of white and Japanese American YWCA social workers. Fifty girls in and outside of Los Angeles attended. They also invited mothers to accompany their daughters. The second summer camp program focused on instilling progressive values, included an array of activities, from social to spiritual hygiene, including morning exercise, tent inspection, Bible study, and a main meeting that focused on world friendship or missions. The camp also provided opportunities for community and friendship building among the girls, including a campfire and a stunt night, where girls performed plays.[74]

As a result of their participation in Girl Reserves, young women were more likely to go on to become cultural ambassadors. Many were likely to be active at their high school, in their church, go on to attend college, and register to vote. The president of the Loha-Tohela Girl Reserves, Charlotte Shimizu, attended University of Southern California and joined the Japanese Trojan Club.[75] She was active at her church and later served as chair of the Young People's Church Federation of Southern California.[76] She later registered as a Democrat.[77] She became a YWCA secretary at the Honolulu branch.[78] The vice president, Terue Miyako, of the Loha-Tohela Girl Reserves participated in community circles.[79] She went to Jefferson High School and joined the Japanese Club and Latin Club. Later, she attended Los Angeles City College; joined the honorary law society, Phi Lambda Sigma; and served as treasurer for the scholastic honor society, Tau Alpha Epsilon.[80]

Even as the Japanese American Girl Reserves movement sought to build bridges with white progressives, immigrant mothers, and young women, these bridges were propped up on class divides and urban markers of respectability. A life of conferences, camps, and banquets could only be possible if families did not need their children to labor in the family business, such as a farm or a shop. Often, only middle-class families (or those aspiring to the middle class) who banked on education as children's primary labor could afford the time and expense of their daughters' participation in the Girl Reserves. Moreover, as the YWCA continued to expand progressive values of social and spiritual hygiene, a hierarchy of womanhood concretized between urban and rural young women. YWCA workers respected women with proper social manners, cleanliness, modern fashion, and of higher education. They looked down on rural women who might appear unkempt, dirty, ill-mannered, and less fluent in English. Much of these impressions carried into World War II, as the YWCA continued its Americanization work in the incarceration camps.[81]

By 1934, when Satow ended her career as the Los Angeles YWCA secretary, she had built a network of people, spaces, and events that developed and empowered the transnational New Women as cultural ambassadors. Under Satow's secretarial work, she expanded the YWCA progressive values in Japanese American communities across Los Angeles through the formation of new clubs. Her list of accomplishments included advising several new Girl Reserves, among them Tri-U, All Around Juniors, SOF Juniors, and helping to organize Calrose and Chalenas. The number of Japanese American Girl Reserves had almost doubled from when she first began in 1926 to when she left in 1934. Moreover, Satow built up interest and attendance around youth summer camps, which recruited future Girl Reserves to the movement.[82] And finally, Satow supported the interracial work of the YWCA by accompanying Japanese American Girl Reserves representatives to predominantly white mainstream GR conferences. Through the Japanese American Girl Reserves movement, Satow defined the transnational New Women as racial progressives who built bridges between white and Japanese American communities of women as well as across old and new generations of Japanese American women.

The Japanese American Girl Reserves project around new womanhood and US Internationalism contrasted from the pianist project of modern womanhood and Japanese imperialism. While the pianist project originated in the Japanese imperial agenda of expanding settler colonialism and the modern woman both domestically and abroad, the Girl Reserves grew out of the US progressive agenda of expanding American imperialism and the New Woman abroad and domestically. While the piano project sought to train a domestic skill through individual discipline and talent, reflecting the race for imperialism and modernity, the Girl Reserves aimed to socialize young women through civic clubs and conferences, mirroring the goal of building bridges in the period of racial exclusion. Moreover, while the piano project focused on women's place in the home, the Girl Reserves emphasized women's place in the public sphere. These contrasting projects of womanhood often led to tensions in the home between mothers and daughters, bound up in disagreements about vocations and intertwined with family economies of debt, sacrifice, and guilt.

Still, while the Girl Reserves provided an expansion of women's roles compared to the classically trained pianist, the modern woman and the New Woman shared and extended similar hierarchies of class and education, an urban and rural divide, and a shortsighted vision of imperialism. Piano training required private lessons or enrollment into private music schools, another expense for aspiring immigrant families. The Girl Reserves also required expense in time and extracurriculars in conferences, camps, and banquets. Moreover, both the trained pianist and Girl Reserves reflected urban elitism over rural culture, as the piano became attached to modern civilized cities and the Girl Reserves provided a characteristic image of city girls whose introduction to "nature" was primarily through camping trips. As a result, young working-class or rural women were viewed as less modern. Finally, Japanese imperialism inhibited a complex identity formation for women like Satow who wanted to emphasize both Japanese and American identities. However, US imperialism also proved limiting because the YWCA often tokenized social workers of color like Satow, who had to do the labor of interracial justice without truly seeing equitable integration.

Epilogue

New women and New Men had been building toward a world where the United States and Japan would have harmonious relations, but that future quickly foreclosed as the United States and Japan went to war with one another. While in the 1920s, Japan had instituted a liberal democracy, by the 1940s, extreme nationalists in the military had taken over the Japanese civilian government and begun the Sino-Japanese War to realize Japan's imperial destiny in Asia. At first, some had justified Japan's aggression in China in order to maintain peaceful relations and to curb anti-Japanese sentiment. Later, as the United States criticized Japanese aggression, many could no longer justify Japan's military rule. Young people retreated from biculturalism. After Japan's attack on Pearl Harbor, the US government followed previous patterns of racial exclusion and passed Executive Order 9066 in February 1942, which unjustly incarcerated Japanese Americans without due process. Unlike the legislation of the 1920s, which had largely aimed to racially exclude immigrants from land ownership, citizenship, and immigration but observed the rights of young people with US citizenry, World War II incarceration targeted all Japanese Americans regardless of citizenship status. At the same time, the bar for US-Japanese friendship building unceremoniously moved from coercive Americanization to compulsory Americanism, forcing many to give up any ties to Japan or Japanese culture. The US government suspected all Japanese Americans as disloyal and demanded strict loyalty.

Being "cultural bridges" and "friendliness builders" in an era of empire building and racial exclusion paved the way toward fervent defense of

Japanese military aggression against the United States or complete cooperation with the US government at their unjust incarceration. In Japan, under military rule, New Men showed their support for Japanese war efforts. For instance, they acted as radio broadcasters to the United States, renarrating US interference and justifying Japanese aggression. In the United States, inside the incarceration camps, New Women and New Men encouraged and participated in various loyalty metrics to the US government. New Women and New Men were the organizers who mediated between detainees and unwelcoming townspeople nearby the camps, camp administrators who worked with the War Relocation Authority (WRA) to create an orderly society, "loyal" detainees cleared to work as incarcerated labor outside the camps, and spiritual leaders navigating between martial law and so-called "enemy aliens." With resistance out of their purview, they instead reached for safety, survival, and resilience.

Susie Yamamoto and John Ando had participated in major organizations that shaped the development of young people and their response to their incarceration. By the 1930s, Yamamoto and Ando sold their hog farms and pursued a new business endeavor—the Snow Queen Soap Company—and continued to be active members of the JACL.[1] In order to encourage young people to buy into immigrant-owned stores and companies in Little Tokyo during the Great Depression, both Yamamoto and Ando were part of the organizing team for developing the Nisei Week festival.[2] Lon Kurashige argues that in the early 1930s, JACLers heralded the Nisei as a new breed of American citizen who was at home in both Japan and the United States, but by the late 1930s retreated from biculturalism. After President Roosevelt issued Executive Order 9066, the JACL directed Japanese Americans to comply and cooperate with the US government. Historian Paul Spickard argues that the men of JACL seized the opportunity to work with the government and disempower the Issei for their own political gains.[3] This distancing from the Issei is rooted in earlier tactics deployed during the anti-Japanese legislation in the 1920s, when elites had blamed farmers for anti-Japanese exclusion laws. They thought that, if they sacrificed some, it might save more. It didn't. Because incarceration was no negotiation. Many criticized the JACL for their failure to stand up for the rights of Japanese American citizens.

Yamamoto and Ando, along with their daughters, Caroline and Mitsuko, were sent to the Rohwer incarceration camp in Arkansas, where detainees faced a particularly hostile environment, as Governor Homer Adkins, a Ku Klux Klan member, instructed colleges to bar resettlers and limited their work on local farms.[4] Many of the state's political leaders made accusations that the incarcerees were coddled, hoarded food, or disloyal, generating resentment among poor white townspeople.[5] In a radio address, the WRA director addressed these rumors that Japanese American incarcerees were receiving same war rations as everyone else. Just as they had served in the Long Beach Rotary Club, Yamamoto and Ando attempted to establish good relations with local rotary clubs in Arkansas. For example, the Yamamoto and Ando served as guest speakers for the local Rotary Clubs on the subject of creating better relations between evacuees and the residents of Arkansas and Mississippi.[6] They invited the Rotary Clubs for a tour of their facilities and activities at Rohwer. During the visit, the hosts made speeches, entertained with a musical program, and shared dinner.[7] Yamamoto helped to build a YWCA at Rohwer and gave an acceptance speech after the dedication of the YWCA Hall for public use. The hall had been furnished by both the incarcerees within the camps as well as YWCA members from outside, including the Hot Springs YWCA and Little Rock YWCA.[8]

Yamamoto and Ando were part of the waves of those deemed "loyal" enough to exit the camps for work during World War II. The WRA announced a "voluntary rehabilitation program" that would bring about "more effective understanding of the Japanese by the public and aid the evacuees in the post-war period."[9] Ando served as part of the relocation efforts, visiting and reporting on St. Louis, Chicago, and Cleveland, as possible sites.[10] Recruitment was gendered: Vegetable farms, as well as the Michigan State College of Agriculture, in eastern Michigan recruited incarcerees, largely men, for agricultural labor.[11] Schools and individual households also recruited women workers as school teachers, nursery assistants, or housemothers.[12] Individual households also recruited couples for domestic work, where women worked in the home and the men operated as gardeners.[13] By June 1943, Yamamoto and Ando relocated to Bloomfield Hills, Michigan, where they worked and lived for a family as domestic laborers.[14]

The movement of Japanese American women into domestic caregiving roles directly coincided with other women leaving domestic labor for better paid wartime work opportunities. At a time when white, Black, Indigenous, and Latinx women were encouraged to temporarily leave their homes in order to step into war work or men's wage-earning roles in defense industries such as the canneries and shipping yards, Japanese American middle-aged women were moving from incarcerated camps into US homes as domestic labor. Domestic labor took on new meaning from when Yamamoto had first worked as a schoolgirl in the 1920s. Whereas once domestic labor was largely seen as a form of Americanization and an economic incentive, Yamamoto had performed domestic work in order to learn proper domesticity to live freely and avoid any missteps, what she coded "not make any breaks." Domestic labor during World War II became the site of rehabilitation where Yamamoto and Ando labored to build a better image to white families and reenter the United States; however, Yamamoto and Ando saw it as paying better than what was available in the camps, allowing the family to stay together, and offering a way to leave the Jim Crow South.

By 1934, Masao Dodo and his family moved to New York, where Dodo worked as the New York correspondent to the Japan-based newspaper, *Tokyo Nichi Nichi*. Dodo continued to serve as a cultural diplomat as tensions escalated between Japan and China. By 1937, Dodo remained steadfast in his support of the Japanese military's actions, primarily because he believed in the Japanese government's newfound mission behind its aggression: Greater East Asia Co-Prosperity Sphere. The Japanese government began to spread the ideology that Japan saw itself as the leader in helping colonized countries and peoples to gain equality with white and colonizing Western countries. This influenced Dodo's understanding of cross-ethnic solidarity, departing from his previous disassociation from Filipinos. Further, he expanded the government ideology from cross-ethnic to cross-racial solidarity in the United States. Literary scholar Etsuko Taketani shows that he defended Japan's actions in China to the African American community.[15] Historian Marc Galliccio reports that by 1937, Dodo gave speeches to the Harlem's Association of Trade and Commerce, promoting that Japan was the only colored nation to challenge the empire of white nations. His message appealed to African Americans who had familiar idioms of Black internationalism.[16] Historian Brian Hayashi writes that Dodo and his family moved to Japan in 1938, where Dodo became a radio correspondent for Japan's Radio Tokyo and beamed wartime propaganda.[17]

Dodo's ideologies and belief systems had a deep impact on youth politics. First, he expressed an early vision of the sociological argument of the model minority: a racial minority that did not rely on US welfare, but through self-help, and a comparably better racial standing than other minority groups. Future sociologists would make a similar argument that Japanese Americans did not rely on government assistance in order to undermine civil rights protests. Second, Dodo represented a growing number of Asian American Christian conservatives. He represented the opinions of many patriarchal men who felt threatened by the changing roles of women. Moreover, he believed that a return to nuclear family Christian morals would resolve and maintain societal order. And finally, more immediately, Dodo expressed an ethnic nationalism, where an individual's actions should serve and reflect the goals of the home community. That brand of ethnic nationalism led Dodo to align with the ideologies undergirding Japanese military aggression in China.

Chiyo Otera and Thomas Sashihara had to auction their drugstores and the five-and-dime.[18] Otera and Sashihara were first sent to the temporary assembly center at the Santa Anita race track and then relocated to Heart Mountain incarceration camp, Wyoming, where white administrators needed to maintain order by electing trusted Japanese Americans to be block managers and council people. Some viewed Japanese American managers and council people as collaborators and sympathizers with white administrators. Others believed that Japanese Americans worked with white administrators to ensure that Japanese Americans contributed to policy- and decision-making. Otera became one of the few women administrators in the camp in the political realm, serving in multiple positions, including at the camp library, on the parent-teacher association of block 25 elementary school, YWCA, coordinating council for girls' clubs and Scouts, and coordinating council for prevention and disposition of juvenile delinquency.[19] Her primary role was doing girl scout work for $16 a month, coordinating girls' troops like the Brownies.[20] Both daughters, Diane and

Maureen, were part of the girl scouts. The community council was a "clearinghouse of complaints" that faced some of the similar issues around women's expanding sexuality in the prewar era. For instance, at one meeting for the coordinating council for prevention and disposition of juvenile delinquency, the council discussed the problem of community dances, which were attended by twelve- and fourteen-year-olds, and discussed the possibility of using police force to block the entry of young boys and girls.[21]

Thomas Sashihara also worked in camp governance. At the Santa Anita assembly center in California, Sashihara was elected mayor. When he and ten other male detainees (six without US citizenship and five with US citizenship) met to request an investigation of the conditions at Santa Anita, particularly their low wages and food quality, and discussed whether to establish a Japanese language component, a scuffle broke out. Camp administrators arrested the five with US citizenship and transferred the six without US citizenship to Tuna Canyon Detention Station, outside of Los Angeles.[22] When he rejoined his family at Heart Mountain Relocation Center, Sashihara became a perfect citizen in the eyes of camp authorities. He served as a representative of the charter commission.[23] Later, he joined the community enterprises board of trustees, where he utilized his business experience at the camp store. However, the operation of the camp store generated controversy, as many of the prisoners could not afford the prices. At Heart Mountain, Sashihara was also a member of the Boy Scout advisory board and Christian church board and president of the YMCA.[24] During one of the draft resistance movement at Heart Mountain, Sashihara was lauded as one of "This Week's Heroes" for his work on resettlement efforts to find suitable agricultural and industrial programs. He joined the WRA staff to help formerly incarcerated to establish businesses and homes in the Great Lakes area.[25]

By 1944, Otera, Sashihara, their two daughters, and son became a poster Japanese American family for the War Relocation Authority Photographic Section (WRAPS). WRAPS selected "loyal Japanese Americans" to model the resettlement process through a commissioned photographic essay, which depicted people being issued war ration books, receiving word of confirmation of employment, checking time for the last payroll, obtaining internal employment clearance, consulting with the property clerk regarding

6.1 Family portrait of the Sashiharas for the WRA plan on resettlement, 1944. Standing: Diane Sashihara, Tom Jr. Sashihara, Maureen Sashihara. Seated: Thomas Tozaburo Sashihara and Chiyo Nina Otera Sashihara. Courtesy of Bancroft Library.

transferring personal property, submitting an application for clothing allowance, filing application for indefinite leave, taking pictures for their identification cards, being issued passes prior to their indefinite leave, packing their clothes and preparing to board the bus for leave. Historian Lane Hirobayashi argues that WRAPs used these staged photos to encourage "loyal" Japanese Americans to reenter society and resettle on the East Coast. Moreover, the other primary purpose of the photos served as public relations packages that invited general US viewers to support loyal but hard-pressed Japanese Americans.[26]

Central to the photographic essay is the portrayal of Otera, Sashihara, and their children as a nuclear family that abided by postwar gender norms (fig. 6.1). After the war, the US government encouraged women in temporary war work to return to their domestic roles in the home. Domesticity was celebrated, and women were asked to forget any professional skills they learned and center their lives around family and the home. At the same time, the US government began entering the Cold War, and in order to spread democracy in Asia, first needed to address racism at home. WRAPS utilized Otera's negotiation of "good wife, wise mother" to promote assimilation to Japanese Americans and combat racism among white Americans. WRAPS portrayed a disciplined transnational new womanhood: a co-optation of "good wife, wise mother" to align with burgeoning postwar gender ideologies that women belong in the home as well as new imperatives of racial equality to legitimize the United States as the global leader of the free world. Other postwar versions of "good wife, wise mother" would appear later as war brides and as the mother of a nuclear family that undergirded the model minority to serve the US liberal imperatives.

Gene Sakamoto was incarcerated at Amache (Granada) incarceration camp in Colorado, then relocated to work as incarcerated labor on farms during wartime.[27] Amache incarcerees hailed from farming communities in California's Central Valley as well the southwestern suburbs of Los Angeles, including the Seinan neighborhood, where many Japanese Americans like Sakamoto lived alongside African Americans and Latinx. Camp authorities recruited detainees as incarcerated labor on the farms that surrounded Amache. For instance, in the fall of 1942, over 140 "volunteers" participated in the "nationwide crop-saving campaign" to aid nearby beet farmers facing a shortage of labor and potential loss of crops. That fall, over 1,200 evacuees made up the "volunteer evacuee army" that labored on the farms in Colorado.[28] By spring of 1943, Sakamoto had applied for leave to work on a farm near Hoehne, Colorado.[29]

In the spring of 1944, Sakamoto was part of recruited incarcerated labor at Seabrook Farms in New Jersey (fig. 6.2).[30] Seabrook Farms was one of the largest producers of frozen and canned vegetables in the nation and became a major food supplier to the US military during World War II. Seabrook laborers drew from many different populations, including Black

6.2 Gene Akira Sakamoto (standing, third from the left) worked in dry goods storage at Seabrook Farms in New Jersey, 1950. Courtesy of Rutgers University Libraries.

migrants from Florida, whites from West Virginia, Kentucky, Tennessee, and Arkansas. Seabrook hired many Japanese Americans recently released from incarceration camps, which aligned with the new policy mandating that Japanese Americans be relocated from the West Coast to the East Coast. Sakamoto was one of the first Japanese Americans to arrive in February 1944; the population grew to 2,500 residents by 1946. Hours were long, work was difficult, and wages started at fifty cents an hour, depending on gender, type of work, and union status.[31] Single men stayed in dormitories while families lived in family-style housing. Sakamoto worked continuously at Seabrook Farms for many years even as Japanese American families moved on.

The ethnic sports leagues and boys' clubs were forced to disassemble in Los Angeles during evacuation and relocation, but recreational leaders and young men quickly reorganized clubs and sports at Heart Mountain, Rohwer, Amache, and Jerome, which served multiple purposes. Historian

Samuel Regalado argues that, while in the prewar years sports had served as a bridge concept, such displays of American patriotism were ultimately fruitless since the US government implemented incarceration based on racist assumptions about their forever foreignness. When they arrived at assembly centers and incarceration camps, recreational leaders requested equipment and uniforms to play sports, WRA officials were surprised at their enthusiasm for US sports.[32] Recreational leaders started from scratch again, with little to no resources in hastily constructed incarceration facilities, but were determined to organize athletic competitions. At Amache, managers planned to organize a touch-football league for adults as well as an intramural football league for junior high schoolers in the fall season.[33] Recreational leaders also organized a basketball league and a table tennis tournament during the winter.[34] In the spring, they organized softball leagues.[35] Just as they had once turned to developing their identities through sports as a response to their national rejection from the body politic, sports became their life support for seeing themselves not how the United States depicted them as the enemy, but as both American and Japanese. Sports provided a link to normalcy in the very first years for the incarcerated, and as the war turned in the United States' favor and relaxed WRA rules, sports provided opportunities for teams to build connections and compete against teams at other incarceration camps. In an environment where the WRA demanded 100 percent Americanism, sports continued to enable Japanese Americans to cultivate Japanese culture or attachment to ethnicity, while maintaining US national ties or displaying patriotism.

Lily Satow and Donald Fujiyoshi had traveled between Hawai'i and Los Angeles, serving as director of the Young People's Society at the Japanese Christian Church in Los Angeles while also starting a family. After receiving a theology degree from the University of Southern California, Fujiyoshi worked for the Hawaiian Evangelical Association.[36] By 1941, both Satow and Fujiyoshi worked with the Young People's Society in Los Angeles at the Japanese Christian Church.[37] Later that year, Fujiyoshi was installed as pastor for the Waimea Japanese Christian Church. In the weeks before Pearl Harbor, authorities arrested the Reverend Paul Osumi of Lihue Christian Church because of his ties with the Japanese Consulate of Honolulu. Osumi insisted that his correspondence was not collusion but assistance in helping Japanese Americans who had dual citizenship to expatriate.[38] After Osumi was incarcerated and then moved to incarceration camps in the States, Reverend Fujiyoshi became pastor of the Lihue Christian Church in 1942.[39] Reverend Fujiyoshi divided his time between two eastern Kauai churches, preaching the morning service at Lihue and then another service at the Kapaa church. At an entirely new location in an unfamiliar community, and with Fujiyoshi's attention turned toward two ministries, Satow was left with the majority of caretaking of their children: Norman, Ron, and Elaine (under one year old).

A few months after they arrived, Japan attacked Pearl Harbor and the US military instituted martial law in Hawai'i five days later, remaining in effect until October 24, 1944. The US Army moved into Kauai. Four incarceration processing centers were set up in Kauai, and over a hundred were detained. Freedoms were curtailed, including living under a curfew and blackout, censorship of press, radio, and telephone calls. The military permanently closed all twenty-two Japanese language schools and fifteen of the nineteen Buddhist temples. All civilians had to carry identification. Additional restrictions were placed on Japanese Americans: they could not travel or change residences without permission, and they were prohibited items considered espionage. Some had to evacuate, fishermen could not go to sea, and many people lost their jobs. Authorities implemented a policy of "selective detention" and investigated those considered disloyal or potentially dangerous; many lived in constant fear of searches, investigations, arrests, interrogations, and incarceration.[40] Japanese American leaders constituted the Kauai Morale Committee, which was tasked with Americanizing the Japanese Hawaiian communities.[41] Christian churches became central to mediating between military rule and the Japanese Hawaiian community.

Social work scholar Yoosun Park argues that social work organizations, including the YWCA, did not support mass incarceration of Japanese Americans but did not take a strong stand against incarceration, either. Rather, they encouraged adjudication of loyalty rather than wholesale removal and cooperated with the government organs that built and maintained incarceration. Park assesses that, as a whole, social workers were complicit with incarceration, but the YWCA was progressive in its vision of racial equality at the time and unique in seeing that incarceration posed an ethical, moral and political implication for their national democracy. The YWCA was present with vocal protests at the beginning, organizations in the camps, and facilitation of resettlement.[42] While the YWCA did its part in mediating the injustice of incarceration, young women utilized the Girl Reserves movement to survive the injustices of incarceration as well as enjoy the expansions of freedom that many (non-incarcerated) women in the United States experienced during World War II. Historian Valerie Matsumoto argues that young women drew from their prewar club activities to provide some amount of fun in a dreary camp environment. Girls' clubs organized dances and sports games. These dances enabled young women to participate in sexual freedoms such as dating, romance, and marriage. Young women took into clerical positions in the camp, and WRA authorities often favored them. Moreover, girls' clubs enabled young women to build morale and support the war efforts.[43]

Young women from Los Angeles revived the Girl Reserves movement where the majority were sent to Heart Mountain, Rohwer, Amache and Jerome, and continued to build on their Y world in hopes of a better future. Because of the prewar relationship between Japanese American Girl Reserves and the YWCA, and the organizing labor of secretaries like Satow, the YWCA organization continued to show up for young women in incarceration camps. At Heart Mountain, thirty-six girls' clubs had registered with the recreation department, and the Heart Mountain branch of the YWCA was recognized by the end of its first year. Girls' clubs planned dances, welcoming committees, carnivals, and organized for a youth center.[44] At Rohwer, the YWCA Board organized Girl Reserves clubs among high schoolers, up to nine clubs that planned activities for up to 150 girls.[45] The YWCA provided "a constant source of pleasant relations with the outside"; for example, the Girl Reserves created essay-writing contests and provided opportunities for girls to visit outside the camps and attend Girl Reserves conferences in the Midwest.[46] At Amache, where Satow's mother was incarcerated, Girl Reserves hosted rallies, dances, sent a number of girls to attend conferences, and participated in war effort activities such as harvest camps.[47] Young women applied the skills they had learned in the Girl Reserves to organize communities of women and forge bridges inside and outside the incarceration camps at the height of racial exclusion and injustice. They performed the care work of maintaining morale in desolate times as well as creating friendlier relations with the world outside. They still held onto the YWCA progressive mission of racial equality. And through social service, young women planted the seeds for revolutionary organizing to come.

NOTES

INTRODUCTION

1 "Life History of a Japanese College Freshman Girl," Box 31, Survey of Race Relations Records. All quotations by Lily Satow are from this source.
2 Tamura, *Americanization, Acculturation, and Ethnic Identity*. Yoo, *Growing Up Nisei*. Imai, *Creating the Nisei Market*.
3 Azuma, *In Search of Our Frontier*.
4 Choy and Wu, *Gendering the Trans-Pacific World*.
5 Ngai, *Impossible Subjects*.
6 Lu, "Good Women for Empire."
7 Nomura, "Voices of Women."
8 Tyrrell, *Reforming the World*.
9 Putney, *Muscular Christianity*. Abe, "Muscular Christianity in Japan."
10 Griffith, *Fight for Asian American Civil Rights*.
11 Threlkeld, "Twenty Years of Worlds of Women."
12 Yasutake, *Transnational Women's Activism*.
13 Alexander, *Guiding Modern Girls*.
14 Matsumoto, *City Girls*.
15 Takezawa and Okihiro, *Trans-Pacific Japanese American Studies*.
16 See for example, Peiss, *Cheap Amusements*; Wheeler, *New Women*; Dumenil, *Modern Temper*; Enstad, *Ladies of Labor*; Matthews, *Rise of the New Women*; Zeitz, *Flapper*.
17 Higginsbotham, *Righteous Discontent*. White, *Too Heavy a Load*. Wolcott, *Remaking Respectability*. Chapman, *Prove It on Me*.
18 Harris, *Sex Workers, Psychics, and Number Runners*.
19 Sueyoshi, *Discriminating Sex*.
20 Oharazeki, *Japanese Prostitutes*.
21 Bernstein, *Recreating Japanese Women*.
22 Bernstein, *Recreating Japanese Women*.
23 Sato, *New Japanese Woman*.
24 Koyama, *Ryōsai Kenbo*.

25 Hinnershitz, *Race, Religion, and Civil Rights.*

26 See Wu, *Color of Success.*

27 Kurashige, *Japanese American Celebration.*

28 Matsumoto, *City Girls.*

29 Yu, *Thinking Orientals.* Griffith, *Fight for Asian American Civil Rights.*

30 Tamura, *Americanization, Acculturation, and Ethnic Identity.* Imai, *Creating the Nisei Market.* Yoo, *Growing Up Nisei.*

31 Wakida, "Through the Fire."

32 Modell, *Economics and Politics of Racial Accommodation.*

33 Matsumoto, *City Girls,* 1.

34 Gretchen Tuthill, "A Study of the Japanese in the City of Los Angeles," MA thesis, University of Southern California, 1924, Box 25, Survey of Race Relations Records.

1. THE RURAL NEW WOMAN

1 "Interview with Susie Yamamoto," Box 25, Survey of Race Relations Records. Unless otherwise indicated, all subsequent quotations by Susie Yamamoto are from this source.

2 Evelyn Nakano Glenn cites that it was common for Issei women to serve as live-in domestic workers and for young Nisei women to serve as schoolgirls (*Issei, Nisei, War Bride*).

3 V. S. McClatchy, "Japan's Peaceful Penetration," *Sacramento Bee,* June and July 1919, Box 22, Survey of Race Relations Records.

4 Irwin, *Seed of the Sun.*

5 "Japanese Barred from Citizenship."

6 "Report on Oriental and Agriculture by Los Angeles Chamber of Commerce," Box 26, Survey of Race Relations Records.

7 Yokoyama, "Japanese Associations of America," 33. Yokoyama argues that the takeover of the Japanese associations by businessmen was not coincidental, as many felt stung by Japan's negotiations with the United States in the Gentlemen's Agreement. In the eyes of Japanese business entrepreneurs, restricting the migration of Japanese laborers hurt their agricultural businesses, since they needed a source of labor for sustaining their agricultural industries; they did not believe that the Japanese consulate was working to protect Japanese immigrant business interests. With business leaders, the Japanese associations established a monopoly of handling the official work previously done by the Japanese consulate.

8 Kanzaki, *California and the Japanese,* 3.

9 Toyama, "Japanese Community in Los Angeles."

10 *Japanese Immigration Hearings, part 1,* 28.

11 Charles H. Sherill, speech at the American-Japan Society Banquet, November 19, 1919, reprinted as Sherill, "American's Plain Speaking." See also "General Sherill

Urges Ladies Agreement with Japan as well as Gentlemen's," *Ellensburg (WA) Daily Record*, December 24, 1919.

12 Shima, "Appeal to Justice."

13 Lee and Yung, *Angel Island*, 132. Since the passports were good for six months, the picture bride system officially came to an end on September 1, 1920.

14 "Japanese in Los Angeles County," *San Bernardino Daily Sun*, September 4, 1920, California Digital Newspaper Collection.

15 "Caution, Caution, Neighbors," *San Bernardino Daily Sun*, October 24, 1920.

16 "Vote on Amendments," *San Bernardino Daily Sun*, November 5, 1920.

17 Azuma, "Nichibei Shimbun." With a peak circulation of 25,000, which included Los Angeles and San Francisco editions, the *Japanese American News* was influential among Japanese American communities, sought harmony with white Americans, valorized social assimilation, and promoted adaptation to white Christian ideals.

18 "Translation from *Japanese New World* and *Japanese-American News*," Box 28, Survey of Race Relations Records.

19 "Phelan Makes Attack on U.S. Orient Policy," *San Bernardino Daily Sun*, March 14, 1924.

20 "Records of the Immigration and Naturalization Service, 1787–2004,". Thanks to Sue Payne at the Arda Haenszel California Room of the Norman F. Feldheym Central Library for locating this from Ancestry.com.

21 Social Security Applications and Claims Index, 1936–2007, Ancestry.com, 2015.

22 San Bernardino County Recorder, *Miscellaneous Record Book V*, 1905–1919, San Bernardino, 185. Thanks to Genevieve Preston at the San Bernardino County Historical Archives for locating this land title. For more on Chinatown in San Bernardino, see Costello et al., "Luck of Third Street."

23 California, Death Index, 1905–1939, Ancestry.com, 2013. Thanks to Sue Payne for locating this.

24 *San Bernardino City Directory, 1920*.

25 Japanese American hog farmers did experience anti-Japanese movements in places like Seattle, Washington. See Blair, "1920 Anti-Japanese Crusade."

26 "Notice," *San Bernardino Daily Sun*, December 30, 1920; "Notice," *San Bernardino Daily Sun*, January 6, 1921.

27 *Twenty-Sixth Annual Session of the Pacific Japanese Mission of the Methodist Episcopal Church*, Seattle, Washington, September 3–6, 1925, Digital Archives of the California Pacific Conference, www.calpacumc.org/archiveshistory/#1561163441732-d51bb61a-788d.

28 "Interview with Susie Yamamoto," Box 25, Survey of Race Relations Records.

29 Glenn, *Issei, Nisei, War Bride*, 124–28.

30 Rabinovitch-Fox, "New Women."

31 Bernstein, *Recreating Japanese Women*.

32 Wakida, "Louise Suski."

33 Wakida, "Julia Suski."

34 "The Girl of Today," *Rafu Shimpo*, February 21, 1926.

35 "Interview with Teru Miyamoto," Box 31, Survey of Race Relations Records.

36 For more on feminism and the politics of fashion, see Rabinovitch-Fox, "This Is What a Feminist Looks Like."

37 "Interview with Miss Esther B. Bartlett of the Y.W.C.A. International Institute," Box 31, Survey of Race Relations Records.

38 "Minutes of Board of Directors, LA YWCA Branch, September 27, 1922," YWCA of Los Angeles Collection.

39 *International Institute of the Young Women's Christian Association*, 1924, YWCA of Los Angeles Collection. The International Institute provided housing to many groups, including giving 1,879 nights' lodging to German, Mexican, and Native American girls.

40 *Young Women's Christian Association Los Angeles Meeting Program*, January 31, 1930, YWCA of Los Angeles Collection.

41 "Miss Yamamoto to Resume Study," *Rafu Shimpo*, May 2, 1926. Hoji Shinbun Digital Collection.

42 "Japanese Pay Charity Quota," *San Bernardino Daily Sun*, November 9, 1924.

43 Garcia, *World of Its Own*.

44 "City Moves to Take Bids for Fixing Bridge," *San Bernardino Daily Sun*, November 18, 1924.

45 "Garbage Collecting in City Will Be Continued," *San Bernardino Daily Sun*, April 26, 1924.

46 "City Garbage Collector Is Given Warning," *San Bernardino Daily Sun*, July 8, 1925. "New Garbage Agreement Is Not in Force," *San Bernardino Daily Sun*, July 10, 1925.

47 1930 US Federal Census, Ancestry.com.

48 "Seeing San Bernardino in Five Minutes," *San Bernardino Daily Sun*, May 25, 1928.

49 "Robert C. Harbison for Congressman," *San Bernardino Daily Sun*, November 5, 1916.

50 "Girl Graduates from Two Colleges Simultaneously," *San Bernardino Daily Sun*, July 31, 1927. "Woman Judge Is Striking against Double Standard," *San Bernardino Daily Sun*, August 11, 1927. "Girl Flier and Pilot in Hawaiian Flight Qualify," *San Bernardino Daily Sun*, August 14, 1927. "Girl Perfects System for Women of Surplus Weight," *San Bernardino Daily Sun*, August 15, 1927.

51 "Girl Makes Success by Operating Hog Ranches," *San Bernardino Daily Sun*, July 20, 1927.

52 *New Castle (PA) News*, July 16, 1927; *Sarasota (FL) Herald*, July 24, 1927. *Dubuque (IA) Telegraph Herald and Times Journal*, July 17, 1927; *Winters (TX) Enterprise*, July 1, 1927; *Nyssa (OR) Gate City Journal*, July 15, 1927; *Emporia (KS) Gazette*, July 27, 1927; *Zansville (OH) Times Recorder*, July 22, 1927; *Brookfield (NY) Courier*, July 20, 1927. *Chilicothe (MO) Daily Tribune*, July 28, 1927; *Kerrville (TX) Mountain Sun*, June 30, 1927; *Washington C.H. (OH) Herald*, August 13, 1927.

53 "Council Urges Show-Down on Drain Project," *San Bernardino Daily Sun*, October 2, 1928.

54 *Daily Sentinel*, July 30, 1927.

55 "Susie Yamamoto Engaged to J. Ando," *Rafu Shimpo*, March 11, 1929; "Card Party Reveals Girls Engagement," *Rafu Shimpo*, March 18, 1929; "Miss Yamamoto Will Marry J. Ando Soon," *Rafu Shimpo*, July 1, 1929.

56 "Many Friends Attend Rites for Yamamoto-Ando Union," *Rafu Shimpo*, July 15, 1929; "Susie Yamamoto Ando Returns from Wedding Trip This Week," *San Bernardino Sun*, July 14, 1929.

57 "Interview with John Ando," Box 34, Survey of Race Relations Records.

58 Kurashige, *Japanese American Celebration*.

59 Modell, *Economics and Politics of Racial Accommodation*.

60 "Forming of Citizens Club Looms as Young People Meet," *Rafu Shimpo*, September 17, 1928.

61 "Citizens to March unto Real Arena," *Rafu Shimpo*, August 11, 1930.

62 "Citizens' League Appoint Executive Body," *Rafu Shimpo*, September 15, 1930.

63 "1932 Confab to Be Held in Los Angeles," *Rafu Shimpo*, September 15, 1930.

64 "Citizen's League Plan for Japan Tour," *Rafu Shimpo*, August 30, 1931.

65 "Big Crowd Enjoys Evening at Gakuseikai Open House," *Rafu Shimpo*, October 17, 1927.

66 "Citizens' League to Hear City Office Candidates," *Rafu Shimpo*, April 20, 1931; "Citizens League to Fight against Segregation Bill," *Rafu Shimpo*, April 20, 1931; "Baker Talks to Citizens on Thursday," *Rafu Shimpo*, September 14, 1931.

67 *Rafu Shimpo*, August 25, 1930.

68 "Citizens League Installs New Officers during July," *Rafu Shimpo*, June 29, 1931; "Citizens' League Will Make Definite Convention Plans," *Rafu Shimpo*, August 31, 1931; "Councilman Will Address Local Citizens' League," *Rafu Shimpo*, September 7, 1931; "Baker Talks to Citizens on Thursday," *Rafu Shimpo*, September 14, 1931; "Citizens League to Vote for Officers at Meeting," *Rafu Shimpo*, October 2, 1932; "Officers for L.A. Clubs during Current Semester," *Rafu Shimpo*, January 1, 1933; "Citizens' League of LA to Aid San Diego Organize," *Rafu Shimpo*, August 6, 1933; "Citizen's League to Usher in First of Autumn Dances," *Rafu Shimpo*, September 24, 1933; "Local Citizens' Body Plans to Introduce '34 Candidates," *Rafu Shimpo*, December 10, 1933.

69 US Department of Agriculture, "1932 Outbreak."

70 "County Refuses to Pay Bill for Guards to Enforce the Quarantine," *San Bernardino Daily Sun*, May 10, 1932.

71 US Department of Agriculture, "1932 Outbreak."

72 "Garbage Collector's Contract Suspended," *San Bernardino Daily Sun*, May 18, 1932.

73 "City Enforces Contract for Garbage Plan," *San Bernardino Daily Sun*, June 12, 1932.

74 "Garbage Collection Issue Serious, Contractor Says," *San Bernardino Daily Sun*, February 24, 1933.

75 "City Takes Action to Bar Collapse of Garbage Collection," *San Bernardino Daily Sun*, February 27, 1933.

76 "L.A. Firm Asks Collection of City Garbage," *San Bernardino Daily Sun*, March 15, 1933.

77 "City Garbage Issue Revived," *San Bernardino Daily Sun*, June 18, 1933. "New Garbage Plan Drafted," *San Bernardino Daily Sun*, June 20, 1933.

78 "City to Levy Garbage Fees," *San Bernardino Daily Sun*, June 23, 1933.

79 "Collection of City's Refuse Topic," *San Bernardino Daily Sun*, July 17, 1933; "Hog Ranch South of City Established," *San Bernardino Daily Sun*, August 19, 1933; "City Garbage Contract Let," *San Bernardino Daily Sun*, July 25, 1933. Seven other bidders included the San Pedro Commercial Co., Municipal Contracting Co., Collins and Harris of San Bernardino, Baker's Duroc Ranch, and Harry V. Herman. The decision to contract with Farrington was not made without controversy. The attorneys for the seventh bidder tried to block the procedure and there were demonstrations against the city council decision.

80 "New City Garbage Law Providing Service Fees Effective within Month," *San Bernardino Daily Sun*, July 27, 1933.

81 "Hog Ranch South of City Established," *San Bernardino Daily Sun*, August 19, 1933.

82 "Garbage Contractor Surrenders Pact," *San Bernardino Daily Sun*, August 2, 1933.

2. THE INTELLIGENTSIA NEW MAN

1 "Short Biography of Mamoru Takada," Box 32, Survey of Race Relations Records. Unless otherwise indicated, all subsequent quotations by Masao Dodo are from this source. The young orphan boy matches the profile of Kay Sugahara, who graduated from UCLA, instituted the Los Angeles Chapter of the JACL, and went on to become a millionaire through his University Foreign Service Company. See Hirahara, *Distinguished Asian American Business Leaders*.

2 Azuma, *Between Two Empires*.

3 Hayashi, *For the Sake*.

4 Williams, *American Sutra*.

5 Sonida, "Decline."

6 "Life History of Masao Dodo," Box 32, Survey of Race Relations Records.

7 Iwai, "Japanese Christianity."

8 Anderson, *Christianity and Imperialism*.

9 Azuma, *Between Two Empires*.

10 For more on Angel Island, see Daniels, "No Lamps."

11 For more on the experience of schoolboys, see Kiyama, *Four Immigrants Manga*.

12 See Andrés, "I Am Almost More at Home."

13 Williams and Moriya, *Issei Buddhism*.

14 Masao Dodo, "The Social Welfare Works of the Japanese M.E. Mission," Box 37, Survey of Race Relations Records.

15 "Miss C.," Box 37, Survey of Race Relations Records.

16 Friese, "Japanese Girls and Women."

17 "The Social Welfare Works of the Japanese M. E. Mission," Box 37, Survey of Race Relations Records.

18 *The Japanese Young Men's Association: A Brief Survey of the Past and Present Activities* (Tokyo: Bureau for Social Work, 1922), accessed on HathiTrust Digital Library. Originating before the Meiji period and designed as a training ground for young boys, the Young Men's Association emphasized military training in the form of Samurai arts as well as intellectual accomplishments, including reading Chinese classics. During the Meiji Restoration, the Young Men's Association reorganized, and many of the men fought in the Russo-Japanese War (1904) and the Great War. By 1918, members were encouraged to cultivate their education, citizenship, literature, physical training, leadership, and reaction to opposition. By 1922, almost 16,700 associations had organized all across Japan. In Southern California had at least six Young Men's Associations: one in Los Angeles had about 150 members, an uptown organization claimed about 50 members, and there were local associations in Gardena, Compton, Oxnard, Long Beach, and the San Gabriel Valley.

19 "The Japanese Young Men's Association: The Translation from the *L.A. Japanese American*," Box 34, Survey of Race Relations Records.

20 "The Japanese Young Men's Association: The Translation from the *L. A. Japanese American*," Box 34, Survey of Race Relations Records.

21 "Japanese Young Men's Associations of Southern California," Box 32, Survey of Race Relations Records.

22 "Young Men to Hold Debate at San Bernardino," *Rafu Shimpo*, August 16, 1926.

23 "Young Men's Hot Debate Ends in Tie," *Rafu Shimpo*, August 30, 1926.

24 "Young People's Week," Box 32, Survey of Race Relations Records.

25 "Young People's Week," Box 32, Survey of Race Relations Records.

26 "Young People's Week," Box 32, Survey of Race Relations Records.

27 "Y. M. Federation," *Rafu Shimpo*, March 28, 1926.

28 "F.Y.M.A. Wants to Help Second Generation," *Rafu Shimpo*, April 25, 1926.

29 Syrett, *Company He Keeps*.

30 "So. Cal Student Club Names New Officers," *Rafu Shimpo*, March 15, 1926.

31 "Trojans Speak at Union Church on Diverse Topics," *Rafu Shimpo*, May 16, 1927.

32 "Japanese Young Men's Associations of Southern California by Hideo Oyama," Box 32, Survey of Race Relations Records.

33 "Many Attend Gakusekai All University Social Meet," *Rafu Shimpo*, March 7, 1927.

34 Griffith, *Fight for Asian American Civil Rights*.

35 See Masao Dodo, "Present Estimated Japanese Population in Los Angeles City and County," Box 30; "What Magazines Do the Japanese Read," Box 30; "A Short Biography of Mamoru Takada, Born in 1909," Box 32; "Life History of Masao Dodo," Box 32; "Miss C," Box 37; "The Japanese Free Methodist Mission of Los Angeles," Box 37; "The Social Welfare Works of the Japanese M.E. Mission," Box 37; "Young People's Week," Box 38, all in Survey of Race Relations Records. Some of these reports are also available in the "Dodo, Masao" folder, Yuji Ichioka Papers.

36 "Occidental Hi-Yi Met Last Monday," *Rafu Shimpo*, April 4, 1926.

37 "Far-Reaching Improvements Definitely Launched," *Rafu Shimpo*, October 14, 1929.

38 "Far-Reaching Improvements Definitely Launched," *Rafu Shimpo*, October 14, 1929.

39 "Aggression? Yes, for Mutual Gain," *Rafu Shimpo*, November 25, 1929.

40 The model minority rose to prominence during the Cold War and civil rights eras. For histories on the model minority, see Cheng, *Citizens of Asian America*; Wu, *Color of Success*.

41 "Police Make 718 Arrests during the Year," *Rafu Shimpo*, November 18, 1929.

42 "Cowardly Neglect," *Rafu Shimpo*, December 9, 1929.

43 "Best to Help Ourselves Is Chest Slogan," *Rafu Shimpo*, November 18, 1929.

44 "We Like to Hear the Answer," *Rafu Shimpo*, November 18, 1929.

45 "Three-Day Marriage and Then What," *Rafu Shimpo*, October 21, 1929.

46 "Where Are You, Flappers and Boobies?," *Rafu Shimpo*, November 11, 1929.

47 "Why So Much about Dancing?" *Rafu Shimpo*, February 17, 1930.

48 "Rosy Future Already Shows Signs of Dawn," *Rafu Shimpo*, December 02, 1929.

49 "Japanese Exempt in Mexico Ban," *Rafu Shimpo*, December 9, 1929.

50 "Why Not Embrace Mexico?" *Rafu Shimpo*, December 9, 1929.

51 See Dewitt, "Watsonville Anti-Filipino Riot."

52 "A Few Lessons from Race Riot," *Rafu Shimpo*, January 27, 1930.

53 "Arrest Four Japanese in Red Roundup," *Rafu Shimpo*, December 2, 1929.

54 "Local Reds Caught in Police Net," *Rafu Shimpo*, March 3, 1930.

55 "Psychology of a Radical," *Rafu Shimpo*, March 3, 1930.

56 "Atrocious Crimes Hurt Racial Pride: 3 Bad News Discredit Local Boys," *Rafu Shimpo*, March 10, 1930.

57 "How Many More Bad News?," *Rafu Shimpo*, March 10, 1930.

58 Azuma, *Between Two Empires*.

59 "Is Japan Justified in Her Policy Toward China?," *Rafu Shimpo*, February 25–28, 1932.

60 "Masao Dodo's Brilliant New Book Digs Deep into the Pacific Era to Analyze Problems of the Future," *Rafu Shimpo*, April 9, 1933.

61 See Taketani, *Black Pacific Narrative*; Gallicchio, *African American Encounter*.

3. THE HIGHBROW NEW WOMAN

1 "Interview with Miss Chiyo Otera," Box 25, Survey of Race Relations Records.

2 "A Social Document by Masami Suzuki," Box 32, Survey of Race Relations Records.

3 "Interview with F. T. Nakaya," Box 28 Survey of Race Relations Records.

4 For more on the Union Church, see Hayashi, *For the Sake*. The Union Church was first built on 227 North San Pedro Street. On March 25, 1923, a new larger church building was dedicated at 120 North San Pedro Street.

5 Gretchen Tuthill, "A Study of the Japanese in the City of Los Angeles," MA thesis, University of Southern California, 1924, Box 25, Survey of Race Relations Records.

6 MacFarland, "Christian Endeavor Movement." See also Clark, *Christian Endeavor Manual*; Erb, "Development"; Clarke, "Christian Endeavor Movement."

7 "Interview with Frank Nakamura," Box 34, Survey of Race Relations Records.

8 "Interview with Miss Hida Watanabe," Box 31, Survey of Race Relations Records.

9 "Interview with Teru Miyamoto," Box 31, Survey of Race Relations.

10 See Ruiz, *From Out of the Shadows*. Historian Vicki Ruiz argues that in the 1930s Mexican immigrant communities in Los Angeles, chaperonage was both an actual and symbolic assertion of familial oligarchy and triggered deep-seated tensions over autonomy and self-determination. She argues Mexican American women challenged chaperonage, but did not change the foundation of the family oligarchy; rather, it was one important step toward the sexual liberation that would arise in Chicana feminism generations later.

11 "Interview with Kyo Inouye," Box 31, Survey of Race Relations Records. Kyo Inouye became a concert singer who later toured Japan in 1931. "Kyo Inouye Sings in Final Concert Before Coast Tour," *Rafu Shimpo*, February 16, 1931.

12 "Interview with Chiyoe Sumi," Box 30, Survey of Race Relations Records.

13 "Interview with Miss Chiyo Otera," Box 25, Survey of Race Relations Records.

14 *Japanese Immigration Hearings, Part I*, 973–76.

15 For more on Kiyo Sue Inui, see Racel, "Inui Kiyosue"; Inui, "California's Japanese Situation."

16 Mrs. K. S. Inui, "The Problems of the Youth Today," *Rafu Shimpo*, April 25, 1926.

17 US City Directories, 1822–1995, Ancestry.com, 2011. "Interview with Miss Chiyo Otera," Box 25, Survey of Race Relations Records.

18 Smith, *Japanese American Midwives*.

19 "Bobbed Hair Is Unsuited for Japanese Modern Girl," *Rafu Shimpo*, March 28, 1927.

20 "Interview with Miss Chiyo Otera," Box 31, Survey of Race Relations Records.

21 "Senior C. E. Name Officers," *Rafu Shimpo*, June 17, 1926.

22 "All Feminine Cabinet to Rule Senior C. E. or Union Church," *Rafu Shimpo*, January 1, 1927.

23 "C. E. Debate Teams Named," *Rafu Shimpo*, May 2, 1926.

24 Matsumoto, *City Girls*.

25 "Letter to the Editor," *Rafu Shimpo*, March 28, 1926.

26 *Rafu Shimpo*, April 4, 1926.

27 Ibid. Sakano's wife wrote a follow-up to his letter, defending him and saying that he suffered from a nervous breakdown because of the criticisms hailed at him. "Letter to the Editor," *Rafu Shimpo*, April 25, 1926.

28 "New Name for Club," *Rafu Shimpo*, March 21, 1926.

29 "Second Generation Problem Brought Up for Discussion," *Rafu Shimpo*, April 4, 1927.

30 "Social Hygiene from Every Angle, Subject of Lecture," *Rafu Shimpo*, April 18, 1927. "Social Hygiene Lecturer Ready to Give Talk Here," *Rafu Shimpo*, May 2, 1927.

31 Wuebker, "Social Hygiene in America."

32 "Divorce Cases in Tokyo City Show Enormous Increase," *Rafu Shimpo*, July 15, 1929.

33 Masao Dodo, "Three Day Marriage and Then What?," *Rafu Shimpo*, October 21, 1929.

34 "3-Fold Object for the Party," *Rafu Shimpo*, June 13, 1926. "Chiyo Otera's Engagement Announced," *Rafu Shimpo*, June 20, 1926.

35 Nicolaides, "Where the Working Man Is Welcomed."

36 Gonzalez, "Odd Man Out."

37 For a post-1965 history of the San Gabriel Valley, see Fong, *First Suburban Chinatown*; Chang, *Changs Next Door*; Nicolaides and Zarsadiaz, "Design Assimilation in Suburbia."

38 1930 US Federal Census, Ancestry.com, 2002. Stewart, "Victorian Sprawl."

39 1930 US Federal Census, Ancestry.com.

40 Hendricks and Patterson, "1930 Census in Perspective."

41 "Personals," *Rafu Shimpo*, September 20, 1926.

42 Stage and Vincenti, *Rethinking Home Economics*. http://hearth.library.cornell.edu (Version January 2005).

43 "Personals," *Rafu Shimpo*, May 9, 1927.

44 "Surprise Birthday Arranged by Wife," *Rafu Shimpo*, February 16, 1931.

45 "Old-Fashioned Party Given Miss Mukaye," *Rafu Shimpo*, August 17, 1931.

46 "Chi Alpha Deltas Hold Christmas Party," *Rafu Shimpo*, December 17, 1933.

47 "Progressive Dinner Given by Pledges," *Rafu Shimpo*, April 14, 1930.

48 "Too Frequent Dancing Discussed in Candid Talks," *Rafu Shimpo*, February, 03, 1930.

49 "Parents and Young List Points for Approval," *Rafu Shimpo*, May 19, 1930.

50 "Our Dance Mad Daughters," *Rafu Shimpo*, April 04, 1932.

51 "Dance Hall Given Permit to Open," *Rafu Shimpo*, April 15, 1929.

52 "Brewin Typs [*sic*]," *Rafu Shimpo*, April 17, 1932.

53 "Bruins Complete Plans for Semi-Formal Dance," *Rafu Shimpo*, February 17, 1930. "Bruin Club Choose Country Club for Semi-Formal Dance," *Rafu Shimpo*, March 30, 1931.

54 "Olympic Dance Expected to Attract Large Crowd," *Rafu Shimpo*, June 12, 1932.

55 "Nikkai Head Nearly Walk Out En Masse at Election," *Rafu Shimpo*, January 28, 1934.

56 "Community Center to Be Established with Tenno's Cash Donation," *Rafu Shimpo*, November 11, 1934.

57 "Y' Doings," *Rafu Shimpo*, February 17, 1934.

58 *National Association of Retail Druggists* (Chicago) 36, no. 15 (July 12, 1923), Los Angeles County Incorporation Records. Iwaki incorporated with other Japanese-owned businesses, including Matsumoto, Tanaka, and Yamamoto under the Japanese Hotel Men's Credit Association of Los Angeles. The Los Angeles County Incorporation Records, Seaver Center for Western History Research.

59 Longstreth, *Cultural Landscapes*.

60 "Very Simple but Delicious," *Rafu Shimpo*, July 3, 1932, and July 10, 1932.

61 *Rafu Shimpo*, November 7, 1933.

62 "Iwaki to Open 5 and 10 Cent Store," *Rafu Shimpo*, May 6, 1934.

63 "One Side of Sports," *Rafu Shimpo*, March 6, 1932.

64 "One Side of Sports," *Rafu Shimpo*, December 27, 1931.

65 "Miss Tokunaga Again Visits Los Angeles," *Rafu Shimpo*, February 27, 1932.

66 "Nisei Employment Bureau Places 34 during Sale Days," *Rafu Shimpo*, August 12, 1934.

67 "Molly Oyama Works at New L.A. Store," *Rafu Shimpo*, May 13, 1934.

68 *Sashihara v. State Board of Pharmacy*, 7 Cal.App.2d 563.

69 "Revision of Laws in State," *Nichibei Shinbun*, June 20, 1935.

70 However, the amendment would not go into effect until 1941, when Tom Otera Sashihara, Ray Fukushima, and Fred Sakuda passed the state board examinations to become full-fledged pharmacists. "Three Southland Japanese Pass Pharmacy Exam," *Nichibei Shinbun*, September 14, 1941.

4. THE MUSCULAR NEW MAN

1 "W. C. Smith Interview with G.S.," Box 25, Survey of Race Relations Records.

2 Kiyoshi K. Kawakami, "YMCA and Japanese: Orientals Find Door to This Christian Brotherhood Closed," *New York Times*, June 11, 1913, 8.

3 Catherine Lee Wahlstrom, "Recreation for Japanese in Los Angeles," Box 34, Survey of Race Relations Records.

4 Gretchen Tuthill, "A Study of the Japanese in the City of Los Angeles," MA thesis, University of Southern California, 1924, Box 25, Survey of Race Relations Records. Wahlstrom, "Recreation."

5 Jenks, "History of Miss Oliver."

6 *Japanese Immigration Hearings, Part I*, 943–46.

7 *Japanese Immigration Hearings, Part I*, 943–46.

8 "Interview with Miss Oliver," Box 35, Survey of Race Relations Records.

9 Jenks, "History of Miss Oliver."

10 See Kurashige, "Re-thinking Anti-Immigrant Racism." The Los Angeles Polytechnic High School was on the corner of Flower Street and Washington Boulevard, between the 110 Freeway and the 10 Freeway.

11 Polytechnic High School Yearbook, 1921, Classmates.com.

12 Frank Sugiyama, "Sportdom's What-Nots," *Rafu Shimpo*, April 5, 1936.

13 "Interview with Frank Nakamura," Box 34, Survey of Race Relations Records.

14 "The Second Generation Japanese by Leo Toyama," Box 32, Survey of Race Relations Records.

15 "Interview with Seiichi Nobe," Box 25, Survey of Race Relations Records.

16 "Good Things for Boys," *Rafu Shimpo*, March 15, 1926.

17 "Announcements: Pasadena Y.M.C.A.," *Rafu Shimpo*, February 21, 1926. Other officers included Shinich Kato, Nobu Kawai, N. Mitsumori, Toshi Kawai, George Nishimoto, Matsui, and Henry Shimanouchi. *Japanese Student* 3, no. 3 (December 1918), Harvard University, digitized by Google Books March 16, 2009, accessed May 1, 2020. Kao, "Permanent Parking Space." See Pasadena Digital History Collaboration Collection for photos and news articles of Jiro Morita.

18 Harold Hubbard, "Pasadena Resident Settles Royal Score," *Pasadena Star News*, (1960?), Pasadena Digital History Collaboration Collection.

19 "Hi-Y Boys Met," *Rafu Shimpo*, March 21, 1926.

20 Griffith, "Where We Can Battle."

21 "World of Thanks from the Editor," *Rafu Shimpo*, December 26, 1926.

22 "Occidental Hi-Y Met Last Monday," *Rafu Shimpo*, April 4, 1926.

23 "The Occidental Hi-Y Club," *Rafu Shimpo*, March 15, 1926.

24 "Good Things for Boys," *Rafu Shimpo*, March 15, 1926.

25 "Many Boys Join YMCA Camp Near Bear Lake," *Rafu Shimpo*, August 16, 1926.

26 "Interorganizational Track Meet Held Tomorrow," *Rafu Shimpo*, May 30, 1927.

27 "Second Generation to Meet Wrestlers," *Rafu Shimpo*, August 1, 1926.

28 "Students of Both Sides of Pacific in Cordial Meet," *Rafu Shimpo*, August 9, 1926.

29 "Open Challenge by Pasadena Y," *Rafu Shimpo*, April 11, 1926.

30 "Hi-Y News," *Rafu Shimpo*, November 22, 1926. "Shimizu Hoopers Win Victory Over Colored Hi-Y Five," *Rafu Shimpo*, January 17, 1927.

31 "Basketball Teams Start Practicing," *Rafu Shimpo*, October 15, 1926.

32 "Bulletin: English Supplement October 21, 1926," West Adams Christian Church Records.

33 "Oliver Club, Jr., Begin Training," *Rafu Shimpo*, July 25, 1926.

34 "Olivers Practicing Hard to Battle Lincoln Indians," *Rafu Shimpo*, February 7, 1927.

35 "Five Wins in Three Nights Toll of Oliver Junior Boys," *Rafu Shimpo*, February 28, 1927.

36 "Plans under Way to Organize So. Calif. Basketball League," *Rafu Shimpo*, December 20, 1926. "Sportitorials," *Rafu Shimpo*, April 11, 1927.

37 Kurashige, *Japanese American Celebration*.

38 "Sportitorials," *Rafu Shimpo*, October 31, 1927.

39 "Waseda Quintet to Arrive in Los Angeles Tomorrow," *Rafu Shimpo*, January 16, 1928.

40 "Hoop Circuit Certainty as Representatives Meet," *Rafu Shimpo*, December 26, 1926.

41 Regalado, *Nikkei Baseball*.

42 "So. Cal Baseball Association Holds First Meet," *Rafu Shimpo*, April 2, 1928.

43 "Summer Baseball League," *Rafu Shimpo*, September 3, 1928.

44 "Baseball Teams Gather for Business and Social," *Rafu Shimpo*, November 19, 1928.

45 "L.A. Nippon Victorious Over Strong Keio," *Rafu Shimpo*, May 7, 1928.

46 "W.C. Smith Interview with G.S.," Box 25, Survey of Race Relations Records.

47 "Oliver Club to Hold Community Sing," *Rafu Shimpo*, March 21, 1926.

48 "Oliver Club News," *Rafu Shimpo*, March 19, 1928.

49 "New Beverly Hills Store to Open Soon," *Rafu Shimpo*, December 23, 1929.

50 "Sun Produce Player Spiked During Game," *Rafu Shimpo*, May 16, 1930.

51 "Savings Association Hold First Meeting," *Rafu Shimpo*, September 23, 1929.

52 Fukuoka, "Mutual Life and Aid."

53 "Savings Union Elects Officers," *Rafu Shimpo*, July 16, 1928.

54 "Two Young Men Honored by Japanese Bruin Club," *Rafu Shimpo*, January 8, 1928. "Berkeley Squad to Tackle Three Local Casaba Teams," *Rafu Shimpo*, January 7, 1929. "Oxy Hi-Y News," *Rafu Shimpo*, March 11, 1929.

55 "Clarence Arima's Impressions of Japan," *Nichibei Shinbun*, November 12, 1925.

56 "Ernest Iwasaki Now Heads Y. P. Society," *Rafu Shimpo*, December 27, 1929. "Young Newlyweds Fete Friends Here," *Rafu Shimpo*, July 30, 1928. Iwasaki spoke at the wedding of Mr. C. C. Fujii, one of the prominent young businessmen of San Luis Obispo.

57 "Arai-Nobe Betrothal Announced at Party," *Rafu Shimpo*, December 2, 1929. "Bruin Club Reception Given Freshmen at Y.W.C.A. Hall," *Rafu Shimpo*, October 3, 1927. "Personals, Et Cetera," *Rafu Shimpo*, November 01, 1926.

58 "Personals et Cetera," *Rafu Shimpo*, September 26, 1927. "Second Generation Golf Exponents Win Handicap Tourney," *Rafu Shimpo*, April 22, 1928. "L.A. Dentist to Wed Girl from Guadalupe," *Rafu Shimpo*, October 14, 1929. "Rainbow Room of Mayfair Set for Poly Dinner-Dance," *Rafu Shimpo*, June 3, 1929.

59 "Bob Kuwahara to Hold Exhibition," *Rafu Shimpo*, February 25, 1929. "Savings Union Elects Officers," *Rafu Shimpo*, July 16, 1928. 1930 US Federal Census, Ancestry.com, 2002.

60 "Savings Club Holds Meeting Wednesday," *Rafu Shimpo*, September 17, 1928.

61 1930 US Federal Census.

62 "Three Young People's Groups Hear University Professor," *Rafu Shimpo*, October 1, 1929.

63 "Savings Association to Hear Market Man," *Rafu Shimpo*, October 13, 1930.

64 Ito, "Naotaro and Tsuruko."

65 "Koku Sugahara Elected Y.M.D. Group President," *Rafu Shimpo*, March 17, 1930. "Savings Association Meet with Y.M.D.'s," *Rafu Shimpo*, March 10, 1930.

66 "Savings Club Hold Game for Members," *Rafu Shimpo*, May 13, 1929.

67 "Savings Association Plans Many Interesting Meets," *Rafu Shimpo*, April 15, 1929.

68 "Savings Association Plan Dinner Instead of Meetings," *Rafu Shimpo*, October 11, 1931. "Social Activities," *Rafu Shimpo*, October 4, 1931.

69 "Bruin-Savings Association Tennis Teams Play Sunday," *Rafu Shimpo*, April 27, 1931. "Social Activities," *Rafu Shimpo*, May 18, 1931.

70 "Organizations," *Kashū Mainichi Shinbun*, November 12, 1931.

71 "Clarence Arima: Savings Association," *Rafu Shimpo*, January 1, 1931.

72 "New Officers Installed by Association at Dance," *Rafu Shimpo*, June 1, 1931.

73 "Savings Association Plan Dinner Instead of Meeting," *Rafu Shimpo*, October 11, 1931.

74 "Savings Association Will Sponsor Educational Film," *Rafu Shimpo*, September 21, 1931.

75 "Consul to Talk about Manchuria," *Rafu Shimpo*, December 6, 1931.

76 "Savings Association Change Dance Locale," *Rafu Shimpo*, April 24, 1932.

77 "Savings Association to Distribute Foods," *Rafu Shimpo*, April 17, 1932.

78 "Can-Didly Speaking," *Rafu Shimpo*, April 24, 1932.

79 "Reminiscences Bye Ye Old Timer," *Rafu Shimpo*, September 3, 1933.

80 "Japanese Athletic Union Ready," *Rafu Shimpo*, September 11, 1932.

81 "J.A.U. to Begin Sport Calendar with Hoop and Diamond Leagues," *Rafu Shimpo*, September 11, 1932.

82 "JAU Set for Honor Award," *Rafu Shimpo*, October 4, 1936.

5. THE PROGRESSIVE NEW WOMAN

1 "Life History of a Japanese College Freshman Girl," Box 31, Survey of Race Relations Records.

2 "Life History of a Japanese College Freshman Girl," Box 31, Survey of Race Relations Records.

3 Yoshihara, *Musicians from a Different Shore*.

4 Howe, "Role of Women."

5 Lu, "Good Woman for Empire."

6 Kawai, *My Lantern*, 143.

7 *Shin Sekai* (*New World*), August 14, 1923.

8 Satow's father, Peter, had come from the farming class and immigrated in the 1890s to the United States. Satow earned enough money to return to Japan; court and match a new partner, Kiyose; and pay for their voyage back to the United States in 1905. Satow made several trips back and forth between San Francisco and Japan. 1910 US Federal Census, Ancestry.com, 2006. US Bureau of the Census et al., *Benevolent Institutions* (Washington, DC: Government Printing Office, 1914), Library of Congress, www.loc.gov/item/14030585/. "Life History of a Japanese College Freshman Girl."

9 "Life History of Mr. and Mrs. F," Box 30, Survey of Race Relations Records.

10 "Some Japanese Families in Southern California by Constance Ricketts," Box 38, Survey of Race Relations Records.

11 "Experience with Orientals," Box 38, Survey of Race Relations Records.

12 "Interview with Peter S.," Box 28, Survey of Race Relations Records.

13 All the Suski sisters played piano at graduation ceremonies in the summer of 1926. See "Graduates of S.B.U.C. Honored," *Rafu Shimpo*, June 13, 1926. Louise Suski played a piano duet with Chiyo Otera. "Young Olivers Give Music and Singing," *Rafu Shimpo*, August 30, 1926. Clara Suski played a piano duet with Yoshiko Ishioka. "High School Graduates in Congratulation Banquet," *Rafu Shimpo*, June 27, 1926. Julia Suski played the piano at the banquet. "St. Francis Xavier School Holds First Graduation," *Rafu Shimpo*, June 27, 1926. Flora and Clara played a piano duet.

14 "At California Art Club Piano Recital Planned," *Rafu Shimpo*, July 10, 1932.

15 "These Spoilt Children," *Japanese American News*, May 20, 1926.

16 *Holly Leaves* 8, no. 17 (November 1, 1919)

17 1920 US Federal Census, Ancestry.com, 2006.

18 "Large Class Will Receive Diplomas at High School," *Rafu Shimpo*, June 8, 1931.

19 Fuji Fujino also received a diploma from the Los Angeles Conservatory of Music. She began teaching piano at home and at the conservatory. See "Personals Et Cetera," *Rafu Shimpo*, February 13, 1928; "Personals Et Cetera," *Rafu Shimpo*, July 11, 1927.

20 "Cosmopolitan Music School Gives Recital," *Rafu Shimpo*, July 2, 1928.

21 1920 US Federal Census, Ancestry.com, 2006.

22 1920 US Federal Census, Ancestry.com, 2006.
23 *Rafu Shimpo*, April 18, 1926.
24 California Voter Registrations, 1900–1968, Ancestry.com.
25 1920 US Federal Census.
26 "Local Talent Gives Rich Piano Recital," *Rafu Shimpo*, September 13, 1926. 1920 US Federal Census.
27 "Japanese Program a Huge Success," *Rafu Shimpo*, April 25, 1926.
28 "Personal Columns," *Rafu Shimpo*, August, 30, 1926.
29 "Young Soprano from North Stages Brilliant Concert," *Rafu Shimpo*, June 4, 1928.
30 "Young Pupils Give Musical Recital," *Rafu Shimpo*, August 27, 1928
31 1920 US Federal Census.
32 Boris, *Home to Work*.
33 "Life History of a Japanese College Freshman Girl."
34 "Life History of a Japanese College Freshman Girl." For more on a daughter's debt, see Ninh, *Ingratitude*.
35 Phoenix, "Not by Might."
36 World Young Women's Christian Association, *Girl Reserve Movement*.
37 "Los Angeles Girl Defends Second Generation," *Japanese American News*, May 28, 1926.
38 "Life History of a Japanese College Freshman Girl."
39 Student: Asilomar region, MS 00324, YWCA of the USA Records.
40 Record group 5: International Work, YWCA of the USA Records.
41 Niiya, "Miya Sannomiya Kikuchi." See also Yamamoto, "Miya Sannomiya Kikuchi."
42 Student: Asilomar region, YWCA of the USA Records.
43 Student: Asilomar region.
44 Student: Asilomar region.
45 Ida Louise Jackson, "Overcoming Barriers in Education," an oral history conducted in 1984 and 1985 by Gabrielle Morris, Regional Oral History Office, San Francisco Views Collection.
46 Student: Asilomar region.
47 Ichioka, "Attorney for the Defense."
48 "Interview with Prof. Y. Ichihashi," Box 32, Survey of Race Relations Records.
49 Student: Asilomar region. Several other guests were invited. Judith Mangino, a government research student in education from Mexico City, served as a resource on Mexico. Elizabeth Curtis, executive of the YWCA work in Estonia and a member of the Foreign Division of the national board, also attended. Finally, Dr. Josephine Kennedy, a formerly medical missionary in China, served as the conference physician.
50 "Students' Conference at Asilomar for Girls Ends," *Rafu Shimpo*, June 27, 1926.
51 Lily Satow, "Doings at the Asilomar Conference for Co-Eds," *Rafu Shimpo*, July 4, 1926.
52 "Life History of a Japanese College Freshman Girl."
53 For more on the Community Chest, see Community Chest and Welfare Federation of Los Angeles Area records.

54 "Chest Gives 20,000 to Lil Nippon," *Rafu Shimpo*, February 24, 1930.

55 "Women Renew Chest Drive," *Rafu Shimpo*, November 17, 1930.

56 "Community Chest Nearing Quota," *Rafu Shimpo*, November 14, 1933.

57 "Inter-Club Council Held at Girl's Camp in Griffith Park," *Rafu Shimpo*, September 19, 1927.

58 "'Treasure of Life' Is Theme of Main Speaker at G. R. Camp," *Rafu Shimpo*, May 20, 1929.

59 Matsumoto, *City Girls*.

60 In 1928, at the first Girl Reserves Conference, they invited Shizu Ishikawa, of the Tokyo Higher Girls' School, who also worked at the YWCA in Japan. Ishikawa was the main speaker on the subject of schools and clubs in Japan. See "G. R. Conference Planned at Griffith Park Camp," *Rafu Shimpo*, March 31, 1930. Harriet Robbins, vice principal of Beverly Hills High School, delivered a speech titled "Follow the Gleam."

61 "Many Applications Made for Girl Reserve Conference," *Rafu Shimpo*, May 13, 1929. "Treasure of Life Is Theme."

62 "Japanese G. R. Conference Held at Griffith Park Camp," *Rafu Shimpo*, May 14, 1928. "Japanese Girl Reserves Conference Well Attended," *Rafu Shimpo*, May 21, 1928.

63 "Emba Club to Install Girl Reserves Club," *Rafu Shimpo*, September 24, 1928. "New G. R. Club Organized," *Rafu Shimpo*, October 8, 1928.

64 Japanese Christian Church newsletter, June 16, 1929, West Adams Christian Church Records.

65 "Japanese Christian Church Bulletin," April 7, 1929, April 21, 1929, April 28, 1929, May 5, 1929, and June 23, 1929, West Adams Christian Church Records.

66 World Young Women's Christian Association, *Girl Reserve Movement*.

67 "Six Girls from Los Angeles to Attend G. R. Conference," *Rafu Shimpo*, June 15, 1931.

68 "Doll Festival Held at Christ Church," *Rafu Shimpo*, March 4, 1929.

69 "Girl Reserves Make Final Plans for Doll Festival," *Rafu Shimpo*, February 23, 1931.

70 "Girl Reserves Choose Cast for Play at Doll Festival," *Rafu Shimpo*, February 16, 1931.

71 "The Japanese Girls Festival," *Rafu Shimpo*, March 3, 1930.

72 Corbett, *Cultivating Femininity*.

73 "Second Annual Family Tea Held by Girl Reserves' Clubs," *Rafu Shimpo*, January 23, 1928. "Many Mothers Are Invited to Girl Reserve Family Tea," *Rafu Shimpo*, January 30, 1928. "Young Girls and Mothers Enjoy Annual Family Tea," *Rafu Shimpo*, February 26, 1928. "Parents Are to Be Invited to Annual G. R. Family Tea," *Rafu Shimpo*, January 7, 1929. "Girl Reserves Sending Out Invitation to Their Parents," *Rafu Shimpo*, January 14, 1929. "Japanese G. R. Set Plans for Third Annual Family Tea," *Rafu Shimpo*, January 12, 1929. "Girl Reserves Family Tea Given at Institute Sunday," *Rafu Shimpo*, January 28, 1929. "Many Mothers With Girls at Annual G. R. Banquet," *Rafu Shimpo*, January 13, 1930. "G.R.'s Hold Successful Mother-Daughter Banquet," *Rafu Shimpo*, January 19, 1931.

74 "Japanese Girls' Camp to Open at Pacific Palisades Aug. 20," *Rafu Shimpo*, August 13, 1928. "Girls' Camp Closes after Active Week," *Rafu Shimpo*, August 27, 1928.

75 School Yearbooks, 1900–1999, Ancestry.com, 2010.
76 "400 Attend as YPCC Conclave Opens," *Nichibei Shinbun*, November 3, 1935.
77 California, Voter Registrations, 1900–1968, Ancestry.com, 2017.
78 "Charlotte Shimizu in New Post at YWCA," *Rafu Shimpo*, September 2, 1937.
79 1930 US Federal Census.
80 School Yearbooks, 1900–1999.
81 Park, "Role of the YWCA."
82 "All YWCA Clubs Join to Honor Lily Satow at Tea This Afternoon," *Rafu Shimpo*, May 27, 1934.

EPILOGUE

1 "Nisei Enters Soap Making Business after Selling His Hog Raising Enterprise," *Rafu Shimpo*, March 24, 1938. "Nisei Soap Factory Center of Attraction," *New World Sun*, September 29, 1938. "John Ando to Head Finance Committee; Chairmen Selected," *Rafu Shimpo*, January 1 and 26, 1941.
2 "History of Nisei Week," Japanese-City.com, www.japanese-city.com/calendar/events/index.php?com=location&lID=839, accessed July 9, 2021.
3 Spickard, "Nisei Assume Power."
4 Niiya, "10 Little-Known Stories."
5 Williams, *Time of Fear*.
6 *Rohwer Outpost* (McGehee, AR), December 9, 1942. Japanese American Internment Camp Newspapers, 1942–1946 Collection.
7 "Answers to the Questionnaires in Community Activities," Rohwer Reconstructed Digital Archive.
8 "Dedication of YWCA Hall Rites to Be Held Today," *Rohwer Outpost*, May 29, 1943.
9 *Rohwer Outpost*, December 5, 1942.
10 *Rohwer Outpost*, May 5, 1943.
11 *Rohwer Outpost*, April 17, 1943.
12 *Rohwer Outpost*, November 24, 1943.
13 See Glenn, *Issei, Nisei, War Bride*. *Rohwer Outpost*, May 29, 1943.
14 *Rohwer Outpost*, June 12, 1943. Final Accountability Rosters of Evacuees at Relocation Centers, 1942–1946, Ancestry.com, 2013. They departed a year and a half later in 1943 for Bloomfield Hills, Michigan.
15 Taketani, *Black Pacific Narrative*.
16 Gallicchio, *African American Encounter*.
17 Hayashi, *For the Sake*.
18 Iwaki Drug Company Auction, Los Angeles Photographic Archive.
19 Kekki, "Life at Heart Mountain." *Heart Mountain (WY) Sentinel*, November 28, 1942. Japanese American Internment Camp Newspapers, 1942–1946 Collection.
20 *Heart Mountain (WY) Sentinel*, August 21, 1943. Chiyo Sashihara, "I Remember," *Breckenridge Beacon*, May 1983, Roger Endo, personal collection.
21 *Heart Mountain (WY) Sentinel*, January 9, 1943.

22 "Names of Detainees," Tuna Canyon Detention Station Coalition, www.tuna canyon.org/names-of-detainees/, accessed July 9, 2021. Linke, "Santa Anita."

23 Thomas Sashihara, "Tozaburo to Thomas," unpublished manuscript, 1985, Roger Endo, personal collection.

24 *Heart Mountain (WY) Sentinel*, September 18, 1943.

25 "Tom Sashihara, Former Resident, Joins WRA Staff," *Heart Mountain (WY) Sentinel*, July 28, 1945.

26 Hirabayashi, Shimada, and Iwasaki, *Japanese American Resettlement*.

27 Final Accountability Rosters of Evacuees.

28 *Granada Pioneer* (Amache, CO), November 14, 1942. Japanese American Internment Camp Newspapers, 1942–1946 Collection.

29 Hayashi, "Chiyoko Sakamoto." Final Accountability Rosters of Evacuees.

30 WWII Draft Registration Cards for California, 10/16/1940–03/31/1947, record group "Records of the Selective Service System," 147, Box 1579, National Archives at St. Louis, Ancestry.com.

31 Nakamura, "Seabrook Farms."

32 Regalado, *Nikkei Baseball*.

33 *Granada Pioneer* (Amache, CO), November 7, 1942.

34 *Granada Pioneer* (Amache, CO), January 6, 1943.

35 *Granada Pioneer* (Amache, CO), June 5, 1943.

36 *Nippu Jiji*, September 2, 1941. See Fujiyoshi, "Study of the Educational Program."

37 *Kashū Mainichi Shinbun*, February 28, 1941.

38 Nakamura, "Paul Osumi."

39 *Nippu Jiji*, October 30, 1941. *Nippu Jiji*, September 18, 1942.

40 Scheiber and Scheiber, "Martial Law in Hawaii."

41 LaVenture, "Sharing War Stories."

42 Park, *Facilitating Injustice*.

43 Matsumoto, *City Girls*.

44 T. J. O'Mara, Heart Mountain Relocation Center Community Activities Section Final Report, August 22, 1944, Bancroft Library.

45 Nat R. Griswold, "Rohwer: From Final Report: Historical Statistical-Functional Report of Community Activities Section," Japanese American Relocation Digital Archive, Bancroft Library.

46 *Rohwer Outpost*, April 14, 1943.

47 Japanese Americans Relocated during World War II, Ancestry.com, 2005. Ogo Shew, "Feminine Identity Confined."

BIBLIOGRAPHY

ARCHIVES

California Digital Newspaper Collection. University of California, Riverside.

Hoji Shinbun Digital Collection. Hoover Institution Archives, Stanford University.

Japanese American Internment Camp Newspapers, 1942–1946 Collection. Library of Congress.

Japanese American Relocation Digital Archive. Bancroft Library, University of California, Berkeley. Calisphere.

Los Angeles County Incorporation Records. Seaver Center for Western History Research. Los Angeles County Museum of Natural History.

Los Angeles Photographic Archive. UCLA Special Collections. Calisphere.

Nathaniel Robadeau Griswold Rohwer Relocation Center Records, MS G88 257. Rohwer Reconstructed Digital Archive. Special Collections. University of Arkansas Libraries.

Pacific Japanese Mission Conference of the Methodist Episcopal Church Journals. Digital Archives of the California Pacific Conference. United Methodist Church, Pasadena, California.

Pasadena Digital History Collaboration Collection. Pasadena City College.

San Bernardino City Directories. Arda Haenszel California Room. Norman F. Feldheym Central Library.

San Bernardino County Recorder. San Bernardino County Historical Archives.

San Francisco Views Collection. Bancroft Library, University of California, Berkeley, Calisphere.

Survey of Race Relations Records. Hoover Institution Archives, Stanford University.

West Adams Christian Church Records. Japanese American National Museum.

Yuji Ichioka Papers. UCLA Library Special Collections.

YWCA of Los Angeles Collection. California State University Northridge.

YWCA of the USA records. Sophia Smith Collection of Women's History, MS 00324. Smith College.

OTHER SOURCES

Abe, Ikuo. "Muscular Christianity in Japan: The Growth of a Hybrid." *International Journal of the History of Sport* 23, no. 5 (2006): 714–38.

Alexander, Kristine. *Guiding Modern Girls: Girlhood, Empire, and Internationalism in the 1920s and 1930s*. Vancouver: University of British Columbia Press, 2017.

Anderson, Emily. *Christianity and Imperialism in Modern Japan: Empire for God*. New York: Bloomsbury Academic, 2014.

Andrés, Benny J. "'I Am Almost More at Home with Brown Faces than with White': An Americanization Teacher in Imperial Valley, California, 1923–1924." *Southern California Quarterly* 93, no. 1 (2011): 69–107.

Azuma, Eiichiro. *Between Two Empires: Race, History, and Transnationalism in Japanese America*. New York: Oxford University Press, 2005.

———. *In Search of Our Frontier: Japanese America and Settler Colonialism in the Construction of Japan's Borderless Empire*. Berkeley: University of California Press, 2019.

———. "Nichibei Shimbun." *Densho Encyclopedia*, May 21, 2013. https://encyclopedia.densho.org/Nichibei_Shimbun_(newspaper)/.

Bernstein, Gail Lee, ed. *Recreating Japanese Women, 1600–1945*. Berkeley: University of California Press, 1991.

Blair, Doug. "The 1920 Anti-Japanese Crusade and Congressional Hearing." Seattle Civil Rights Labor History Project, 2006. https://depts.washington.edu/civilr/Japanese_restriction.htm.

Boris, Eileen. *Home to Work: Motherhood and the Politics of Industrial Home Work in the United States*. New York: Cambridge University Press, 1994.

Chang, Wendy. *The Changs Next Door to the Diazes: Remapping Race in Suburban California*. Minneapolis: University of Minnesota, 2013.

Chapman, Erin. *Prove It on Me: New Negroes, Sex and Popular Culture in the 1920s*. New York: Oxford University Press, 2012.

Cheng, Cindy I-Fen. *Citizens of Asian America: Democracy and Race during the Cold War*. New York: New York University Press, 2013.

Choy, Catherine Ceniza, and Judy Tzu-Chun Wu, eds. *Gendering the Trans-Pacific World: Diaspora, Empire, and Race*. Leiden: Brill Press, 2017.

Clark, Francis E. *The Christian Endeavor Manual: A Textbook on the History, Theory, Principles, and Practice of the Society, with Complete Bibliography and Several Appendixes*. Boston: United Society of Christian Endeavor, 1903.

Clarke, Francis E. "The Christian Endeavor Movement." *North American Review* 161, no. 466 (1895): 287–96. www.jstor.org/stable/25103578.

Corbett, Rebecca. Introduction. In *Cultivating Femininity: Women and Tea Culture in Edo and Meiji Japan*, 1–24. Honolulu: University of Hawai'i Press, 2018.

Costello, Julia G., Kevin Hallaran, Keith Warren, and Margie Akin. "The Luck of Third Street: Archaeology of Chinatown, San Bernardino, California." *Historical Archaeology* 42, no. 3 (2008): 136–51. www.jstor.org/stable/25617517.

Daniels, Roger. "No Lamps Were Lit for Them: Angel Island and the Historiography of Asian American Immigration." *Journal of American Ethnic History* 17 (Fall 1997): 3–18.

Dewitt, Howard A. "The Watsonville Anti-Filipino Riot of 1930: A Case Study of the Great Depression and Ethnic Conflict in California." *Southern California Quarterly* 61, no. 3 (1979): 291–302.

Dumenil, Lynn. *The Modern Temper: American Culture and Society in the 1920s*. New York: Hill and Wang, 1995.

Enstad, Nan. *Ladies of Labor, Girls of Adventure: Working Women, Popular Culture, and Labor Politics at the Turn of the Twentieth Century.* New York: Columbia University Press, 1999.

Erb, Frank Otis. "The Development of the Young People's Movement." *Biblical World* 48, no. 3 (1916): 129–92. www.jstor.org/stable/3142079.

Fong, Timothy P. *The First Suburban Chinatown: The Remaking of Monterey Park, California.* Philadelphia: Temple University Press, 1994.

Friese, Margaret. "Japanese Girls and Women." *Women's Home Missions* 37, no. 10 (October 1920): 11.

Fujiyoshi, Donald. "A Study of the Educational Program of the Church School of the Japanese Christian Church and Institute of Los Angeles." Master's thesis, University of Southern California, 1942.

Fukuoka, Fumiko. "Mutual Life and Aid among the Japanese in Southern California with Special Reference to Los Angeles." Master's thesis, University of Southern California, 1937.

Gallicchio, Marc. *The African American Encounter with China and Japan: Black Internationalism in Asia, 1895–1945.* Chapel Hill: University of North Carolina Press, 2000.

Garcia, Matt. *A World of Its Own: Race, Labor, and Citrus in the Making of Greater Los Angeles, 1900–1970*. Chapel Hill: University of North Carolina Press, 2002.

Glenn, Evelyn Nakano. *Issei, Nisei, War Bride: Three Generations of Japanese American Women in Domestic Service*. Philadelphia: Temple University Press, 1988.

Gonzalez, Elwing Suong. "Odd Man Out: Shifting Notions of Culture, Community, Marginalization in the Power of Struggle for Alhambra, 1940s to 1970s." Master's thesis, California State University Los Angeles, 2009.

Griffith, Sarah. *The Fight for Asian American Civil Rights: Liberal Protestant Activism, 1900–1950*. Urbana: University of Illinois Press, 2018.

———. "'Where We Can Battle for the Lord and Japan': The Development of Liberal Protestant Antiracism before World War II." *Journal of American History* 100, no. 2 (September 2013): 429–53.

Harris, LaShawn. *Sex Workers, Psychics, and Numbers Runners: Black Women in New York City's Underground Economy*. Urbana: University of Illinois Press, 2016.

Hayashi, Brian. *For the Sake of Our Japanese Brethren: Assimilation, Nationalism, and Protestantism among the Japanese of Los Angeles, 1895–1942*. Stanford, CA: Stanford University Press, 1995.

Hayashi, Kristen. "Chiyoko Sakamoto." *Densho Encyclopedia*. https://encyclopedia.densho.org/Chiyoko%20Sakamoto. Accessed July 22, 2021.

Hendricks, David, and Amy Patterson. "The 1930 Census in Perspective." Genealogy Notes 34, no. 2 (Summer 2002). www.archives.gov/publications/prologue/2002/summer/1930-census-perspective.html.

Higginsbotham, Evelyn. *Righteous Discontent: The Women's Movement in the Black Baptist Church, 1880–1920*. Cambridge, MA: Harvard University Press, 1994.

Hinnerschitz, Stephanie. *Race, Religion, and Civil Rights: Asian Students on the West Coast, 1900–1968*. New Brunswick, NJ: Rutgers University Press, 2015.

Hirabayashi, Lane Ryo, Kenichiro Shimada, and Hikaru Iwasaki. *Japanese American Resettlement through the Lens: Hikaru Iwasaki and the WRA's Photographic Section, 1943–1945*. Boulder: University Press of Colorado, 2009.

Hirahara, Naomi. *Distinguished Asian American Business Leaders*. Westport, CT: Greenwood Press, 2003.

Howe, Sondra Weland. "The Role of Women in the Introduction of Western Music in Japan." *Bulletin of Historical Research in Music Education* 16, no. 2 (1995): 81–97. www.jstor.org/stable/40214860.

Ichioka, Yuji. "'Attorney for the Defense': Yamato Ichihashi and Japanese Immigration." *Pacific Historical Review* 55, no. 2 (1986): 192–225.

Imai, Shiho. *Creating the Nisei Market: Race and Citizenship in Hawaii's Japanese American Consumer Culture*. Honolulu: University of Hawai'i Press, 2010.

Inui, Kiyo Sue. "California's Japanese Situation." *Annals of the American Academy of Political and Social Science* 3 (January 1921): 97–101.

Irwin, Wallace. *Seed of the Sun*. New York: George H. Doran, 1921.

Ito, Roy T. "Naotaro and Tsuruko, My Issei Parents." Discover Nikkei, November 28, 2008. www.discovernikkei.org/en/journal/article/2799/.

Iwai, Shuma. "Japanese Christianity in the Meiji Era: An Analysis of Ebina Danjo's Perspective on Shintoistic Christianity." *Transformation* 25, no. 4 (2008): 195–204. www.jstor.org/stable/43052742.

"Japanese Barred from Citizenship." *Literary Digest*, December 2, 1922.

Japanese Immigration Hearings Before the Committee on Immigration and Naturalization, July 19, 20, and 21, 1920. Washington, DC: Government Printing Office, 1921.

Jenks, Hillary. "History of Miss Oliver and the Oliver Clubs." Discover Nikkei. www.discovernikkei.org/en/nikkeialbum/items/879/. Accessed May 1, 2020.

Kanzaki, Kiichi. *California and the Japanese*. San Francisco, 1921.

Kao, Mary Uyematsu. "A Permanent Parking Space for Jiro Morita." *Amerasia Journal* (blog), September 13, 2012. www.amerasiajournal.org/blog/?p=1840.

Kawai, Michi. *My Lantern*. Tokyo: Kyo Bun Kwan, 1939.

Kekki, Saara. "Life at Heart Mountain: A Dynamic Network Model of Japanese American Community during World War II." PhD diss., University of Helsinki, 2019.

Kiyama, Henry. *The Four Immigrants Manga: A Japanese Experience in San Francisco, 1904–1924*. Berkeley, CA: Stone Bridge, 1999.

Koyama, Shizuko. *Ryōsai Kenbo: The Educational Ideal of 'Good Wife, Wise Mother' in Modern Japan*. Leiden: Brill, 2012. ProQuest Ebook Central.

Kurashige, Lon. *Japanese American Celebration and Conflict: A History of Ethnic Identity and Festival, 1934–1990*. Berkeley: University of California Press, 2002.

———. "Re-thinking Anti-Immigrant Racism: Lessons from the Los Angeles Vote on the 1920 Alien Land Law." *Southern California Quarterly* 95, no. 3 (Fall 2013): 265–83.

LaVenture, Tom. "Sharing War Stories: Five-Year Study Leads to Museum Updating Exhibit of Internment of Japanese Americans." Discover Nikkei, January 3, 2014. www.discovernikkei.org/en/journal/2014/1/3/sharing-war-stories/.

Lee, Erika, and Judy Yung. *Angel Island: Immigrant Gateway to America*. New York: Oxford University Press, 2010.

Linke, Konrad. "Santa Anita (Detention Facility)." *Densho Encyclopedia*. https://encyclopedia.densho.org/Santa%20Anita%20(detention%20facility. Accessed July 29, 2021.

Longstreth, Richard W. *Cultural Landscapes: Balancing Nature and Heritage in Preservation Practice*. Minneapolis: University of Minnesota Press, 2008.

Lu, Sidney Xu. "Good Women for Empire: Educating Overseas Female Emigrants in Imperial Japan, 1900–1945." *Journal of Global History* 8 (2013): 436–60.

MacFarland, Henry B. F. "The Christian Endeavor Movement." *North American Review* 182, no. 591 (1906): 194–203.

Matsumoto, Valerie J. *City Girls: The Nisei Social World in Los Angeles, 1920–1950*. New York: Oxford University Press, 2014.

Matthews, Jean. *The Rise of the New Women: The Women's Movement in America, 1875–1930*. Chicago: Ivan R. Dee, 2004.

Modell, John. *The Economics and Politics of Racial Accommodation: The Japanese of Los Angeles, 1900–1942*. Urbana: University of Illinois Press, 1977.

Nakamura, Kelli. "Paul Osumi." *Densho Encyclopedia*. https://encyclopedia.densho.org/Paul%20Osumi. Accessed July 23, 2021.

———. "Seabrook Farms." *Densho Encyclopedia*. https://encyclopedia.densho.org/Seabrook%20Farms. Accessed July 22, 2021.

Ngai, Mae. *Impossible Subjects: Illegal Aliens and the Making of Modern America*. Princeton, NJ: Princeton University Press, 2004.

Nicolaides, Becky M. "'Where the Working Man Is Welcomed': Working-Class Suburbs in Los Angeles, 1900–1940." *Pacific Historical Review* 68, no. 4 (1999): 517–59.

Nicolaides, Becky M., and James Zarsadiaz. "Design Assimilation in Suburbia: Asian Americans, Built Landscapes, and Suburban Advantage in Los Angeles's San Gabriel Valley since 1970." *Journal of Urban History* 43, no. 2 (March 2017): 332–71.

Niiya, Brian. "Miya Sannomiya Kikuchi." *Densho Encyclopedia*. https://encyclopedia.densho.org/Miya%20Sannomiya%20Kikuchi/. Accessed February 11, 2020.

———. "10 Little-Known Stories about Rohwer Concentration Camp." *Densho* (blog), July 7, 2020. https://encyclopedia.densho.org/Miya_Sannomiya_Kikuchi/.

Ninh, erin Khuê. *Ingratitude: The Debt-Bound Daughter in Asian American Literature*. Minnesota: University of Minnesota Press, 2011.

Nomura, Shiori. "The Voices of Women on Birth Control and Childcare: A Japanese Immigrant Newspaper in the Early Twentieth-Century USA." *Japan Forum* 21, no. 2 (January 2010): 255–76.

Ogo Shew, Dana. "Feminine Identity Confined: The Archaeology of Japanese Women at Amache, a WWII Internment Camp." Master's thesis, University of Denver, 2010.

Oharazeki, Kazuhiro. *Japanese Prostitutes in the North American West, 1887–1920*. Seattle: University of Washington Press, 2016.

Park, Yoosun. *Facilitating Injustice: The Complicity of Social Workers in the Forced Removal and Incarceration of Japanese Americans, 1941–1946*. New York: Oxford University Press, 2020.

———. "The Role of the YWCA in the World War II Internment of Japanese Americans: A Cautionary Tale for Social Work." *Social Service Review* (Chicago) 87, no. 3 (2013): 477–524.

Patterson, Martha H. *Beyond the Gibson Girl: Reimagining the American New Woman, 1895–1915*. Urbana: University of Illinois Press, 2005.

Peiss, Kathy. *Cheap Amusements: Working Women and Leisure in Turn-of-the-Century New York*. Philadelphia: Temple University Press, 1986.

Phoenix, Karen E. "'Not by Might, nor by Power, but by Spirit': The Global Reform Efforts of the Young Women's Christian Association of the United States, 1895–1939." PhD diss., University of Illinois at Urbana–Champaign, 2010.

Putney, Clifford. *Muscular Christianity: Manhood and Sports in Protestant America, 1880–1920*. Cambridge, MA: Harvard University Press, 2003.

Rabinovitch-Fox, Einav. "New Women in Early 20th-Century America." *Oxford Research Encyclopedia of American History*, August 22, 2017.

———. "This Is What a Feminist Looks Like: The New Woman Image, American Feminism, and the Politics of Women's Fashion, 1890–1930." PhD diss., New York University, 2014.

Racel, Masako N. "Inui Kiyosue: A Japanese Peace Advocate in the Age of the 'Yellow Peril.'" *World History Bulletin* 31, no. 2 (2015): 9–14.

Regalado, Samuel. *Nikkei Baseball: Japanese American Players from Immigration and Internment to the Major Leagues*. Urbana: University of Illinois Press, 2013.

Ruiz, Vicki L. *From Out of the Shadows: Mexican Women in Twentieth-Century America*. New York: Oxford University Press, 2008.

Sato, Barbara Hamill. *The New Japanese Woman: Modernity, Media, and Women in Interwar Japan*. Durham, NC: Duke University Press, 2003.

Scheiber, Jane, and Harry Scheiber. "Martial Law in Hawaii." *Densho Encyclopedia*. https://encyclopedia.densho.org/Martial%20law%20in%20Hawaii. Accessed July 27, 2021.

Sherill, Charles H. "An American's Plain Speaking in Japan." *Harvey's Weekly*, December 27, 1919.

Shima, George. "An Appeal to Justice: The Injustice of the Proposed Initiative Measure." 1920. UCLA Special Collections. Online Archive of California. https://oac.cdlib.org/view?docId=hb9r29p5zr&brand=oac4&doc.view=entire_text.

Smith, Susan. *Japanese American Midwives: Culture, Community, and Health Politics, 1880–1950*. Urbana: University of Illinois Press, 2005.

Sonida, Hidehiro. "The Decline of the Japanese Warrior Class." *Japan Review*, no. 1 (1990): 73–111.

Spickard, Paul R. "The Nisei Assume Power: The Japanese Citizens League, 1941–1942." *Pacific Historical Review* 52, no. 2 (1983): 147–74.

Stage, Sarah, and Virginia Vincenti, eds. *Rethinking Home Economics: Women and the History of a Profession*. Ithaca, NY: Cornell University Press, 1997.

Stewart, Eric. "Victorian Sprawl: Streetcar Technology and the Suburban Ideal in Los Angeles, 1870–1920." *California History* 93, no. 2 (2016): 17–30.

Sueyoshi, Amy. *Discriminating Sex: White Leisure and the Making of the American "Oriental."* Urbana: University of Illinois, 2018.

Syrett, Nicholas. *The Company He Keeps: A History of White College Fraternities*. Chapel Hill: University of North Carolina Press, 2009.

Taketani, Etsuko. *The Black Pacific Narrative: Geographic Imaginings of Race and Empire between the World Wars*. Hanover, NH: Dartmouth College Press, 2014.

Takezawa, Yasuko, and Gary Y. Okihiro, eds. *Trans-Pacific Japanese American Studies: Conversations on Race and Racializations*. Honolulu: University of Hawai'i Press, 2016.

Tamura, Eileen. *Americanization, Acculturation, and Ethnic Identity: The Nisei Generation in Hawaii*. Urbana: University of Illinois Press, 1994.

Threlkeld, Megan. "Twenty Years of Worlds of Women: Leila Rupp's Impact on the History of U.S. Women's Internationalism." *History Compass* 15, no. 6 (2017). https://doi.org/10.1111/hic3.12381.

Toyama, Chotoku. "The Japanese Community in Los Angeles." MA thesis, Columbia University, 1926.

Tyrrell, Ian. *Reforming the World: The Creation of America's Moral Empire*. Princeton, NJ: Princeton University Press, 2010.

US Department of Agriculture. "The 1932 Outbreak of Foot and Mouth Disease in Southern California." Washington, DC: US Department of Agriculture, August 1933.

Wakida, Patricia. "Julia Suski." *Densho Encyclopedia*. https://encyclopedia.densho.org/Julia%20Suski. Accessed November 9, 2021.

———. "Louise Suski." *Densho Encyclopedia*. https://encyclopedia.densho.org/Louise%20Suski/. Accessed August 28, 2019.

———. "Through the Fire: Louise Suski." Discover Nikkei, March 3, 2012. www.discovernikkei.org/en/journal/2013/4/23/louise-suski/.

Wheeler, Marjorie Spruill. *New Women of the New South: The Leaders of the Woman Suffrage Movement in the Southern States*. New York: Oxford University Press, 1993.

White, Deborah Gray. *Too Heavy a Load: Black Women in Defense of Themselves, 1894–1994*. New York: W. W. Norton, 1999.

Williams, Duncan Ryūken. *American Sutra: A Story of Faith and Freedom In the Second World War*. Cambridge, MA: Belknap Press of Harvard University Press, 2019.

Williams, Duncan Ryūken, and Tomoe Moriya. *Issei Buddhism in the Americas*. Urbana: University of Illinois Press, 2010.

Williams, Sue, dir. *Time of Fear*. Documentary, 56 min., 2005.

Wolcott, Victoria. *Remaking Respectability: African American Women in Interwar Detroit*. Chapel Hill: University of North Carolina Press, 2000.

World Young Women's Christian Association. *The Girl Reserve Movement: A Manual for Advisers*. Y.W.C.A. New York City: Publication Department, National Board, Young Women's Christian Associations, 1921.

Wu, Ellen. *The Color of Success: Asian Americans and the Origins of the Model Minority*. Princeton, NJ: Princeton University Press, 2014.

Wuebker, Erin. "Social Hygiene in America." *Public Health Archives*: Gale, 2020.

Yamamoto, Eriko. "Miya Sannomiya Kikuchi: A Pioneer Nisei Woman's Life and Identity." *Amerasia Journal* 23, no. 3 (Winter 1997): 72–101.

Yasutake, Rumi. *Transnational Women's Activism: The United States, Japan, and Japanese Immigrant Communities in California, 1859–1920*. New York: New York University Press, 2004.

Yokoyama, Hidesaburo. "Japanese Associations of America." Master's thesis, University of Chicago, 1921.

Yoo, David. *Growing Up Nisei: Race, Generation, and Culture among Japanese Americans of California, 1924–49*. Urbana: University of Illinois, 1999.

Yoshihara, Mari. *Musicians from a Different Shore: Asians and Asian Americans in Classical Music*. Philadelphia: Temple University Press, 2007.

Yu, Henry. *Thinking Orientals: Migration, Contact, and Exoticism in Modern America*. New York: Oxford University Press, 2002.

Zeitz, Joshua. *Flapper: A Madcap Story of Sex, Style, Celebrity, and the Women Who Made America Modern*. New York: Crown, 2006.

INDEX

CPSIA information can be obtained
at www.ICGtesting.com
Printed in the USA
BVHW080336150522
636924BV00004B/13

9 780295 750521